BOOKBINDING & CONSERVATION BY HAND.

A WORKING GUIDE

LAURA S. YOUNG

ILLUSTRATIONS BY
SIDONIE CORYN

PHOTOGRAPHS BY
JOHN HURT WHITEHEAD III

R. R. BOWKER COMPANY

NEW YORK & LONDON, 1981

Published by R. R. Bowker Company
1180 Avenue of the Americas, New York, N. Y. 10036
Copyright © 1981 by Laura S. Young
All rights reserved
Printed and bound in the United States of America

Library of Congress Cataloging in Publication Data

Young, Laura S.
    Bookbinding and conservation by hand.

    Bibliography: p.
    Includes index.
    1.   Bookbinding—Handbooks, manuals, etc.
I. Title.
Z271.Y68   686.3'02   81-7669
ISBN 0-8352-1375-7   AACR2

DEDICATION
Posthumously to my son, my only child,
Robert Starbuck Young

Contents

Preface

This book is designed as a working guide in the field of hand bookbinding and book conservation. It is intended as a practical manual for teachers and their students; as an instruction guide to be followed by the beginner attempting to learn binding on his or her own; and as a ready reference for experienced binders, book collectors, book dealers, and librarians. Although a book is an inanimate object, it has a life expectancy, and it has integrity. The survival of both its integrity and its continuing usefulness as a tool in human pursuit of knowledge rests largely in the hands of librarians, book conservators, and restorers.

Hand bookbinding in the United States has been influenced primarily by the English, French, and German schools of binding. The techniques described in this volume follow in principle the German school; to the best of the author's knowledge, this is the first time that these binding practices have appeared in print in English.

The heart of this working guide is the three chapters dealing with techniques and the chapter on conservation. Basic techniques (Chapter 5) detail the fundamental skills that are applicable to all hand bookbinding. General techniques (Chapter 6) include those practices that, with minor variations, cover the early stages in all types of bindings. Specific techniques (Chapter 7) describe the steps primarily used in producing a specific type of hand binding. These chapters have been arranged to avoid duplication and to facilitate the logical and orderly progression of the work.

The basic principles of conservation work (Chapter 11) cover one of the more important areas in the field of hand bookbinding today. They are dealt with in some detail, omitting only those materials or techniques that are in the author's judgment too new in the overall picture to have proven themselves. The great amount of research and experimental work presently going on in this area has far-reaching significance and should be followed closely by the interested student and teacher. Until the results of these findings are proven, they are more appropriately reported in serial publications where controversial issues can be aired and inevitable changes can reach the interested public with reasonable promptness. A list of publications that customarily carry such articles appears in the Bibliography.

All instructions throughout this book have been tested at the bench by at least one person, in addition to the author, for clarity and completeness. Where feasible and appropriate, a list of materials needed precedes the step-by-step instructions for a given section or technique. These lists will allow the binder to gather together all materials and equipment to be used before beginning work on any phase of the project. In some instances, especially in those sections where alternate methods or materials are suggested, or where remedies to correct errors are detailed, materials or equipment are noted along with the instructions as part of the text (rather than in a preceding list). Heavy equipment such as presses do not appear in the lists of materials, even when they are to be used, since it is assumed that the binder will be doing any binding work in an area where such equipment is always available. The use of heavy equipment, however, is detailed in Chapter 3 and where appropriate in the text.

Measurements and dimensions for all work are given in inches and feet, followed, where possible, by metric measurements. Measurements less than ½ inch are not given in metrics. Metric conversion charts also appear in the Appendix.

All technical terms are explained when they first appear in the text. The Appendix contains supply sources, tests on leather, and recipes for making pastes and other bookbinding needs in the workshop.

The history of bookbinding, making of decorated papers, and listing of historic paper sizes and instructions for folding a printed signature are not covered in detail in this guide, contrary to the usual practice of other authors in the field. Both the history and techniques involved in making decorated papers are specialized fields in themselves, and few hand binders today receive unfolded sheets from the printer. Readers who wish to explore these areas of hand binding will find references to them in the Bibliography.

Acknowledgments. The author is grateful to all of her students who have read the manuscript and to those who have tested the techniques as written and offered helpful suggestions; to Virginia Wheeler, an interested friend, for her objective evaluation; posthumously to Mary S. Coryn, a colleague, whose interest and encouragement were an inspiration; to Sidonie Coryn, the illustrator, for her ability and cooperation; to Susan Schulz, for her assistance in the parchment/vellum nomenclature research; to John Hurt Whitehead III for his excellent photographs; to Maria Grandinette, who meticulously and methodically executed every step as written in the instructions, and whose findings and suggestions have made this a better book; and to Jerilyn G. Davis (Jeri), my able assistant for more than fifteen years, for her sustained interest and continuous help during the period that the manuscript was in process.

Introduction

Hand bookbinding is an old and honorable craft that has served society well for many centuries. Several hundred years ago, binders held an important place in the literate life of the community, and in university circles they were reputedly afforded the honor of participating, appropriately robed, in the institution's formal academic processions. Although time has brought many changes, scholars in particular owe much to these early craftspeople, whose work made possible the survival of many volumes that are currently invaluable in our pursuit of knowledge.

The advent of the machine age, an inevitable evolvement in a growing world, in a sense made obsolete the people who worked by hand. At best, their efforts became secondary to the machine, and these hand craftspeople viewed with suspicion and contempt those whose inventive abilities produced the mechanical "things" that placed the hand worker's livelihood in jeopardy. Hand craftspeople, however, have survived, and to a large extent, ironically perhaps, they owe their survival to the machines, for they could not possibly have coped with the pressures of mass book production.

With the passage of time, the books produced by some of those early machines have proven to be inferior—a fact that cannot be blamed on the machines themselves. The fault lies with the use of poor quality goods in the search for new sources of raw materials to keep the machines in operation.

The brittle, crumbling paper and the leather that has turned to "red rot," both products of accelerated processes during the infancy of the machine age, have turned out to be costly mistakes for libraries and book collectors. The current and growing concern in coping with these problems has, however, again set the stage for the hand bookbinder to assume an important role in the area of book conservation, or restoration. The machine cannot deter or repair the deterioration and destruction that its use has inadvertently brought about.

In recent years, the term *hand bookbinding* has taken on a somewhat ambiguous meaning. To many people, it brings to mind the elaborately decorated and bejewelled bindings of the sixteenth and seventeenth centuries that, supposedly, were done only in monasteries. To the casual observer, hand binding may be a "dying art," but that is decidedly not so. A number of craftspeople active today are quite capable of producing work comparable to that of the early hand binders, as long as there are patrons willing to support it.

To "purists" in the field, hand bookbinding means adhering closely to the early techniques of sewing on cords, lacing the cords into the boards, and covering the whole in leather, using the tight back method of construction. To them, no book is "bound" unless done in this manner. With the great variety of books that are produced today, ranging widely from those excellently designed and printed on good paper to rather commonplace productions of indifferent or poor quality, it is unrealistic to restrict the definition of the term to the established techniques of three or more centuries ago.

To the modern practitioner, amateur and professional, the term means custom work. In satisfying one's self or one's clients, the hand binder has a wide choice of techniques and materials; a binding can be simple or elaborate, traditional or modern, based on the quality of the book, its contents, and its anticipated use; and, of course, the personal tastes of the binder or those of the client.

Hand bookbinding is an exacting craft. To learn it properly, one must first master the seemingly simple tasks of measuring accurately, cutting straight, and pasting neatly. Binders must familiarize themselves with the materials with which they will work, for the behavior of materials can be quite different; what is suitable for one job may be very inappropriate for another. From an historical point of view, especially important in conservation work, the binder should know something about the periods in history when the use of certain materials was first introduced.

It is true that books have been bound from instructions in do-it-yourself kits or oversimplified volumes. Directions of this type, however, hardly scratch the surface, and the work that results is seldom satisfying to the binder after the initial excitement has waned. Such publications do serve a useful purpose in providing a starting point, but it is unfair and misleading to encourage would-be binders to believe that they can produce work of "professional" calibre in a short period of time. The great masters in all handcraft fields served long apprenticeships, followed by years of independent work before gaining recognition for their ability.

Hand bookbinding is a rewarding craft when pursued with seriousness. In these times when people live with so many material things, the workings of which we accept but do not always understand, any object that we fashion properly with our own hands can, and does, become a stabilizing and satisfying experience.

To a person with artistic talent and ability, once these techniques are mastered, hand binding offers a challenging medium for creative and artistic expression, within the limits imposed by the book itself. The binder, unlike the artist, does not have free reign; he or she starts with a product from skilled hands and should never overlook or underestimate the talents of the author, illustrator, designer, and producer whose efforts made the book possible. The binder should also remember that a book, if properly used, consists of movable parts—in contrast to a painting that is hung on the wall and seldom touched. If in the interest or originality or creativity, the binder produces a binding that is so fragile or so perishable as to render the book useless, it is an ill-conceived and poorly designed binding, no matter how artistic or beautiful it may be as an object of art.

To the book lover with a more practical than artistic approach, hand bookbinding offers the rewarding opportunity to rebind, restore, or refurbish the items in his or her own library. Or it will provide the knowledge that puts the book lover in a position to deal intelligently with any professional binder that he or she might employ.

To the person who wishes to pursue an independent career, hand binding offers a number of advantages—the satisfaction of doing work one enjoys, the freedom that comes with controlling one's own time, and the ability to live almost anywhere.

Hand bookbinding is very much alive and thriving today.

1 The Makeup of the Book

Anyone interested in hand bookbinding is, of course, familiar with the outward appearance of books, but surprisingly few people have any knowledge of the way a book is constructed or of the possible variations in binding styles. Figure 1-1 shows various external parts of a book for tight back and case and Bradel bindings (bindings are described in Chapter 2), and Figure 1-2 indicates the internal parts of book construction. Although this chapter is not a detailed description of the intricacies of book production, it does point out a few of the practices in the making of a book that have significance to the hand bookbinder.

Construction, Pagination, Dating, and Size

For many years, books were printed on sheets of paper large enough to hold a number of pages. The printer's type or plates were so arranged in or on the press that when the sheet was printed and folded, the pages fell into proper numerical sequence. A group of folded pages is referred to as a signature, a section, a gathering, or a quire. The use of the term *signature* reputedly predates the printing press when all books were handwritten and scribes were required to sign the portions for which they were responsible either with their initials or some symbol assigned to them.

With the advent of printing in the fifteenth century, the sheets on which the book was printed were marked in some way on what would be, when folded, the first page of each signature. This mark usually appeared in the center or right-hand corner at the bottom of the page. The pages were marked either with Arabic numerals or letters of the alphabet in proper sequence. If the number of signatures exceeded the number of letters in the alphabet, the letters were repeated in duplicate, triplicate, and so on. There were many variations in this practice. These numbers or letters served as a guide in the folding and collating of the book, and they were useful to the binder in taking a book apart and putting it back together. This marking practice has given way in recent years to a coding on the folded edge of each signature, which shows at a glance, after the pages are folded and gathered, whether they are in proper order (Fig. 1-3).

The pagination of preliminary material, or front matter, such as the preface, introduction, and table of contents, is usually in lowercase Roman numerals. These are sometimes taken into account in numbering the first page of the text. If, for example, the first page of the text is 9, this means that there are 8 pages of preliminary material. This system of numbering is helpful in checking the completeness of a volume. Unfortunately, this system is not in universal use; the first page of text in many books is 1, giving no clue to the number of preliminary pages.

1

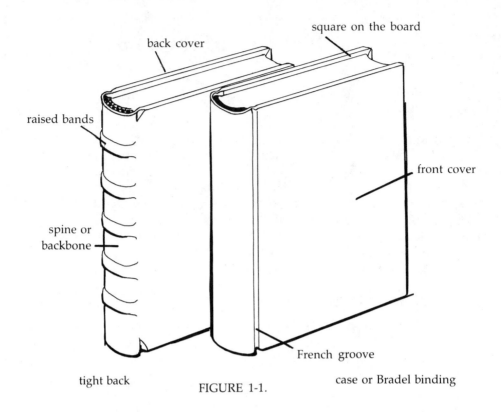

FIGURE 1-1.

Because the choice of binding style should be governed to some extent by the date of publication, hand binders should know something about the dating of books. In many books, the publication date appears on the title page, or, if not there, in the copyright information on the verso of the title page, or at the end of the preface. (Verso is the left-hand page of an open book or manuscript; recto, a right-hand page.)

Copyright laws did not, however, exist until the eighteenth century. Before formal laws, the author's rights were protected in Europe by printing guilds and in England by a common law that protected the author against publication of the work without his or her permission. Once this permission was granted, however, the author ceased to have control of the work. England's first copyright act was passed in 1710. The first American copyright statute was passed in 1790, following Article 1, Section 8, of the U.S. Constitution. Most of the major countries in the world today adhere to the Berne Convention, whose copyright rules became effective in 1887. This represents reciprocal protection for the author or publisher in the countries that signed this agreement (the United States did not).

Occasionally, one finds a puzzling date on the title page of an old volume. (The following key is useful in converting these to more conventional dates: C, 100; IƆ, or D, 500; CIƆ or M, 1,000; IƆƆ 5,000; CCIƆƆ 10,000; IƆƆƆ 50,000; CCCIƆƆƆ 100,000. Thus, CIƆ IƆ CLXXXVIII—1688.

After the French Revolution and France became a republic, some

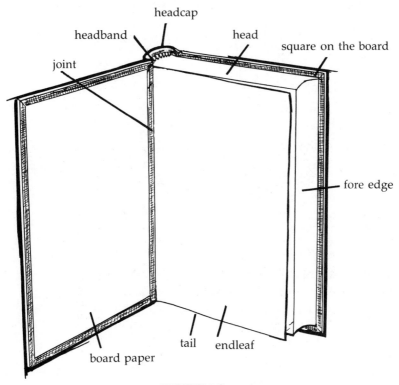

headcap

headband

head

square on the board

joint

fore edge

tail   endleaf

board paper

FIGURE 1-2.

books printed in that country were dated to indicate the age of the republic, for instance, "An. XIII" = 1805, that being the thirteenth year of the republic, which began in 1792 (from Nicholson, *A Manual of the Art of Bookbinding*, see Bibliography under Instructional Manuals).

The book sizes customarily used by catalogers and bibliographers originally referred, not to the actual size of the book, but to the number of times the sheet on which it was printed had been folded. This applied when books were printed on a more or less standard size of paper. For many years, however, paper has been made in a great variety of sizes, and these terms have lost their true meaning. They are used today primarily to indicate the approximate size of a book, regardless of the number of folds or the number of pages in a signature. These terms are listed below. (It should be noted that most library catalog cards carry the size of books in centimeters.)

Broadside A sheet of paper, especially of large size printed on one side only (no standard size).

Folio A sheet of paper folded once to make 2 leaves or 4 pages of a book (half the size of the original sheet).

Quarto A volume printed from sheets folded twice to form 4 leaves or 8 pages; book size about 9 1/2 × 12 inches (24.1 × 30.5 cm); abbr. 4to or 4°.

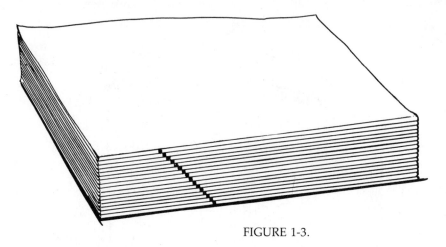

FIGURE 1-3.

Octavo A book size about 6 × 9 inches (15.2 × 22.8 cm) determined by printing on sheets folded to form 8 leaves or 16 pages; abbr. 8vo or 8°.
Duodecimo A book size about 5 × 7 1/2 inches (12.7 × 19 cm) determined by printing on sheets folded to form 12 leaves or 24 pages (4 leaves or 8 pages must be cut off the sheet and folded separately to arrive at this number of pages in a signature); abbr. 12mo or 12°.
Sextodecimo A volume printed from sheets folded to form 16 leaves or 32 pages, approximately 4 × 6 inches (10.1 × 15.2 cm); abbr. 16mo or 16°.

What Is a Rare Book?

Webster gives many definitions for the word *rare*. The ones that seem most applicable to books are *not frequent; unusual; unusually excellent;* and *fine.* The Rare Book Division of one of the country's great libraries uses as a basis for selection the words *important; scarce;* and *in demand.* Meeting these requirements, historically, are books printed in Europe before 1600, in the British Isles before 1640, and in the Americas before 1800. Limited editions that are examples of fine printing and private press books, by definition, are included without regard to publication date.

Much of the ephemeral material published in the past finds its way into rare book collections because it is "not frequent, unusual, or scarce." Few copies of many of these items have survived, due no doubt to the fact that little importance was placed on their value at the time they were issued. Some 2- or 5-pence publications of the early nineteenth century, however, are bringing handsome prices in today's marketplace. Another group that is in demand by those interested in rare books are association copies. An otherwise commonplace volume, carrying the signature of a well-known public figure, becomes "unusual and in demand" overnight.

Many rare book libraries and collectors have different criteria as a basis for selection. They are in all probability, however, governed to some degree by the criteria given above. This brief overview is intended only to give the potential binder some background information that might be helpful in the selection of books to be bound and in reaching a decision as to how they should be treated.

2 Bindings and Book Design

Types of Hand Bindings

There are, broadly speaking, two types of hand bindings: a tight back (sometimes referred to as a fast back) and a hollow back. In a tight back binding, the covering material is attached firmly to the spine of the book. When the book is opened, the covering material on the spine arches with the spine of the book. In a hollow back binding, the covering material is free from the spine. When the book is opened, the spine of the book arches and the spine of the binding lies flat on the table. A case binding, a Bradel, an English split board, and a German tube are all hollow back bindings.

Another distinction between types or styles of bindings are those with a visible joint, or French groove, in which the covering boards are offset from the edge of the spine, and those that have no visible joint and with relatively little space between the edge of the spine and the edge of the board. Those with the visible joint include a case binding, a Bradel, and an English split board. Those without the visible joint include the tight back and the German tube. (Refer to Fig. 1-1 and Fig. 1-2 for some of these distinctions.) Still another variation is between the binding that is built up on the book step-by-step and the one that is prepared in 1 series of steps and the cover made in a separate series; when book and cover are complete, they are brought together. Bindings built up on the book include Bradel, English split board, tight back, and German tube. Only in a case binding are the book and the cover prepared or constructed separately. The table on Binding Characteristics shows the different characteristics of each binding type discussed here.

In this book, instructions are given for three hollow back bindings—case, Bradel, and German tube—and the tight back. The English split board (a hollow back) is well covered in a number of English publications and will not be discussed here. The rest of this chapter includes detailed descriptions of the four styles of binding, with suggestions for appropriate use. These four styles or types of bindings are those most commonly encountered and used by hand binders today. It should be noted, however, that there is some revival of interest in the early bindings of the Coptic period, and some research and work are being done in this area by a number of present-day binders.

Case Binding

A case binding (sometimes called a casing) is a hollow back binding with a visible joint, or French groove. It resembles a hardcover edition binding (one with stiff covers). The basic differences between a machine-edition binding and a handmade case binding are in the treatment of

5

Binding Characteristics

	TIGHT BACK	HOLLOW BACK			
		Bradel	Case	English Split Board	German Tube
Covering material attached to spine	X	—	—	—	—
Covering material free from spine	—	X	X	X	X
Visible joint	—	X	X	X	—
No visible joint	X	—	—	—	X
Bindings built up on book	X	X	—	X	X
Book and cover prepared separately	—	—	X	—	—

the endsheets and in the sewing. In a hand casing, the endsheets are customarily prepared as separate or additional signatures and are sewn along with the book onto tapes. In machine casings, the endsheets routinely consist of folded sheets, which are attached to the first and last signatures of the book by a narrow line of adhesive, and the book is sewn—if at all—without tapes.

The book is prepared in 1 series of steps, and the case—or cover—is made separately. The book is then attached in the case by hinges or pasted-down board papers and pressed between brass-bound boards. The protruding brass edge on these boards, along with the offset covering board, produces the visible joint.

A case binding is the simplest of hardcover bindings. It is a suitable and adequate binding for a large percentage of the books produced in the last half or quarter of the nineteenth century and in the twentieth century. It is not, generally speaking, a proper binding for earlier books, nor would it be appropriate for a book on which the binder wished to execute an elaborate hand-tooled design.

Almost any material suitable for binding can be used for a case binding, with many attractive possibilities. Made cloth or leather headbands are recommended; sewn silk ones seem out of place and pretentious in a binding of this style. When properly constructed, with materials of good quality used, the case is a sound binding for quartos and smaller volumes.

Bradel Binding

A Bradel binding, often referred to as a bonnet or bristol board binding, resembles a case binding in that it has a hollow back and a visible joint. It is, however, built up on the book and is comparable in some respects to the English split board binding. Thought to be of

German origin, it was used in France by Alexis-Pierre Bradel, from whom it gets its name. Little is known about the date of its introduction, but it would probably be appropriate for late nineteenth- and twentieth-century volumes.

The Bradel is considered by some binders to be stronger than a case binding and thus more appropriate for heavy volumes such as reference books that will be subject to frequent and heavy wear. It also is useful when a rounded spine is desired and the paper on which the book is printed is too soft or spongy to hold a normal rounding. Like a case binding, the Bradel can be executed in a variety of materials or combinations, and sewn headbands are not recommended.

German Tube Binding

A German tube binding is a hollow back with no visible joint. It differs from other hollow backs primarily in the construction of the tube, which is routinely made from durable paper and is solidly constructed. It can be executed with a smooth spine or raised bands. Both the tube and the binding are built up on the book. Although generally referred to as of German origin, it is said to have been first used by J. Smits of Zurich, Switzerland, whose students introduced the technique into Germany.

The German tube is a suitable binding for books of the twentieth century. Like the tight back, it is executed primarily in leather or vellum, and its headbands are routinely sewn. Books bound in this style usually open well, although the ease with which a bound book opens is due to some extent to the quality of the paper on which it is printed. This is a durable, well-constructed binding and appropriate for creative designs.

Tight Back Binding

A tight back binding, sometimes referred to as a fast back, has the covering material attached solidly to the spine and has no visible joint. It is built up step-by-step on the book. The tight back is considered by many people, including binders, to be the most durable of hand bindings and considered by some to be the only *true* hand binding.

The tight back is an appropriate binding for most books published over the last few centuries. It can have a smooth spine or raised bands; it is executed almost exclusively in leather or vellum; and its headbands are customarily sewn or worked in either silk or linen thread.

Small-format books bound in this style do not open easily, so its use should generally be restricted to large volumes. The tight back lends itself well to tooled decorations, inlays, onlays, and other ornamentation.

Selecting Books for Binding or Rebinding

The first step in the binding process is the selection of suitable books. Sewn paperbacks are excellent for the beginner. If hard covers are desired, the ideal ones to start with are average-size octavo volumes that need attention; that have no great intrinsic value, but deal with subject matter of interest to the owner; that are in signatures and were originally saddle sewn (sewn through the center fold); that do not require extensive page repair; and that can be completely rebound without destroying a binding of interest.

Do not undertake as a first project the family Bible, Grandma's original cookbook, a volume damaged by a pet puppy, or one that should be restored and not rebound. Examples of books that should be restored, if possible, rather than rebound are first editions, private press books, association and autographed copies, incunabula (books printed before 1500 from movable type), early manuscript volumes, or a volume of any period whose binding is distinctive either for its excellence or as an oddity. (There is a growing belief among conservators that many of these items should not be rebound or restored, but rather preserved in their existing condition in a protective case. This would assume that their projected use is nominal and that they are not in a state of deterioration.) At any rate, only when familiarity with techniques increases and skills improve, is it time for projects of this nature.

If there is any doubt as to the proper treatment of a volume—and give it some thought—wrap the volume carefully in acid-free paper and put it away until some later date. Much of the history of bindings has been destroyed inadvertently because of indiscriminate rebinding.

It is recommended that a beginner select three books that can be carried along together through the various steps. Repeating a step rather quickly is a help in remembering it. And there are a number of stages when the work of one book must stop to allow for drying time or time in the press.

Designing a Binding

Design is "an outline or pattern of the main features of something to be executed." Any object fashioned by people is designed.

After selecting the books to be bound, design the bindings. Give consideration to the quality of the paper and typography, as well as the book's date of publication, size, and anticipated use. Do not, for instance, waste good leather on a book poorly printed on cheap paper. Do not put a cloth case binding on a seventeenth-century volume, or raised bands on a thin book with a long title, or a tight back binding on a small thin book that will be used frequently, or a dainty patterned paper on a somber tome, or a light-colored perishable material on a volume that will receive hard or constant use. Taking these warnings into consideration, decide first on the type of binding (as discussed earlier in this chapter), then on the style—full leather, full cloth, and so on.

Materials Needed

Pleasing combinations of both textures and colors that are in keeping with the character of the book are desirable. If it is difficult to visualize the finished product, make a small sample board or a dummy. Illustrated exhibition catalogs are also an aid in showing how materials or combinations of materials look on a finished binding. (See under Illustrated Works in the Bibliography.)

Once these decisions are made, choose the materials needed and be sure that you have the necessary quantities on hand or know that they are available. Do not begin the work until the materials are assembled. There is often a marked variation in color between two different dye lots. Among the possibilities for covering material are vellum, full or half-leather, full or half-cloth; two-tone in the same material or in combinations of materials, or full paper.

Flyleaves It is desirable that these match as near as possible the book stock in color, texture, and weight.

Board papers and endleaves These can be the same paper as that selected for the flyleaves, or a solid color, or a decorated paper. They should be chosen with the covering material in mind.

Hinges These are customarily made from the same material as that chosen for the cover, or if a two-tone binding, the material selected for the spine.

Headbands Whether leather, cloth, or silk thread, select a color or colors that complement the other materials.

Patch title label For a leather binding, select a leather contrasting in color to the binding itself. It should, however, be the same type of leather, unless a definite contrast in texture is part of the design. For a cloth binding, this can be either leather or paper. If leather, it is customary to match leather headbands—if any.

Title The selection of type and titling is discussed in detail in Chapter 8; however, some thought should be given to this now, because the selection has a bearing on the binding style. For example, if the title is too long to fit well horizontally in one space between raised bands, then raised bands should not be used. Vertical titling between traditionally spaced raised bands is not generally considered an acceptable practice, although it has been done.

Finishing Although this, too, is described in detail in Chapter 8, it is a good idea at this time to make a preliminary sketch of any proposed tooling or other decorative motif in order to check the availability of the tools and materials.

Binding Styles

The definitions of 3 styles of bindings—one-quarter, one-half, and three-quarter—discussed here vary somewhat, so a number of authoritative sources were consulted for a majority opinion. The sources were 2 dictionaries (Century and Webster), 2 glossaries (Carter and Glaister), and 3 bookbinding manuals (Cockerell, Diehl, and Town). With the exception of the dictionaries, these sources are listed in the Bibliography.

Quarter binding was defined by only 5 of the sources, and 3 agreed that it is a two-tone binding. The material covering the spine comes over onto the boards, and the remainder of the boards are covered in a different material. Two sources said the material covering the spine must cover the boards 1/4 to 1/3 of their width.

All 8 sources defined the one-half binding. Three described it in substance as a binding where the leather (cloth) covers the back (spine) and only part of the sides, the rest of the sides being covered with a different material. This is similar to 3 definitions given for a quarter binding. One gave a similar definition, but added "and sometimes the corners." Two said "leather covers the spine and 1/4 to 1/3 of the board width with leather corners or a fore edge strip." Two agreed in principle that it is a book having the back (spine) and corners covered in one material and the sides in another.

Three-quarter binding was defined by 5 of the sources. Two said that it is similar to a half binding, except that a larger portion of the material covering the spine extends onto the boards and corners. Two gave a similar definition, but did not mention corners. And one said "material covering the spine extends on to the boards for 1/3 their width."

The conclusion is that there is no overriding majority in favor of any one definition for any of these terms. But some standardization of terminology seems highly desirable in this area, not as much for the binder, perhaps, as for the cataloger, bibliographer, book collector, and book dealer.

3 Equipping a Workshop

The primary considerations in setting up a shop are the ambitions and ultimate objectives of the binder. If these objectives do not extend beyond a part-time avocation as an amateur, satisfying work can be done successfully with a relatively small amount of equipment. When time and efficiency are not of overriding concern, many things can be improvised that would be impractical for the professional binder.

When possible, the beginner should visit a hand bookbinding shop and discuss possible equipment purchases with an experienced binder. If, however, your information must come from a manual, first read the manual completely, then decide what type or style of binding is most appealing and buy only the equipment necessary to produce it. As interest and experience increase, additions can be made. If the objective is a professional career, buy the most efficient equipment obtainable. Good equipment, if treated with reasonable care, has a long life. The cost prorated over a period of years generally makes it both a modest and a good investment.

Space is, perhaps, the next consideration. Obviously, do not buy equipment if you have no space to house it. The space, large enough to house the equipment, should also be dry, adequately heated, equipped with several conveniently located electrical outlets, and reasonably accessible to running water.

At least one good sturdy table or work surface, about 4 or 5 feet long and 2 feet (1.2 or 1.5 m × .6 m) wide, is desirable in a one-person shop. Its surface should be smooth and not easily damaged. Height should be such that it is comfortable to work at either in a standing or sitting position. If a person is, for example, 5 feet 4 inches tall (162.5 cm), a table that is 35 inches (89 cm) and a stool or chair 26 inches (66 cm) in height serve well.

Adequate storage space for materials is not only desirable but economical, for materials properly housed remain in usable condition for a long time. Stored improperly, materials soon become dirty, wrinkled, faded, and unusable. Boards and papers are best stored flat. Open shelves are adequate for boards; blueprint cabinets are good for paper. A series of large tubes, 3 or 4 inches (7.6 or 10.1 cm) in diameter, work well for the storage of book cloth and leather, both of which should be stored rolled, with the finished or right side inside. Shallow shelves or some type of cabinet are useful for the storage of miscellaneous supplies and work in progress. Pegboard, with its variety of hooks, keeps small tools in order and accessible.

And last, but by no means least, is money. If funds are limited, make purchases accordingly. Under tight money circumstances, however, it is doubly important that every purchase be a wise and sound investment.

Most, if not all, of the items described in this chapter are available either new or secondhand. When looking for heavy equipment, first check the Yellow Pages of the local telephone book for dealers in binding, box making, or printing equipment who are nearby. The expense involved in crating and shipping presses, cutters, and other items for any appreciable distance can sometimes almost equal its cost. A want ad in the local newspaper for heavy equipment or small hand bookbinding tools sometimes brings rewarding results. Due to overzealous purchasing, bookbinding equipment is doubtless stored in many attics. Some effort and ingenuity may prove well worth the time spent.

The items pictured (except for the plough) and described here are in the author's workshop and represent some 40 years of accumulation. There is no intent to imply that this is the only equipment available or that it is the best. Rather it is to give an idea of what types of things one should look for. Also included are some suggestions for improvising certain pieces of equipment. The equipment is divided into the following groups: heavy equipment, wooden equipment, gluing and pasting equipment, tools for paring leather, and miscellaneous items. In general, their use is discussed in this chapter, but in some cases, where a specific technique or operation represents its primary use, it is listed in the appropriate chapter along with the technique. All tools used specifically for finishing are pictured and described at the beginning of Chapter 8.

Heavy Equipment

This section covers board shears, guillotine, plough and press, French press, standing press, job backer, stamping press, and paring machine. Of these pieces, the only 2 that are highly desirable—if not essential—in a small home workshop are board shears and a standing press.

Board shears (Fig. 3-1) This is a paper cutter that works on the principle of a pair of scissors. The blades or knives are ground with a rather broad edge. One blade is attached to the board in a fixed position; the other blade is movable, thus providing the cutting action. Many of these cutters are equipped with a pressure bar, which holds the material to be cut in position, preventing it from shifting when the blade strikes it. They are also equipped with 2 gauges, 1 on the board or table; the other, or outside gauge, is on the right-hand side of the knife. Attached in a fixed position to the end of the board (where the operator stands) is a stop, which is usually marked off in inches and serves also as a ruler. The 2 gauges are parallel to the cutting edge, and the stop is at right angles to all 3 of these. Both gauges can be set and locked, or tightened, for repetitive cutting.

These cutters are made in a wide range of sizes, in floor and table models, and with the pressure bar controlled by a foot pedal or a hand lever. The 2 gauges are desirable features, and the pressure bar is almost essential in the accurate cutting of binder's board.

The smaller cutters, sometimes referred to as photographic cutters,

FIGURE 3-1. Board Shears.

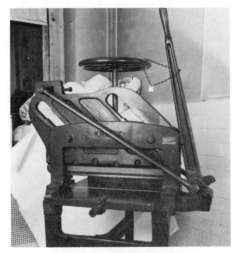

FIGURE 3-2. Guillotine.

which have no pressure bar and no real gauges, are satisfactory for cutting lightweight materials. A large shears will cut anything from the thinnest tissue to heavy binder's board. It is probably the most versatile and the most used piece of equipment in a hand binding shop. When properly adjusted and properly used, it is a very accurate cutting device.

Guillotine (Fig. 3-2) This is a paper cutter and is used by most hand bookbinders primarily for cutting the edges of a book after it has been sewn and the spine glued. (Its use is described in Chapter 6 on Treatment of Edges.) The knife is ground to a very keen, sharp edge, and even a small machine of this type has great cutting power. Every safety precaution should be taken in using it. Do not attempt to use it without first getting proper instruction from someone experienced in its operation.

Plough and press This piece of equipment has been used by hand bookbinders for several centuries and is probably the oldest cutting device other than a knife. It has a heavy lying press, one side of which rests on a sturdy wooden stand commonly known as a tub. In some, the framework of the stand is open; in others it is enclosed, forming a boxlike structure that serves to catch the cuttings when the plough is in use. On 1 jaw of this press is a channel, made by the attachment of 2 strips of hardwood. The left-hand jaw of the plough moves in this channel. The plough is a smaller press with a center-threaded wooden screw with a handle, which controls the movement of the knife. Provision is made in the jaw on the right-hand side to take the knife in a horizontal position; this is an inset metal channel fixed in position so that the exposed side of the knife is flush with the bottom of the jaw. The plough is moved in only 1 direction with the hands, and the wooden screw advances the knife as the cutting progresses. For a clean-cut edge, the knife must be kept sharp and properly adjusted.

The author has had virtually no experience in working with a plough. But in checking through the literature in the field, the author found that Laurence Town, in *Bookbinding by Hand*, seems to give the most detailed

FIGURE 3-3. French Press.   FIGURE 3-4. Standing Press.

instructions for its use (see Bibliography). Many binders swear by them as the only way to cut the edges of a book properly—and many swear at them. Dard Hunter, in *Early Papermaking* (see Bibliography), said: "When the deckle edges were left undisturbed by the printer they often suffered at the hands of the binder, . . . The weapon with which the binder dealt the most deadly blows was the 'plough,' with which he cut away the margins, placing the printing in a false position on the page of the book, and often denuding the volumes of a portion of the very text."

The plough is reputedly an all-purpose cutting device that serves both as a board shears and a guillotine. It is neither recommended nor not recommended. With the plough removed, the lying press serves as a backer and as a general utility press.

French press (Fig. 3-3) This is a standing press constructed largely of wood; in design it is reputedly a very old press. Its threaded screw and the wheel that controls it are metal. The percussion feature permits much greater pressure than can be had with the average standing press. It is also a handsome piece of furniture.

Standing press (Fig. 3-4) This press is made in a variety of styles and sizes. Some are all metal and others a combination of metal and wood. A press with a 12 × 18 inch (30.5 × 45.7 cm) base platen and 12 inches (30.5 cm) or more of daylight between this and the movable plate or platen that is controlled by the threaded screw is an average and useful size. The movable platen should have some kind of guide rods or grooves to hold it steady in its up-and-down motions.

FIGURE 3-5. Job Backer.

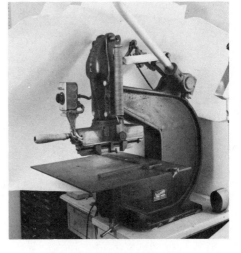

FIGURE 3-6. Stamping Press.

Job backer (Fig. 3-5) This is a useful piece of equipment, particularly in a professional shop. It consists of a heavy metal vise. One jaw is fixed in position, and the other is movable and controlled by a threaded screw with a wheel on the free end. The whole thing is mounted on a wooden stand, or if the stand is metal, the stand and the fixed jaw are cast in 1 piece. The work done in it can be done, however, in a lying press or a German backing press.

Stamping press (Fig. 3-6) This machine is used primarily for titling and die stamping. It does in essence what can be done with a hand pallet and type or handle letters. A number of makes and models are available. Desirable features are accurate gauges, thermostatically controlled heat, ability to adjust the pressure, and capacity for stamping more than one line at a time. Its use is described in Chapter 8.

Paring machine (Fig. 3-7) This is sometimes referred to as a skiving machine. One of the best-known types is the German-made Fortuna. It is designed primarily to pare edges and small pieces of leather. It has a cylindrical or circular knife that revolves at high speed and an emery feed roll that carries the leather into contact with the knife, thus splitting the leather. It is readily adjustable and can be set to thin a piece of leather evenly or produce a gradual thinning or bevelled edge. It pares rapidly and evenly when properly adjusted and is a time-saver in a professional shop.

Wooden Equipment

The pieces of equipment discussed in this section are available in varying sizes. The sizes noted here are average or usual.

Sewing frame (Fig. 3-8) This consists of a flat board, 2 uprights, and a crossbar (24 inches, or 60.9 cm, between uprights). Its construction has changed little over the centuries. The basic purpose of this frame is to

FIGURE 3-7. Paring Machine.

FIGURE 3-8. Sewing Frame. (1) Lay cords.

hold the tapes or cords (see lay cords, Fig. 3-8) on which a book is to be sewn in a fixed and upright position. The threaded posts permit the raising or lowering of the crossbar to which the tapes are attached, and the cutout area in the board keeps the tapes in a vertical position. A satisfactory substitute can be easily fashioned by anyone reasonably handy with woodworking tools; the threaded posts are not an essential feature.

Lying press and German backing press (Fig. 3-9) These presses are vises (18 inches, or 45.7 cm, between screws). They are used primarily for the backing of a book. They are also useful for simply holding a book firmly in position when working on its spine or edges, although they are unnecessarily heavy for many jobs.

Finishing press (Fig. 3-9) This is a very useful press (14 inches, or 35.5 cm, between screws). It is relatively light and easy to handle, and its depth makes it particularly useful in the titling and tooling of a book spine. It is not heavily enough built, however, to be used in the backing of a book. Two pieces of 3/4 inch (1.9 cm) plywood, about 12 inches (30.5 cm) long and 7 inches (17.7 cm) wide, and 2 large C-clamps make a reasonable substitute for this and the lying and German backing presses, although they are not too easy to work with.

Pressboards (Fig. 3-10) These are rectangular pieces of wood. Traditionally they have been made of seasoned cherry, 3/4 inch (1.9 cm) thick, with the ends routed out and a small piece of wood (going in the opposite grain direction) set in to prevent warping. Three-quarter inch (1.9 cm) plywood—preferably a hardwood—if cut smoothly and accurately makes satisfactory pressboards. Tempered Masonite (1/4 inch) also works well; if both surfaces are smooth, they are more useful. Several pair of boards in a range of sizes are desirable, such as 6 × 9, 8 × 11, 12 × 18 inches (15.2 × 22.8, 20.3 × 27.9, 30.5 × 45.7 cm).

Brass-bound boards (Fig. 3-10) These are similar to pressboards with the addition of a protruding brass edge about 1/16 inch deep. They are

FIGURE 3-9. Wooden Equipment. (1) Lying Press,
(2) German Backing Press, (3) Finishing Press.

FIGURE 3-10. Pressing Equipment. (1) Pressboards, (2) Brass-bound
boards, (3) Gilding boards, (4) Zinc sheets.

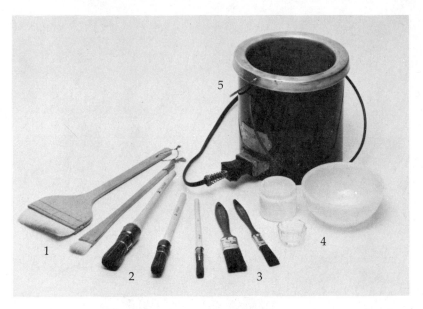

FIGURE 3-11. Equipment for Pasting and Gluing. (1) Japanese brushes, (2) Glue brushes, (3) Paste brushes, (4) Paste bowls, (5) Glue pot.

made with all 4 edges bound in brass, which extends beyond the surface of the board on both sides, and they can be purchased with brass on only 1 edge, which meets most requirements. These are certainly desirable, if not actually necessary, in the production of a case binding. One pair 8 × 11 inches (20.3 × 27.9 cm) will serve the needs of most small shops. This, however, varies with the type of work planned.

Backing boards These are narrow wedge-shaped boards with the broad edge bevelled. They are used by many binders in the backing of a book.

Gilding boards (Fig. 3-10) These are similar in shape to backing boards except that the broad edge is straight or square. They are useful in the treatment of the edges of books, particularly the fore edge.

Gluing and Pasting Equipment

Glue pot (Fig. 3-11) A thermostatically controlled electric pot is the most satisfactory. It maintains a constant temperature ranging between 140° and 150° F (60°–66°C). They are made in a variety of sizes from 1-quart capacity up. This is adequate for the small shop, for it is advisable to make fresh glue frequently. A double boiler serves as a satisfactory substitute, but it should be used in conjunction with a cooking thermometer such as that used in making candy. It is important not to overheat glue.

Glue brushes (Fig. 3-11) The best glue brushes are made from pig bristles, round in shape, and wire-bound. These are made in a variety of sizes and are sold by number. A no. 2 is 1/4 inch in diameter, no. 4, 3/8 inch; no. 8, 5/8 inch; no. 14, 1 inch (2.5 cm); and so on. A range of sizes is desirable.

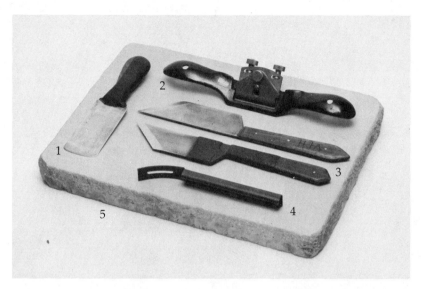

FIGURE 3-12. Tools for Paring Leather. (1) French paring knife,
(2) Spoke shave, (3) German or English paring knife (right and
left handed), (4) Skife, (5) Lithographic stone.

Paste bowls (Fig. 3-11) Almost any type of bowl with a wide top that
holds approximately 12–16 ounces (354–473 ml) is suitable. For small
amounts of mixed pastes, use discarded cosmetic jars that have smooth
vertical inside walls—for easy cleaning—and are deep enough for a
small brush to stand in.

Paste brushes (Fig. 3-11) One inch (2.5 cm) flat paintbrushes are satisfactory, and some type of stiff artist's brush about 1/4 inch in width is
handy for small tip-on jobs.

Tools for Paring Leather

German or English paring knife (Fig. 3-12) These knives have a diagonal cutting edge that is bevelled on the front or top and flat on the back
or the side that rests on the leather when in use. They are designed
primarily for edge paring. The diagonal cutting edge can be ground for
use with either the right or left hand. The German knife is usually
equipped with wooden handles; the English is a bare piece of steel.

French knife (Fig. 3-12) This knife is also bevelled on the top side and
flat on the back. Its rounded cutting edge is designed for use in the
overall thinning of a piece of leather.

Spokeshave (Fig. 3-12) This is just what its name implies, a woodworking tool. It is, however, used by many binders in the overall thinning of
leather. It has a removable blade for ease in sharpening, but it is not as
expendable or easily replaceable as many removable blades. The depth
of cut can be adjusted.

Skife (Fig. 3-12) This is an all-metal tool curved at one end. Its cutting
edge consists of removable narrow razor blades, similar to those used in
an injector razor. It serves as an all-purpose parer.

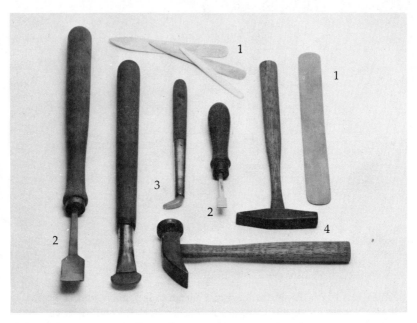

FIGURE 3-13. General Tools. (1) Bonefolders, (2) Metal burnishers,
(3) Agate burnishers, (4) Backing hammers.

Small Tools and Other Items

Backing hammer (Fig. 3-13) Some type of hammer with a rounded head
is needed in the backing of a book. These hammers are made in a
variety of weights and shapes; many are unnecessarily heavy for hand
work. Select one that feels comfortable in the hand.

Bonefolders (Fig. 3-13) These are shaped pieces of bone, as the name
implies. They are fashioned in a variety of sizes and shapes and have
many uses. A large one is useful in the folding of paper, smoothing out
slight wrinkles when pasting and gluing; and a small one is helpful in
turning corners, setting headcaps, and in drawing off lines to be tooled.

Burnishers There are two types of burnishers, metal and agate (Fig.
3-13). Like most small tools, they are both made in various shapes and
sizes. Metal burnishers are used hot in ironing out small wrinkles,
building up a German tube, and polishing leather. One about 1 inch
(2.5 cm) in width is a good average size for many jobs; for polishing
leather a wider one, 2 to 2 1/2 inches (5 to 6.3 cm), is more serviceable.
Agate burnishers are used primarily in the polishing of book edges after
gilding; an inch (2.5 cm) in width is a good average size.

Dividers (Fig. 3-14) A pair of 5 or 6 inches (12.7 × 15.2 cm) long with fine
points and an adjustable screw for setting will serve most purposes. They
have many uses in checking and transferring measurements.

Knives Several types of knives are desirable. A mat or utility knife (Fig.
3-15) is good for cutting paper and board; its blades are easily changed
or replaced, thus ensuring a sharp edge when needed. A surgeon's
scalpel (Fig. 3-15), also with replaceable blades, is excellent for jobs that
require a thin, sharp blade. A no. 4 handle and a no. 23 blade make a

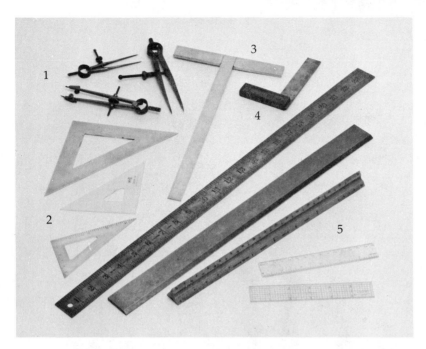

FIGURE 3-14. Tools for Measuring. (1) Dividers, (2) Triangles, (3) T-square,
(4) Right-angle square, (5) Rulers and straightedges.

serviceable combination. For safety's sake, scalpel blades should be changed with a pair of thin-nosed pliers. The traditional bench knife (Fig. 3-15) has many uses where extreme sharpness is not required, or, of course, it can be ground or honed to a very keen edge.

Rulers (Fig. 3-14) Rulers of varying lengths are useful, and at least one with the metric scale should be on hand. If made of steel, these can also serve as a straightedge in cutting.

Scissors (Fig. 3-15) The use of scissors is obvious. One 8 inch (20.3 cm) pair with offset handles and a small pair with fine points should serve the needs of most binders.

Straightedge (Fig. 3-14) This is just what its name implies, a straight-edge. One made of stainless steel is the most useful and versatile. Plastic ones are useful for drawing lines, but they should not be used for cutting against. Eighteen or 24 inches (45.7 or 57.6 cm) in length will serve most purposes.

Triangles (Fig. 3-14) Several sizes are useful. A small right-angle one (Fig. 3-14) is especially useful in mitering corners, and if made of metal, it can be used to cut against.

T-square (Fig. 3-14) This tool is useful in checking right angles, drawing parallel lines, and, if metal, as a straightedge. A rigid stainless steel or chrome-plated T-square with the crosspiece heavier than the upright is preferable to one made of plastic or aluminum.

Band nippers (Fig. 3-15) This is a plierlike tool whose chief use is in shaping and sharpening raised cords after backing and raised bands after the leather has been applied.

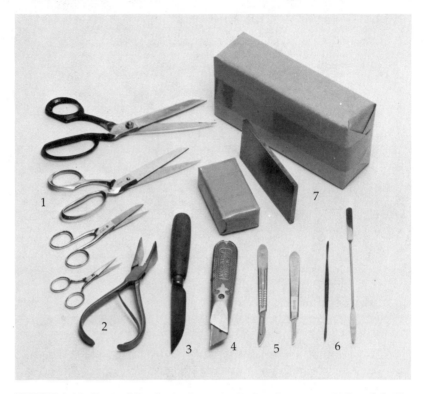

FIGURE 3-15. General Tools. (1) Scissors, (2) Band nippers, (3) Bench knife, (4) Mat knife, (5) Scalpels, (6) Spatulas, (7) Weights (lead, brass, brick).

Spatulas (Fig. 3-15) Several sizes are useful, particularly in lifting materials where a rigid, thin blade with a dull edge is needed.

Plate glass A piece is useful in pasting guard strips. Try using a medicine cabinet shelf.

Weights A number of weights (Fig. 3-15) of various sizes are desirable. Lithographic stones (Fig. 3-12) make excellent weights and are also a good surface on which to pare leather. Ordinary bricks wrapped in newspaper and covered with kraft paper are useful. Lead makes good small weights. The size and shape are not particularly important; they, like bricks, should be wrapped.

Zinc sheets (Fig. 3-10) About 20–25 gauge and 8 × 11 inches (20.3 × 27.9 cm) are handy when the signatures of an entire book require pressing.

Shallow pan A rectangular pan, such as a roasting pan, is necessary for the soaking or washing of pages.

4 Materials and Their Use

One of the basic requirements of good handcraftspeople is that they know—or learn to know—the materials with which they work—their quality, durability, appropriateness, and reaction when handled. They must also know what materials are available and where they can be purchased.

Centuries ago, when the choice of materials was limited and all were made by hand, there was no real problem of selection. The binders used what was available or what they could produce themselves. Updating the picture, the situation has changed considerably. Handmade materials of known quality are becoming increasingly scarce, and hand binders are confronted with a wide choice of materials of unknown quality in almost every phase of their work.

In general, the experienced hand bookbinder realizes that materials of acknowledged quality and durability should be used in his or her work, and the binder doubtless has, through trial and error, built up a personal list of supply sources, seeking help only when the source of some particular item "dries up." The cost of the most expensive and presumably the best materials is small when compared with the knowledge, time, and effort required to produce even the simplest hand binding.

A student, studying with a teacher, usually relies on the teacher for materials or for information as to where they can be purchased. The beginner, attempting to learn alone, probably turns first to the list of supply sources in the manual that he or she is using and then to local suppliers. Unless beginners know reasonably well what they are looking for, they can easily be misled, not only by advertisements but by well-intentioned, but not necessarily well-informed, clerks as well.

A selected list of supply sources appears in the Appendix. In using it, bear in mind that addresses can change in a relatively short period. Even the oldest and best-established firms merge or move, and younger, less stable concerns seem constantly on the go. Telephone directories are probably the most accessible and reliable sources for current addresses. Almost all local telephone offices and many public libraries keep on file a number of current out-of-town directories. Information operators will not give addresses, and telephone numbers frequently remain the same although addresses have changed. It is always a good idea to verify addresses before placing orders.

It is also a good practice to keep a record of all materials purchased: name and address of the supplier, description and name of the material, date purchased, and price. Putting the acquisition date on papers, binder's boards, leathers, and such other items that might be in stock for sometime also proves helpful in the long run.

In this chapter, materials commonly used by the hand bookbinder are discussed. An attempt has been made to give some identifiable information about them as to quality, sizes, weights, how packaged or sold, and the like to serve as a guide in locating suitable materials. Most of the materials listed here can be bought in small quantity from retail bookbinding supply houses or packaged from the manufacturer or a distributor. If not available from these, a suggested source is noted.

Leather

Traditionally, leather has been an important covering material for books. For centuries it was apparently available in sufficient quantity, it was easy to work with, lent itself readily to tooled decoration both blind and gold, and in its early use was a strong and durable material. It is, today, perhaps the most sought-after and the least understood of all hand bookbinding materials. Many people believe that no books are quite so beautiful or elegant as those bound in leather and decorated in gold.

The term *genuine leather* stamped on so many items currently available really only means that the product is made from the hair or grain side of an animal skin or hide. The manufacturer who so stamps the product hopes, perhaps, that the term will imply elegance to the consumer, although no such claim is actually made. Leather carrying this stamp can, of course, be the finest of leathers, although these seldom require assurance. The term, however, can just as honestly be applied to the top split of a cow hide, artificially embossed, and pigmented to look like goat, pig, alligator, or any other animal that is extant or extinct.

Both the composition of animal hides or skins and the chemicals used in their tanning are complex, and a book on bookbinding is not the place to describe in detail these many complexities. General information about the production of leather does, however, have significance in a work of this kind.

The first thing that should be understood about leather is that it is not just tanned, but that it is tanned to meet the specific requirements of the many manufacturers who fashion it into consumer goods. There are in common use today several basic tanning methods—alum, chrome, vegetable, and combination tannages such as alum-vegetable or chrome-vegetable. The skins are first treated with a liming solution of varying strengths, followed by one or more of a great variety of tanning agents, or tannins, and added syntans, governed by the desired end product.

Today, most of the leather tanned, except for industrial uses in the form of pulley belts and such, goes into the production of items that by their very nature have a relatively short useful life. Thus, in the tanning, dyeing, and finishing of these leathers, appearance often, and quite reasonably, takes precedence over durability. One does not, for instance, buy a pair of boots in anticipation of using them for a lifetime and bequeathing them to an heir. Books, however, are leather-bound in the hope that they will survive indefinitely. It is desirable—in fact, necessary—if modern leather bindings are to survive for centuries, as their early predecessors have done, that the leather used in their production be tanned in a manner that reasonably will ensure its longevity.

Leather bindings held up very well for many centuries before the first quarter of the nineteenth. Leather tanned in the second quarter of the nineteenth century became increasingly susceptible to rapid deterioration. This deterioration manifested itself in three ways: Calf skins, thought to have been tanned with oak bark as the tanning agent, became very dry and hard—almost horny; the top surface of other leathers cracked and scaled off in small pieces; and still others were reduced to a red powdery dust, commonly referred to as "red rot."

In England, concern was expressed about these conditions as early as 1840. Professor James Faraday conducted one of the earliest and probably the first serious study of the causes of leather decay. His findings, reported in 1842, sparked further interest and brought about a number of individual and informal research studies. After a few years, these individual researchers realized that the problem was far more serious than originally thought and that organized help from experts was needed. The Society of Arts in London was prevailed upon to undertake a thorough investigation. A committee was formed composed of leather manufacturers, leather dealers, librarians, bookbinders, and members of the society. After some years of research, the findings of the committee were published in 1901, and this report has served as the foundation for most of the subsequent research on bookbinding leathers.

According to the report, the type of skin and the tanning agents used had some significance, but of overriding importance—and the chief culprit in leather deterioration—was the introduction of sulfuric acid in the tanning process or in the dyeing, where it added brilliance and clarity to the colors. With this knowledge, English tanners, who were represented on the research committee, agreed to undertake the vegetable tanning of leather without the use of sulfuric acid. In the various tests made by the committee, goatskins stood out as one of the most durable of the leathers tested. Goatskins imported from Africa in a cured or pickled state were tanned and dyed in England according to the recommendations of the committee.

So, with the problem of leather deterioration "solved," binders used these newly tanned skins with assurance and complacency. It was discovered, however, in a relatively short period of time that these leathers, which had been so conscientiously produced, were deteriorating at only a slightly slower rate than the leathers that had been produced before all the concern and research. Continued study uncovered the fact that these skins, which had left the tannery with a satisfactorily high pH, when tested some years later, showed a lower pH, or a more acid condition (see the Appendix). The acid condition indicated only one thing: In the course of time, the skin had undergone some chemical change. It was generally agreed that this change was brought about by the absorption of sulfur dioxide from the fumes in the air. The iron impurities, apparently present in all tanned skins, served as a catalyst in causing a chemical reaction between the sulfur dioxide (SO_2) and the moisture in the air, producing sulfurous acid (H_2SO_3). Further exposure to atmospheric conditions converted the H_2SO_3 to H_2SO_4, or sulfuric acid.

In the early 1930s, R. Faraday Innes began to study this problem at the request of the British Leather Manufacturers' Association. His findings showed that leather tanned before 1800 had remained chemically inert; it still contained certain water-soluble salts that were not present in the more recently tanned skins. The conclusion was that these soluble salts, or nontans, had protected the leather from chemical attack, and that in the more recent tannages, the salts had been dissolved out either in the washing of the skins preparatory to dyeing or in the change from dyeing by sponging to "drum" dyeing, which required complete immersion in the dyeing solution. Innes discovered that the equivalent of the protective salts inherent in the skin could be returned to it by sponging or spraying with a 7 percent aqueous solution of potassium lactate. He also developed the Peroxide or P.I.R.A. accelerated test (see the Appendix), which when applied to a sample of vegetable-tanned leather will show within a week whether the leather is resistant to sulfuric acid. If a skin resists this test, or shows no adverse effects as a result of it, that particular skin is considered durable.

Between 1933 and 1936, 300 books were bound in a variety of leathers, some buffered and some left untreated. They were placed on open shelves in the British Museum Library. In 1945, the books were inspected, and the leathers that had been treated with potassium lactate seemed to have held up very well. So again it appeared that the problem was solved. This resulted in Plenderleith's *Preservation of Leather Bookbindings* (see Bibliography), which placed faith in the P.I.R.A. test and advocated the use of potassium lactate. In 1970, 35 years after the books were bound, they were again inspected, and the P.I.R.A. test was shown to be an unreliable guide to long-term durability.

Current research shows that sumac-tanned goatskins are the most durable, that potassium lactate should be used only on vegetable-tanned leathers, and that reducing the thickness of a skin by half reduces its strength by 5/6. Research also brought to light other interesting information, which perhaps has more significance for the leather chemist than for the bookbinder, but it does make this complex problem more understandable. No two skins taken from animals of approximately the same age in the same herd have exactly the same chemical makeup. The climate in which the animal is raised has a direct bearing on the type of leather produced from its skin. The skin of an animal raised in a temperate or hot climate produces a firmer, stronger leather than does one raised in a cold climate, where self-preservation means that it will develop longer hair and a fattier skin for warmth. Diet seems to have some significance, but its exact role is difficult to appraise. More understandable to the layperson, and perhaps of more relevance to the bookbinder, is the fact that young animals produce skins of a smoother texture in which the natural grain is less pronounced; these skins are also thinner by nature, so they require less paring (or thinning). The skin of older animals, the goat, for instance, has a much deeper and coarser grain, particularly in the area of the backbone. This is often so different from the rest of the skin that it cannot be used for bookbinding.

Alum-tawed skins reputedly hold up very well. Tawing, however, is not recognized as a true tannage for it consists of applying alum and salt to the skin. Its durability is thought in part to be due to its high salt content. Chrome-tanned skins are also durable. They are less subject to deterioration from atmospheric conditions and more resistant to molds and mildew than are vegetable-tanned leathers. They do not, however, absorb moisture readily, are intractable to work with, and difficult to tool by hand. So, from the hand bookbinder's point of view, they are not desirable. The combination chrome-vegetable tannage holds some promise for suitable bookbinding leather. If the least desirable characteristics in both methods of tanning can be suppressed and the advantages in each brought out, a good, durable product would reasonably be the end result.

Although much has been learned over the years, research chemists seem to agree that no leathers tanned today can be unqualifiedly considered durable over a long period of time, and that there is still need for research in this area. Unfortunately, there is little commercial interest in the longevity of leather because the consumer market for such leathers is so small. Any research will doubtless have to be funded with public or foundation monies.

To encourage further research, and thus hasten the arrival of durable leathers, bookbinders and others concerned with the problem should let their interests be known when purchasing leather. A known demand may bring about fund-raising to continue the necessary research.

Bookbinding leathers are generally sold by the skin and priced by the square foot. In determining the number of square feet in a given skin, all irregularities in shape are included. It would be difficult to arrive at a figure without the use of a measuring machine built for this purpose. This machine consists of a series of closely spaced wheels, which revolve as the skin is passed under them. The revolutions are picked up by a battery of fewer and larger wheels, and, finally, the total footage is recorded on a single dial.

For the beginner or the amateur whose production will not be great, small skins are probably more desirable, for the binder can purchase a greater variety of colors or types of leather without undue expense. For the professional binder, larger skins are considered a better buy. Two average-size octavo volumes or 1 quarto can be cut from a flawless 4 foot (1.2 m) skin, and the 3 volumes can be produced from a 7 foot (2.1 m) skin, if it has no major flaws. The cuttings or scraps are useful for half-leather bindings, labels, headbands, inlays, onlays, and such.

Books have been bound, and probably will continue to be, in the skins of a great number of animals, tanned in a variety of ways. Among them are artificially grained alligator (it is illegal to hunt alligators in the United States), deer, horse, kangaroo, ostrich, seal, shark, sheep, and skunk. With the exception of sheep, these skins are not generally tanned with the bookbinder in mind, so unless there is some particular reason to use them, it is not advisable to do so. Sheep is not recommended because of its softness and its tendency to scuff readily. It is also a good idea to stay away from pigmented and artificially grained or embossed leathers. Their surfaces are resistant to moisture, making them difficult to work with.

The more conventional and most commonly tanned leathers for book-binding are listed below.

Calfskin As its name implies, it is the skin of a calf. It has a smooth surface with very little evidence of graining. Calfskin is available in varying thicknesses and in a variety of colors. The skins range in size from about 8 to 12 square feet (.74 to 1.1 sq m).

Chieftan This is the trade name for a type of goatskin tanned in Scotland. It is fairly thick and coarsely grained and available in a variety of colors. The skins range in size from 7 to 9 square feet (.63 to .81 sq m).

Levant Originally from Levant, this is the skin of a large goat and deeply grained. Over the years it has been considered by many binders to be the most elegant of the goatskins. Unless greatly thinned (which no leather should be), its use should be restricted to large volumes. It is produced in a variety of colors, and the skins range in size from 9 to 12 square feet (.81 to 1.1 sq m).

Morocco A sumac-tanned goatskin originally from Morocco. This is an evenly grained, firm, and flexible leather. It is believed to have been prepared first by the Moors. Today, morocco is a generic name meaning any goatskin or skin embossed to look like morocco. There is no readily available information as to the size of real or true morocco skins or where they can be obtained.

Niger This is a goatskin tanned in Nigeria. The graining is rather uneven, as is the dyeing. It has a limited color range—natural or buff, red in varying hues, and green, which is rarer than the other 2. They range in size from 4 to 7 square feet (1.2 to 2 sq m), but are not in plentiful supply.

Oasis niger These are Nigerian goatskins shipped in a pickled state to England, where they are tanned and dyed. They are considered by many binders to be the most desirable of the goatskins. Their graining is somewhat shallow or smooth and somewhat irregular, and they sometimes have scars or blemishes indicative of the animal's unsuccessful encounter with a thorny bush or a barbed fence. They are produced in a wide choice of colors, and range in size from about 4 to 7 square feet (1.2 to 2 sq m).

Pigskin Alum-tawed skins are the only pigskins generally used by binders. They are produced in limited quantities and not always available. Pigs raised for their hides are reputedly kept in enclosures that present no physical hazards and are said to be washed daily. The skins are rather evenly grained and can easily be identified by the hair follicles that penetrate the entire skin. When held up, light can be seen through these pinlike holes. This is one of the most durable of leathers in its undyed state. It is heavy and tough to work. Its use should be confined to large volumes where it will require minimum paring. Because of the many little holes in the skin, paring weakens it greatly. The undyed skins are a deep buff in color, and they range in size from 8 to 15 square feet (.72 to 1.3 sq m).

Many of these skins are produced abroad and are available through suppliers in their country of tannage or through bookbinding supply houses in the United States that have distributorships for the products from certain tanneries. Domestic leathers, although few, if any, are presently considered suitable for fine work, are also available through bookbinding supply houses, dealers in leather, and stores selling craft supplies.

Parchment and Vellum

Parchment and vellum are animal hides that are preserved by liming and prepared for use by dehairing, scraping, buffing, and washing. Their only resemblance to leather is that they are also made from the skins of animals. They vary in color from a brilliant white to a light cream, and in texture from a rather thick, stiff—almost horny—skin to a thin, pliable one. They are the most durable of the skins used by bookbinders and have been used for bindings for more than 3 centuries, first for limp bindings and later over boards.

What is the difference between parchment and vellum? The answers to this frequently asked question in bookbinding circles, can be found in a number of authoritative sources, spanning a period from 1755 to 1971. The earliest source is the first edition (1755, reprinted by AMS Press) of Samuel Johnson's *Dictionary of the English Language*, which defines the words quite simply as "Parchment. The skin of a sheep dressed for the writer" and "Vellum. The skin of a calf dressed for the writer." The latest source (1971, Oxford University Press) is *The Compact Edition of the Oxford English Dictionary*, which defines parchment as "the skin of the sheep or goat, and sometimes that of other animals, dressed and prepared for writing, painting, engraving." Vellum is "a fine kind of parchment prepared from the skins of calves (lambs or kids) and used especially for writing, painting or binding."

Both Lalande (1762) and Peignot (1812) say that vellum is made from the skin of calves 6 weeks old or younger, and parchment is made from the skins of sheep and goats. (See Bibliography under Historical for these references.) The Encyclopedic, Universal, and Webster dictionaries all define vellum as a fine parchment made of calfskin. The other 5 sources included under vellum the skins of kids, lambs, and goats as well as calves. All 8 references included in their definitions for parchment the skins of sheep, and some added ewes, lambs, goats, and calves. The *Glossary of Terms* published by the British Standards Institution, defines parchment as the flesh split of sheep, goat, or ass skins; generally refers to the flesh split of a sheepskin; and vellum as made from unsplit calf, sheep, and other skins. The best vellum is made from calf. This is primarily a distinction based on whether the skin is split or unsplit, and not on the animal of origin. This definition seems to be unique to England at the present time.

The conclusions we can draw from this research are that there is no hard and fast distinction between the 2 terms; that parchment has become a general term applied to any animal skin that is preserved by liming; that skins to which the term is specifically applied are cream in color, rather thick and stiff, and are usually made from the skins of sheep and goats. Vellum is made (by the same process) from the skins of young calves (6 weeks old or younger), lambs, kids, stillborn, and uterine off-spring of the cow, ewe, and goat; it is brilliant white and thinner and more pliable than the skins of older animals. The definition from the British Standards Institution will doubtless stand on its own merits.

Paper

Before the introduction of the papermaking machine, around the turn of the nineteenth century, all paper was, of course, made by hand. Its chief ingredients were pulped linen or cotton rags and water. It was then sized with a gelatine size for writing and printing purposes. Paper is still being made by hand in pretty much the same way, although not in such quantities. The bulk of today's paper is made by machine. Rags are still used, but because of their short supply, with the introduction of synthetic fabrics, they are being supplanted by cotton linters, made from raw cotton, and from cellulose fibers extracted from wood pulp. As with rags, the longer the fibers the stronger and more durable the paper. Machine-made papers are also sized, although gelatine is no longer the primary sizing material.

There are basically 2 types of paper—wove and laid. A *wove* paper is produced on a closely woven mold or screen and shows no impression from the mesh of the screen. A *laid* paper is produced on a coarser screen or mold supported by wires. These wires are usually placed about 1 inch apart—although this varies—and are oriented vertically. Both the wires and the woof of the screen are impressed on the sheet of paper, leaving slight impressions. The impressions made by the wires are known as chain lines, and the more closely spaced lines are called laid lines.

There are an infinite variety of papers in a number of finishes made today. Antique and matte are slightly rough, dull finishes; plate and calendered, smooth and somewhat shiny; and coated or filled, smooth and glossy. Since most hand binders and conservators, when introducing new paper in a job, try to match the book stock (the paper on which the book is printed) or the original they are replacing, it is desirable to have on hand a variety of papers. The quantity and assortment needed in any shop depend, of course, on the volume and variety of work anticipated.

Text papers meet this requirement very well. Because so many papers are produced domestically, it is impossible to mention them all. A few of the mills known for producing quality papers are Curtis, Mohawk, Strathmore, and Warren. A good way to become familiar with these and other papers is to acquire sample books from the mills or paper merchants. These books are sometimes for sale, not distributed free of charge. Other domestic papers that can be used are those made primarily for artists, such as charcoal papers. Many are available in solid colors in addition to white and cream. A number of imported papers are useful: from France, the papers made by Arches, Canson and Montgolfier, and Rives; from England, those made by J. Barcham Green, and from Italy, the Fabriano mills.

In purchasing any of these papers for incorporation in a binding, choose ones with a neutral or near neutral pH; this means they will be free or nearly so of acidity.

Kinds of Papers

Decorated papers A number of techniques are used to decorate paper by hand. Marbling is probably the oldest and still the most popular. There are also paste papers, papers printed with linoleum blocks and silk screens, and those made with stencils and ruling pens. The techniques used in making these papers are obvious by their names, with the exception of marbling. Briefly, *marbling* is a process whereby colors in solution are floated on a slightly gelatinous aqueous solution and moved around to obtain a desired pattern. A sheet of paper is then laid down on the surface of the solution and immediately lifted off. The paper on contact with the solution picks up the design.

Most of the decorated papers available in this country used to be imported from England, France, Italy, and Sweden. There are, however, several accomplished marblers and other decorated papermakers working successfully in the United States today. When making a selection of decorated papers, in addition to choosing appealing designs, give some consideration to the quality of the paper stock used in their production. It is also a good idea to purchase a minimum of 2 sheets of any pattern selected.

Japanese tissues These papers play an important role in the work of the hand binder, for they have many uses. They are for the most part long-fibered and so are remarkably strong in comparison to thickness. Many of these tissues are on the market and are similar in weight and color, but sold under different names. Those described here and mentioned throughout the text are representative of those in general use by binders. *Usugami* (cream) and *Sekishu* (white and natural) are good light- to medium-weight tissues for guarding folds, re-edging pages, and backing pages. *Okawara* (cream) is heavier than the above tissues and is useful for inner hinges and the hinging of large plates. *Lens tissue* (white) is very thin and is used primarily in the laminating of torn or deteriorating pages. *Hosho* (white) is a heavy soft tissue used chiefly in lining up spines.

Newsprint This is the paper on which newspapers are printed, often referred to as "unprinted news." It is a cheap wood-pulp paper and should not be used in any binding job. It does, however, serve as an inexpensive clean work surface and a surface on which to paste and glue. It is packaged in 100 pound (45 kg) bundles in sheet sizes of 23 × 34 inches (58.4 × 86.3 cm) or in the form of large tablets, although the sheets are smaller in size.

Bond paper Two weights of bond are useful. A 20 pound (9 kg) weight is a good average weight for lining out boards, boxes, and the like. If it is to be incorporated in a finished job, it should be a good quality paper, preferably acid-free. A lighter weight bond—8 or 10 pound (3.6 × 4.5 kg)—is useful in making design patterns and rubbings.

Blotting paper White, unembossed blotting paper is useful in the pre-liminary drying of sheets that have been washed or soaked.

Silicone release This paper is nonsticking, which makes it useful when recently pasted work requires pressing while still damp, such as a page backed or laminated.

Wax paper The ordinary household variety is useful as a moisture barrier and in many incidental ways in a shop. It should not, however, be used next to recently pasted work where pressure is involved.

It is a good idea to save the endleaves and board and covering papers that are removed from books to be rebound. These are frequently useful in replacing missing corners in future jobs. Generally, they can easily be removed from the boards by soaking in a pan of lukewarm water for several hours. They should then be put under light weight to dry.

In addition to the usual paper sources, other possibilities are art supply stores, stationery stores, small specialty shops, job printers known for quality work, and, for newsprint, suppliers to nursery schools and kindergartens.

Of all the papers discussed here, perhaps the most difficult to buy in small quantities are domestic text papers. They are generally available from paper merchants, but many of these houses today sell only in packaged lots. One possibility is cooperative buying among friends in a limited geographic area, where repacking and shipping would not be involved in the division and distribution.

Boards

Binder's board The most readily available board in the United States is made by Davey Company, which has many distributors nationally. The board is gray in color and bears the tag "red label board." It is made in a variety of sizes and weights and packaged in 50 pound (22.5 kg) bundles. The heavier the board, the fewer in a bundle; 26 × 38 inches (66 × 96.5 cm) is a stock size. These boards are calipered in 1/1000th of an inch. Thus, an .059 board is 59/1000th of an inch; for practical purposes, it is 1/16th inch thick. It is considered a lightweight board. This and an .082 or .090, medium-weight boards, should serve most needs. If a heavier board is needed, it can be made by gluing 2 or more boards together to produce the desired thickness. In such a case, cut 1 of the boards to the desired or correct size and the other board or boards slightly larger. Apply glue to both boards and put in the press until dry. The surplus on the larger board can then be cut away. Repeat this process if a third board is added. If both boards are cut to the exact size needed and one slips in the pressing process, they are useless; and if both are cut oversize, it is difficult to get a clean-cut edge on the double or triple thickness.

French carton bleu, English millboard, and Davey "green label"—a dense black board—are considered superior to the red label board, but they are somewhat difficult to locate. Perhaps they will become more plentiful in the future. Some binders have found a satisfactory substitute for these boards in a made or laminated board consisting of several sheets of an all-rag, acid-free mounting board. The most economical way to buy binder's board is by the bundle, if storage space is available and anticipated use warrants it. They are, however, available by the board or in broken bundles from suppliers and in some art supply stores and probably in local trade binderies. Because of weight and cost of shipping, it is always advisable to try to locate a source for all types of board near at hand.

Pulpboard This board has many uses in a workshop. It is a cream-colored, smooth finished board made from wood pulp. It makes a good work surface for a table top and is useful to press pages and to protect the sides of a book while in a finishing press. A stock size is 33 × 44 inches (83.8 × 111.7 cm). It is made in a variety of weights and is calipered in 1/1000th of an inch. An .045 is a useful weight. Generally sold in bundles of 100 sheets, it is available from some paper merchants, although it is not always easy to locate. Any type of inexpensive, undyed, lightweight board that has a smooth surface is a reasonable substitute. Chipboard—the kind that laundries use in folding ironed shirts—works well for many small jobs. Pulpboard and the other boards should not be incorporated in a binding or a protective case. They have virtually no strength and become quite acid in a short time.

Bristol board There are many types and qualities of bristol. The one recommended here has a smooth or plate finish and a near neutral pH. A good average weight is a 220M (this designation means that 1,000 sheets 20 ×26 inches, or 50.8 × 66 cm, weigh 220 pounds, or 99 kg). It is used as the spine in case and Bradel bindings and is incorporated in other bindings in a number of ways. It is also useful as a moisture barrier in some pressing jobs. An additional source is art supply stores.

Sewing Materials

Tapes An unbleached linen tape 3/8 to 1/2 inches wide is lightweight and durable. One manufacturer refers to it as a "stay" tape. It is suitable for most jobs where tape is required and is preferable to either bleached linen or cotton. It is packaged in small yardage or can be bought by the gross yards. Notion counters are an additional source.

Cords For use in raised bands, unbleached hemp and flax twines are considered the best and most durable materials, made in a variety of diameters and packaged in 1/2 and 1 pound (.22 and .45 kg) balls. Cords 1/16 and 1/8 inch in diameter should serve most needs. Stores specializing in packaging materials are an additional source, but don't be persuaded to buy sisal.

Leather or vellum thongs These can be made by pasting together strips of these materials in the desired width and thickness.

Sewing thread An unbleached linen thread is advisable for hand sewing. This comes in a variety of weights and is generally packaged in 2-ounce skeins or half-pound spools. It is sold by number and the number of cords or threads that are twisted together to make up the single thread. The higher the number the thinner the thread. No. 30/2 cord is a good average weight for most volumes, unless the signatures are exceptionally heavy, in which case use an 18/2 cord. Quartos and folios, although large in page size, have few sheets to the signature, so they do not generally require a heavy thread. A possible additional source is stores that specialize in shoe findings and supplies.

Needles One does not need to buy "bookbinder's needles." A package of darners 1/5 contains 10 needles—2 each of 5 sizes—with eyes large enough to take the sewing threads suggested above. These are available at notion counters and dime stores.

Headbands A polished cotton string or cord serves well for the core of the headbands. An all-purpose one would be about 1/16 inch in diameter. This is generally available in any store that sells wrapping materials. The traditional cloth headband is made of a narrow or pin-striped all-cotton shirting or calico. It is most likely found in a yard goods department or a store specializing in yard goods, although it is not always too easy to find.

Silk A twisted silk thread is necessary for working headbands. Available in a variety of colors, it is packaged on small paper spools in quantities of about 8 yards (7.2 m).

Button-hole twist This is a fine silk thread suitable for working headbands on small books. It is readily available in most stores that sell thread—just be sure it is silk.

Embroidery silks Wash twist and purse silk, which used to be readily available, are increasingly difficult to locate. A possible source might be someone who used to embroider.

Linen thread The unbleached linen sewing thread described earlier is suitable for headbands. Colored linen threads are also available in some specialty shops. Rayon and cotton embroidery threads are not recommended for this purpose. Rayon is not durable, and cotton lacks the luster a headband should have. The core for worked headbands can be a hemp cord or strips of vellum pasted together.

Woven Materials

Book cloth This term applies to woven material made from either cotton or flax and sized to prevent adhesives from oozing through the threads. It comes in a variety of weights, finishes, and colors. *Buckram* is a slightly textured cloth; *linen* or *vellum-finish* cloths are smooth surfaced and somewhat shiny; *natural finish buckram* is a coarse-textured cloth with no apparent sizing on the surface or right side. For handwork, a medium-weight, starch-filled cloth is recommended. The thin cloths made primarily for use on case-making machines do not have sufficient body to be handled easily. Pyroxilin-filled, or impregnated, cloths reputedly do not wear as well as do the starch-filled cloths. Coated cloths that "look like leather" are not recommended for hand bindings.

Practically all manufacturers have discontinued some of their better quality cloths and reduced the range of colors in other lines. A few will still sell a minimum of 10 yards (9.1 m) of 1 color to the small consumer. The only sources for smaller yardage are retail bookbinding supply houses. Fabrics other than conventional book cloths can be used successfully if properly handled. Choose a medium-weight, closely woven material for best results.

Miscellaneous materials *Lawn* is a closely woven, lightweight, slightly sized cotton material useful in lining up spines, reinforcing paper hinges, and such. It is preferable in handwork to the loosely woven super or mull used in edition binding. It is generally available in fabric shops or the yard goods section of department stores. It is, however, becoming increasingly hard to find, as synthetic fabrics are predominant today. *Organdy* or any thin, closely woven cotton fabric, preferably white, is a reasonable substitute. *Airplane linen* is also called boiled or brown linen. It is an unbleached, natural color, closely woven, lightweight material useful for cloth hinges or reinforcing paper hinges on large books. It is available from some supply houses. Handkerchief linen is an adequate alternative, available in yard goods departments or stores. Other materials that are useful in the bindery and that can be found in yard goods stores or counters are canton and outing flannel, used for lining up spines of heavy volumes and for polishing leather bindings, and cheesecloth for straining paste or as a polishing cloth.

Adhesives

The trend today among many hand bookbinders is to move almost completely into the field of synthetic adhesives, abandoning the traditional hot hide glue and wheat paste. There are a number of reasons for this shift, and many of them doubtless have validity. There are also a number of tests and evaluations currently being made by chemists and others, with varying results.

Hundreds, possibly thousands, of adhesives are on the market, and for every type there are both good and bad products. The characteristics one should look for in adhesives are stability, durability (retention of adhesive qualities), and reversibility, that is, the adhesive can be removed without damage to the material to which it has been applied. This is particularly important in bookbinding, for books that are used are going to wear out and require rebinding.

A good quality hot hide glue and a pure starch paste—wheat or rice—meet the requirements of good adhesive characteristics. Experienced binders have seen many examples where glue and paste have held up well over the centuries. They have also seen examples where they have failed. With no documented evidence, it is unreasonable to condemn all such adhesives because of the failure of some, with few if any clues as to the reason for failure. Some of the synthetics, polyvinyl acetates, and others, might in the course of time prove to be excellent adhesives, but none around today has survived for three centuries.

In this book, the principal recommended adhesives are: hot hide glue, wheat starch paste, and water-soluble PVA.

Hot hide glue Suggested for gluing up the spines of books, for work with starch-filled book cloth, and for setting slipcases and protective cases together, a good quality hide glue is obtainable from some supply houses, hardware stores, and from stores catering to cabinetmakers. It is sold in both sheet and granular form and usually by the pound. It is mixed with water—3 parts water to 1 part glue—heated to melt the glue, and kept hot while in use. It can be diluted as required. (See glue pot under Gluing and Pasting Equipment, Chapter 3.)

Wheat paste This is recommended for most work with paper and leather. Some binders prefer a rice starch paste for page repair. A commercially prepared wheat paste, if made from pure cellulose, works satisfactorily for most jobs. This is sold in powder form, having been cooked and dehydrated in a vacuum, and can be readily prepared by adding the powder to warm water and stirring. For a workable paste, the proportion is about 4 parts water to 1 part paste. It can be thinned with water or can be made thicker by adding a bit more powder. Many binders prefer to make their own paste; see the Appendix for the recipe.

PVA This synthetic adhesive is generally used in a 50–50 mixture with wheat paste for small tip-on jobs. It has the advantage of drying faster and not introducing as much moisture into the materials as straight paste would do. It is referred to throughout this text as *mixture*. PVA is a white, viscous adhesive, having somewhat the consistency of marshmallow whip. It is available from supply houses and hardware stores. Check to see if it is water-soluble. Unless the anticipated use is great, buy in small quantities because most of these adhesives have a rather short shelf life. (PVA—polyvinal acetate—is a thermoplastic resin.)

Other Adhesives

Flexible glue This is a hide glue to which glycerine or sorbitol terpineol has been added. The additive slows up the drying a bit and reduces the amount of pull to a minimum. It is useful in making large portfolios, but it is not recommended as an all-purpose adhesive. This glue remains flexible, or pliable, in its cold state, but not in condition for use. It, like straight hide glue, should be soaked in water, heated, and kept hot while in use. It is available from some supply houses and is sold by the pound.

Fish glue This is a liquid glue in its cold state, used primarily by the binder in the mounting of dies for hot stamping. Some supply houses stock it, but it is more generally available in hardware stores and houses catering to cabinetmakers.

Glycerine paste This is wheat paste to which glycerine has been added (see the Appendix for recipe). It has the advantageous characteristic of creating virtually no pull. Glycerine is available in drugstores and chemical supply houses.

5 Basic Techniques

The key to success in the field of hand bookbinding, as in any skill or craft, is the mastery of basic techniques. If you cannot measure correctly, cannot cut straight and accurately, cannot apply an adhesive properly, you will never have a satisfying end product. The first step to mastering any field is to lay a firm foundation on which to build. All the basic techniques in hand bookbinding are relatively simple, and if learned properly at the start, they soon become routine. Before beginning actual work on a book, take some time to practice these techniques. A familiarity with both materials and techniques will, in the long run, prove to be time well spent.

Measuring

A ruler is the basic tool for measuring, and its use is essential if you need the exact size in inches or fractions. In bookbinding, however, you do not often need the exact size in inches. The objective in measuring is to make sure the material fits the book. This can be done simply and accurately by laying the material against the book and marking the cutting points (Fig. 5–1).

Most American rulers indicate inches, halves, quarters, eighths, sixteenths, and so on. So do some rulers of English make; others are marked in tenths and twentieths. Some rulers also carry the metric system of centimeters and millimeters, and some indicate only the metric system. Because the divisions on rulers do vary, the beginner should determine what system to use and then always measure with the same ruler.

Dividers are useful in transferring narrow measurements. They can be set at the desired width and the cutting points marked. A few of the areas where they are useful are in cutting guard strips with a knife, evening the margin of material on the inside of covers, determining the position of raised bands, and finding the exact center on a spine strip.

Strips of paper and board can be used to transfer measurements. An easy and accurate way to find the center of a piece of material is to cut a strip of paper its exact width and fold it in half. A strip of board cut to the desired length is an excellent way to determine the proper position for the materials in a two-tone binding. Once the position is decided, lay the strip even with the fore edge of the binder's board, mark it, and cut to the determined length. The strip can then be used to mark all cutting points on both front and back boards. A narrow strip of paper can also be used in determining the exact width of a spine. Lay the paper across the spine, hold it firmly, and mark the points where it crosses the edge of the spine on both sides.

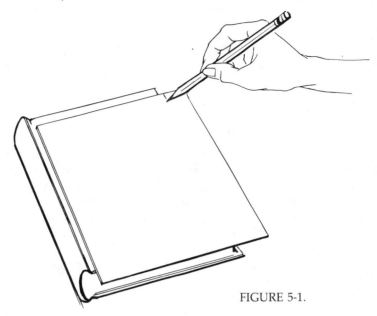

FIGURE 5-1.

Cutting

It is impossible to note all available cutting tools, but several methods of cutting with different tools are described here; at least 1 of them will be helpful in developing the skill necessary for accurate cutting.

Regardless of the equipment or tools used, before attempting to cut material to an exact size, first get 1 straight edge or 1 square corner, whichever is required. Mark this corner or edge in some way (a small penciled cross is adequate), and make all measurements using this as a point of departure. It is very difficult to cut a piece of material accurately to a given size without an accurate point from which to start.

A board shears is the ideal cutting tool for most materials. Its usefulness, however, depends on the user's understanding of its capabilities and limitations (see Chapter 3).

The outside gauge is useful for cutting strips from 1/32nd of an inch or less to about 2 inches (5 cm). To adjust it for a given width, place a ruler on the board and extend it beyond the cutting edge to the desired width. Hold the ruler in position with the pressure bar and bring the gauge in until it makes contact with the ruler. Tighten the gauge and remove the ruler. Slide the material to be cut under the pressure bar, pushing it through until it makes contact in its entire length with the outside gauge; hold in position with the pressure bar, and cut. As many strips as needed can be quickly cut with this 1 setting.

The gauge on the board is used for repetitive cutting of materials wider than 2 inches (5 cm). You can get a straight edge by making 1 cut and a square or right angle by first getting a straight edge, then laying the edge against the stop on the board, and making a second cut. This should produce a right angle. Set and tighten the gauge at the desired width; place the right-angle corner in the right angle made by the gauge and the stop or ruler on the end of the board. With a board shears, if the material is to be cut at right angles, only 1 mark need be made, and this to indicate the cutting point. If, however, the material is to be cut off-square or on the diagonal, a mark should be made at each end of the material and the cut made between the 2 points.

In using a paper cutter with no pressure bar and no gauges, hold the material firmly in position with the hand, or weight it down with a brick. For repetitive cutting, a right-angle square can be laid in the desired position against the stop and weighted down, or if a large number of pieces the same size are needed, fix the square in position with a C-clamp.

When the only available cutting tool is a knife, considerably more time will be required to master its proper use. Probably the best knife to use is a mat or utility knife (see Chapter 3 under Small Tools and Other Items); a metal straightedge should always accompany the knife. In cutting with a knife, 2 cutting points should be marked, 1 at each end of the material. Remember to get a straight edge or right-angle corner before attempting to cut material to size. From this edge or corner, mark the desired size at 2 points with a well-sharpened pencil, holding it at the same angle each time. Lay the material to be cut on some smooth surface such as a piece of clean wasteboard. Place the straightedge in position on the marks, keeping it on the same side of each mark (the thickness of a pencil mark can throw a cut off-square). Hold the straightedge firmly, place the knife blade against it in a vertical position, and, at about a 25–30 degree angle, pull it along the straightedge (Fig. 5-2).

When cutting paper, pull the knife gently or lightly. Too much pressure on the blade will pull the paper rather than cut it cleanly. While holding the straightedge firmly, check to see that the surplus has been cut away. If not, repeat until this is accomplished. Binder's board is cut in the same manner, but more pressure will be needed on the blade, and it is doubly important to hold the blade in a vertical position. If tilted in either direction, the end result will be a bevelled edge, not a straight one. Other materials are cut in the same fashion, following these general rules—the blade should be sharp, the straightedge held firmly, and the pressure on the knife light for lightweight materials.

After cutting materials to the desired size, always check to be sure that they are correctly cut before proceeding with the work. Note that all material is easier to cut with the grain direction than cross-grain. No further specific cutting directions are given in this text. Only the word *cut* or the phrase *cut to size* is used.

Pasting and Gluing

These are techniques used from nursery school onward, but experience has shown that while everyone can handle a brush, few people know how to handle it properly in applying adhesives. The object is to have the adhesive evenly spread over the desired surface, while keeping the other side of the material completely clean. Evenness is particularly important when a water-soluble adhesive is used, for unless the material is equally moist, wrinkles will develop.

Place the material to be pasted or glued on a piece of clean wastepaper that can be easily changed. Put only a small amount of adhesive

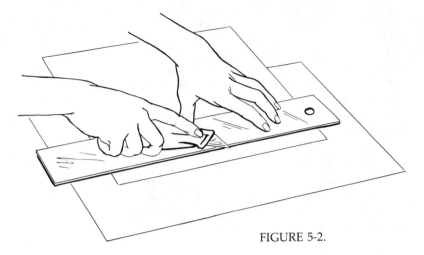

FIGURE 5-2.

on the brush. Start in the center of the material and work out toward the edges in cartwheel fashion; hold the brush lightly and apply the adhesive in short strokes, backtracking a bit with each stroke. Hold the material firmly in position with the fingertips; if it slips, change the wastepaper at once.

Keep adhesives free of foreign matter and thin enough so that they spread easily. One that is too heavy or used excessively will cause ridges or bumps in the finished product.

Most papers will begin to curl as soon as paste is applied. The tendency is to attempt to pick them up quickly and get them in position before they curl more; this seldom works satisfactorily. In fact, they are very likely to curl back on themselves, staining the right side. Stay calm: Hold the paper firmly in position and continue to brush it. If it is adequately covered with paste, do not add more, but keep the brush moving over it from the center outward in every direction. When the paper has evenly absorbed the moisture in the paste, it will relax and lie flat. It can then be picked up and laid in position rather easily.

A general rule is that the adhesive should be applied to the thinner of the 2 materials to be put together. Starch-filled book cloth is glued because paste tends to dissolve the filling and the cloth becomes very limp and hard to handle. Leather and paper are generally pasted because they are easier to handle—particularly in large pieces. The drying time is longer and adjustments, if necessary, can be made.

Determining Grain Direction

Almost all materials used by hand bookbinders, with the exception of leather, have a grain direction. In parchment and vellum, the grain direction runs from head to tail, or in the direction that the animal moves. In book cloth and other woven fabrics the grain direction runs with the finished or selvage edge, or with the threads that make up the warp on the loom.

In handmade paper the grain direction is determined by the way the fibers are laid down on the mold. The vatman, the person who shakes the mold, shakes it first from right to left and then from front to back. Because of the motion in both directions, the fibers are laid down in both directions. The right-to-left motion is reputedly the more vigorous, and the first, so the grain direction will be in the direction of the front-to-back motion. Many authorities feel that handmade paper has no grain direction. Admittedly, it is not very pronounced, but it does, from the hand binder's point of view, exist. In machine-made paper, the grain is usually more pronounced. As the screen on which the pulp is laid moves forward, it is shaken mechanically from left to right or right to left, so the grain direction follows the forward motion of the screen.

The grain direction in paper can be determined in several ways. The first method is the bending or rolling test. Fold the paper loosely, and with the hand, press on it to test the resistance it gives to the pressure; repeat this in the other direction. The way that sets up the least resistance indicates the grain direction (Fig. 5-3a). Another way is to fold the paper sharply in 1 direction, then the other. The fold made with the grain direction will usually be clean and smooth; the fold made against the grain will look crackly and uneven (Fig. 5-3b). A third way to test grain direction is to cut a swatch of the paper and cover it with hot glue; it will immediately curl with the grain direction (Fig. 5-3c).

In heavier materials such as binder's board, the grain direction can generally be determined by the bending test. The way it bends easiest indicates the direction of the grain. In making this test, however, be sure to use approximately the same length of board, for the longer the board the easier it will bend. A piece of board 4 inches (10.1 cm) long will be more difficult to bend with the grain than will a piece 15 inches (38.1 cm) long against the grain. If uncertain, apply hot glue to the board; when it dries it will bend with the grain direction.

Once grain direction is determined on a board or piece of paper,

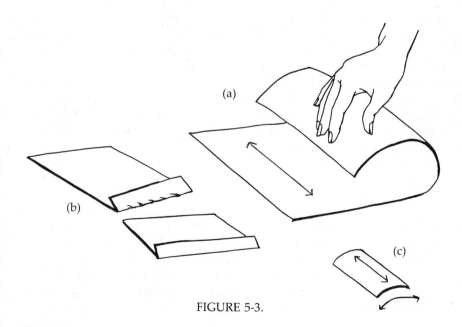

FIGURE 5-3.

mark it lightly with a little penciled arrow. It is a good idea always to leave 1 selvage edge on woven materials from which pieces will be cut from time to time.

The significance of determining the grain direction is discussed next.

Balancing the Pull

All materials with a grain direction stretch more cross-grain than they do with the grain when a water-soluble adhesive is applied. For this reason it is important to know the grain direction, to use all materials in the same direction, and to have the grain direction oriented with the vertical measurement of the book.

Most materials expand when moistened and contract in drying; this tends to warp or pull the material to which it is attached, regardless of whether it is another sheet of paper or a binder's board. Therefore, this "pull" must be balanced. The board paper in a binding, for instance, counteracts the pull of the covering material and should result in a flat, unwarped board.

If all materials are used in the same grain direction, and if for each piece of material that is attached to one side of a binder's board, a piece is attached in the same fashion to the other side, no warpage is likely to develop. An exception is when the 2 materials vary greatly in their pull. A thin paper will pull more than a heavier one because it absorbs more moisture, or gets wetter, from the adhesive. If you are uncertain, or if using unfamiliar materials, make up a sample and see what happens. If one pulls more than the other, balance it with a lining of bond paper or an additional sheet of the same paper. Another exception is when the adhesives vary in their reaction. Hot glue and wheat paste react similarly in this respect, but a PVA might not pull as much as either of them. So, here again, it is a good idea to make up a sample.

If, however, some materials are cut in one grain direction and others are cut in the opposite direction in an attempt to make the most economical use of materials, or a board is lined out with 2 or 3 sheets of paper on either the outside or the inside when the opposite side has no such lining, the board will warp. It can be made to lie flat under pressure, but as soon as the pressure is removed, it will revert to its warped condition.

Once the pull is properly balanced, no amount of normal heat, cold, or humidity will change it. If warpage occurs, and it shouldn't if proper care is taken, it is considered by some binders to be less offensive if the boards warp inward—hugging the book.

Leather Paring

Most leathers that are tanned especially for bookbinding have been somewhat thinned by the tanner, either by deliberate splitting of very heavy skins or in the process of producing a smooth finish on the inner or flesh side of the skin. Additional thinning, however, is usually desirable in the areas where the leather turns over the edges of the boards, at the head and tail in the spine area, at the corners, and in the joints (this is usually done by sanding).

The amount of thinning is determined to some extent by the original thickness of the skin and the size of the book and its anticipated use. The objective is to have the leather thin enough to work easily and not create a bulky appearance in the specific areas mentioned, while at the same time not thinned to the extent that its strength and durability are appreciably reduced. For neatness and elegance, the leather should be fairly thin at all turning points. These are, however, the points that get the greatest wear, so, to some extent, appearance against durability must be weighed in the hope of striking a satisfactory compromise. One solution is to use small skins—those from young animals, which by nature are not unduly heavy—on small books.

There is a knack to paring, and some time should be spent practicing on scraps before paring a large piece cut out for the cover of a book. Experience can also be gained by paring pieces that can be used for headbands or patch labels, with little waste if unsuccessful.

Paring is a slicing motion. The blade of the knife is kept in constant motion as it is drawn across the area to be pared. The leather should always be on a smooth surface—a lithographic stone or a piece of polished marble. Glass is not good because it is harder than the steel of the knife and tends to dull the blade quickly. Care should always be taken to keep the surface on which the paring is being done free of any paring crumbs or other foreign matter. The smallest bit of trash will raise the leather sufficiently to cause the knife to cut deeper than intended. For successful paring, it is essential that the knife be kept sharp while in

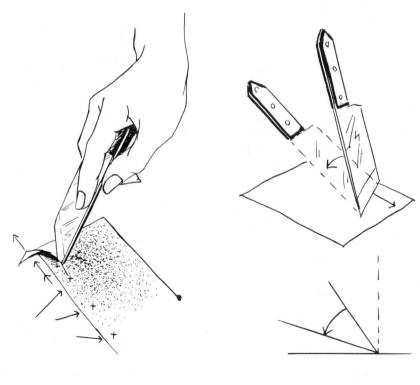

FIGURE 5-4.   FIGURE 5-5.

FIGURE 5-6.

use, so frequent honing or sharpening is necessary. The fibers in leather are surprisingly tough, and the knife dulls very quickly.

An English or German paring knife is recommended for edge paring. With the leather on a smooth surface, begin the paring at the very edge of one side and pare the entire edge to the desired thickness (Fig. 5-4). Hold the knife at sufficient height in starting so that it gets a hold, or bite, on the leather, and as the knife is drawn along lower it or level it off; otherwise it will go right through the leather. After an entire edge is pared, start back a little farther on the skin and pare the entire length again. This time use only the heel of the blade and keep the point of the knife on the stone. This gives some control to the amount cut away and keeps the bevel at an even thickness. Repeat this until the desired width of bevel is obtained (Fig. 5-5).

The French paring knife, with its rounded end, is used primarily to thin a whole cover or areas other than the edges. The work should begin at the edges, which can be started with an edge paring knife and worked back toward the center from all 4 edges. Again, the knife is held at 2 different angles, as for edge paring.

A spokeshave can also be used successfully in thinning an entire piece of leather and is considerably faster than the French knife, once the technique is mastered. The leather must be firmly attached to a smooth surface; a large lithographic stone is ideal, for its weight will keep it from shifting. It must, however, be large enough to allow space for the leather to be clamped to it, without the clamps coming in contact with the leather. Two C-clamps big enough to fit over the edge of the stone and a strip of wood will be needed. Lay a portion of the leather on the stone, place the strip of wood on it at the edge of the stone and attach the clamps—1 at each end (Fig. 5-6). The edge of the stone to which the clamps are attached must extend beyond the edge of the table on which it rests. The blade should be reversed from its usual position so that the beveled edge is down, and the corners of the blade should be rounded. Use both hands on the spokeshave and start the paring near the edge of the piece of wood and work outward in a radial pattern, using a slicing motion. When 1 area is pared, move the leather, clamp it again, and proceed.

The skife with its curved shape can be used both as an edge parer or for paring the entire surface. The trick is to learn to hold it consistently at the same angle so that the paring remains even. A new blade will ensure a sharp edge.

All areas pared, regardless of the method used, should in their finished state be very smooth. The least irregularity will be noticeable when the leather is pasted down. If difficulty is experienced, the finishing can be done effectively by sanding. This is somewhat slow, but it does work with little element of danger, if the leather is on a smooth surface and the area to be sanded is held firmly.

6 General Techniques

This chapter deals with the techniques that apply in general to the binding of a book, regardless of the covering material or binding style. It begins at the starting point of checking the book for completeness, followed by techniques that concern the treatment of pages—guarding, hinging of plates, single pages, repairing torn pages, re-edging, replacing missing corners, wormholes, backing a page, heat set tissue, laminating a page, and removing stains. Other general techniques covered include inner hinges, endsheet sections, treatment of edges, sewing, attaching endsheets, reducing swell, and gluing and rounding the spine. Where the techniques vary for the 4 styles of binding described in this book, instructions are given first for the simplest type of binding, in the belief that the beginner should always start with the simplest method. Then follow instructions for more detailed and complicated techniques.

The beginning of the description or instructions for each technique contains information on what the technique is applicable to or what it covers. Variations, possible pitfalls, and suggested remedies follow the descriptions. Read the entire section on any 1 technique before starting work in that particular area. In the lists of materials specifically needed for a job, which precede a technique where appropriate, large equipment and such small tools as scissors, knives, bonefolders and the like may not be included since it is assumed these items are readily available.

Worksheets It is sound practice for a binder to keep a worksheet on each book handled. The worksheet should include the name of the author, title, publisher, date of publication, condition of the book when received or before any work begins, style of binding, nature of covering material, type of sewing, headbands and the like, date the book was received, date work was started, work proposed or recommended, work actually done, and an identifiable description of all materials used, including types of Japanese tissues, names of adhesives, and so on, and a pattern of titling and decorating, indicating the name of the typeface, its point size, width or number of fillets used, and the like. These things may seem easy to remember, but they are forgotten surprisingly quickly. In the course of time, worksheets make an interesting record for the amateur and a desirable and useful one for the professional, who might also include on the worksheet the fee received for the work.

Checking and Taking the Book Apart

Checking the book for completeness is the first step in rebinding a book. It is particularly important if the sewing is broken and pages are

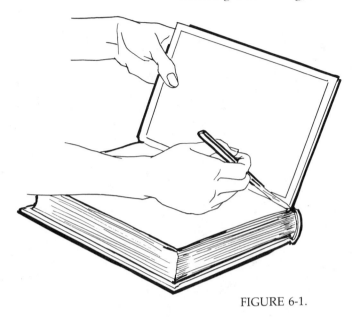

FIGURE 6-1.

loose, or if there is any indication that plates have come loose. Page through the book. If there is a list of plates in the table of contents, check the plates in the book against it. Plates that are printed on a paper different from the book stock and tipped in generally are not included in the pagination of the book. Record this on the worksheet.

The following instructions for taking the book apart apply to a book that requires resewing and will be rebound preserving no part of the original binding. The objective in this step is to separate the signatures and remove from them all remnants of the earlier binding.

Open the book and cut the board paper in the joint, first 1 side, then the other (Fig. 6-1). This will free the book from its covers if it is a hollow back. If a tight back, it will free the covers but not the spine. Place the book between clean protective boards (the covers just removed will serve) and put it in a finishing press with the spine exposed. Carefully remove from the spine as much of the lining material as possible in a dry state, prying it up with the point of a knife and pulling it away. In a hollow back, this usually consists of a piece of paper, a piece of lawn or super (cloth), headbands, and a layer of glue; in a tight back, it will consist of the covering material, some type of paper, headbands, and glue.

If it is not possible to remove these materials in their dry state, use a knife to carefully scrape away as much as can safely be removed. Then apply a generous layer of rather thick wheat paste; let this stand for about 5 minutes. If a thin paste is used, there is danger that the paper will absorb too much moisture from the paste, which can result in ugly stains in the gutter margin of the pages. (The gutter margin is the left-hand margin, or the margin nearest the spine.)

Next, use a bonefolder to scrape away the paste, taking with it as much of the lining material as has been loosened. Keep a piece of

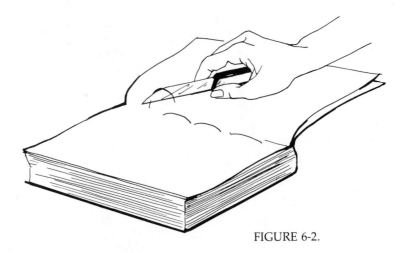

FIGURE 6-2.

wastepaper at hand on which to deposit the debris. Repeat this process until the spine is clean. The more often this is done and the longer the spine stays in a moistened condition, the softer the book pages will become, so the scraping should be done with a light hand.

When the spine is clean, remove the book from the press, and while the spine is still damp, "pull" the book—that is, take it apart signature by signature. Start at the back of the book and, omitting the tipped-on flyleaf, count the number of pages until you reach the center of the signature. Threads from the sewing will be exposed in the center of each signature. Cut the threads (Fig. 6-2). Count off the same number of pages on the other side of the sewing. This should be all of the pages in the last signature.

If there is a small arabic numeral, a letter, or letters of the alphabet at the bottom of the recto side of the last page that was counted, you know that the signature is complete. The signatures in all books are not, however, so marked. When the signatures are not marked, another way to check the number of pages in a signature is to count the leaves between the center of 1 signature and the center of the next. If there are 8 leaves, that is the number to a signature—4 on each side of the center. Unless the total number of pages in the book is evenly divisible by the number of pages in a signature, either the first or last signature of the book will probably not have the same number of pages as the other signatures. Proceed with caution until the number of pages in the bulk of signatures is definitely ascertained. The separating or tearing apart of a few pages in a given signature is no great tragedy, but it does make additional work in the repair.

Frequently, the last page of 1 signature and the first page of the next are attached at the gutter margin. This is the result of the original gluing. Hold the book firmly with 1 hand, grasp the entire signature to be removed in the other hand, and gradually ease it free (Fig. 6-3). Continue until all signatures are separated.

Next, take the signatures 1 at a time, lay them on a piece of waste-board in their folded state, and with a scalpel or sharp knife, push off

FIGURE 6-3.

any remaining glue. Do this first on 1 side, then turn the signature over and repeat (Fig. 6-4). If glue is embedded in the holes made by the earlier sewing, pull it out with the point of a knife or the fingers.

Work out or flatten the fold or crease made when the book was originally backed. Backing is the fanning out of the signatures to create a shoulder or joint against which the covering boards rest. If it is not too pronounced, flatten it first by bending the creases in reverse and rubbing it on a flat surface with a bonefolder. Then press the book as follows. Lay a few signatures—4 or 5—on a pressboard or a zinc sheet; add another board, a few more signatures with the spine or folded edge oriented in the opposite direction. For proper pressing the signatures

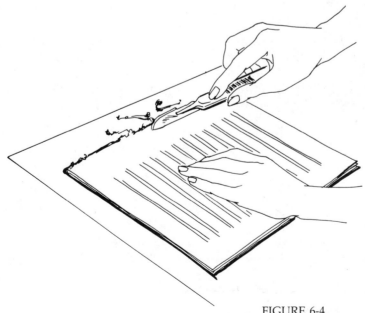

FIGURE 6-4.

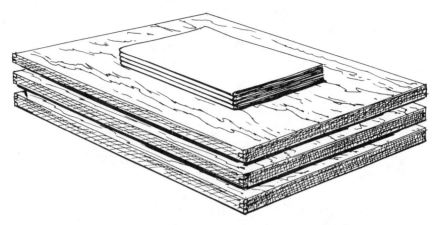

FIGURE 6-5.

should be piled exactly on top of each other (Fig. 6-5). Continue until the entire book is between boards. Place it in the press and screw the press down tight. Leave under pressure, preferably overnight, but at least 2 hours. If sufficient pressboards are not available, or the clearance of the press is inadequate, the pressing can be done in stages.

Sometimes a book has been overbacked and the folded edges of the signatures are badly creased and wrinkled. In that case, as they are piled up for pressing, moisten the wrinkled area with a piece of damp cotton (Fig. 6-6). Only the outside pages of each signature have to be moistened. Some papers might water stain from the moisture, so before trying this remedy, test it on the last signature of the book. Coated papers should never be moistened and pressed in this way.

Guarding

This is the term used for repairing the damaged folds of book pages. The objective is to strengthen the fold, or if 2 pages are completely separated, to make them into a folded sheet again, at the same time keeping bulking in the spine area at a minimum. Frequently, only the outside pages of each signature need attention. If so, there is generally no problem with bulking or excessive swell. If the damage is extensive,

FIGURE 6-6.

however, consideration should be given to the potential use the book will receive, and the tissue selected for the guards should be as thin as safety permits.

Any dry cleaning, washing, deacidifying, and such that seems advisable should be done before the pages are guarded. (These techniques are discussed later.) Here the instructions apply to pages that are in good condition except in the area of the folds.

Materials Needed

Plate glass or piece of nonabsorbent smooth material
Wheat paste thinned to smooth, pureed-soup consistency
Japanese tissue Usugami is a good average weight and color
Newsprint 2-inch (5 cm) wide strips unprinted news, 2 inches longer than book page
Pulpboard 2-inch (5 cm) wide strips of clean, slightly absorbent board, 2 inches longer than book page
Pressboard
Bristol board
Brick
Wasteboard

The width of the guard strips is dependent on the extent of the damage and on the thickness of the signatures—5/8 to 3/4 inch is average. They should be about 1 inch longer than the book pages, and the grain direction in the tissue should run with the vertical measurement of the pages. Check through the book and estimate the number of pages that need attention.

Cutting guards If a board shears is available, set the outside gauge to the desired width and cut a few more strips than you think will be needed. If using a knife, take several sheets of tissue or 1 large piece folded the required length twice, and mark the desired width with dividers at each end of the sheet (Fig. 6-7). Lay a straightedge between the points marked. Hold the straightedge firmly. With a sharp knife cut the strips, putting light pressure on the knife. It is a good idea to leave the strips attached at 1 end. This keeps them together, and they can be pulled away or torn off as needed.

Two methods of guarding are described here: one for pages on which the edges will not be cut, the other for pages where trimming is anticipated (see Treatment of Edges later in this chapter).

For pages that are not to be cut, guard the damaged folds on the outside with the signature in its folded position. If pages other than the outside leaves of the signatures need attention, start with the innermost damaged pages in each signature.

Lay the page on a piece of board with the folded edge off the board and the edge of the board extending beyond the edge of the table. Weight it down. Place a guard strip on the glass; apply paste evenly but lightly (Fig. 6-8). Pick it up by the ends and lay half of its width on the

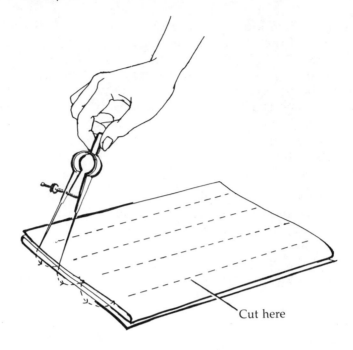

Cut here

FIGURE 6-7.

edge of the top page. Rub gently with the fingers; then fold the other half underneath so that it catches the page on the bottom (Fig. 6-9). Turn the page over and rub the tissue, gently pulling it snugly against the fold. As the pages are guarded, place them between the strips of pulpboard already prepared and weight them down with the press-

FIGURE 6-8.

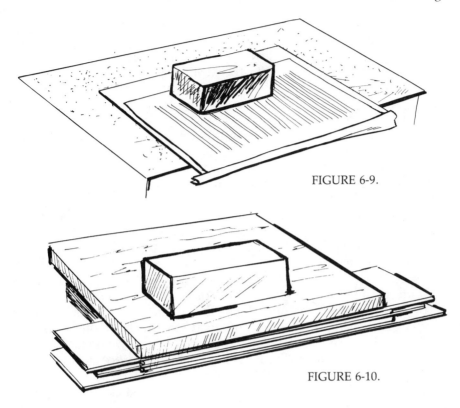

FIGURE 6-9.

FIGURE 6-10.

board and brick (Fig. 6-10). These can be piled up one on top of the other. When picking up the guards, hold them loosely while laying in position. If pulled taut they will tend to curl and become hard to handle, and if stretched while moist, they will shrink in drying and tend to wrinkle the pages.

When the fold is completely broken, take care to align the edges of the pages on both front and back with the edges of the rest of the signature before attaching the guard strip. This will help to keep the edges of the book even.

First guard all of the inner pages of each signature requiring attention. When these are dry, open the pages flat on a suitable cutting surface (a piece of clean wasteboard) and cut off the excess tissue, both top and bottom, even with the edges of the page. This is best done by placing a small metal straightedge evenly along the edges of the pages and cutting with a scalpel. When this is completed, return the repaired pages to their proper position in the book. Repeat the process with the next innermost pages that need attention.

After guarding the entire book and the guards are dry, the excess tissue cut away, and the pages back in proper order, place the book in the press for several hours, stacking the signatures as previously described.

Guarding with pages opened flat This method is generally used when you expect to trim the edges of the entire book. Go through the book and remove all pages that need attention. It saves time later if both the pages that are to be guarded and those that are laid aside are kept in proper numerical order.

Lay a strip of unprinted news on the table, open up the folded page, and lay the folded area on the strip of paper with the inside of the fold facing up (Fig. 6-11). The method of handling the guards is the same as described above, except that they are laid flat on the opened pages, centered on the inside of the fold. When all necessary pages are guarded and the guards are dry, remove them from the unprinted news strips. Run a small bonefolder gently between the paper strip and the page. Then cut away the excess tissue at the ends, fold the pages, reassemble the book in its proper order, and press as described earlier.

The strips of unprinted news keep the working surface clean and prevent excess tissue at each end from sticking to the pulpboard strips while piling up the pages. Pick this strip up along with the page when stacking them to dry.

If it is difficult to remove the pages from the newsprint or pulp-board, either the paste is too heavy or was applied excessively. If gentle pressure with the bonefolder will not free it, rather than force it and endanger tearing the page, cut away as much of the strip as is free and moisten the area of the guard that remains stuck. It should then pull free from the strip. If damaged in the process, add a new guard. If the guard strips do not stick, not enough paste is the cause. Remove the guard and start over. Or if it fails to stick in small areas, put a bit of paste on a small strip of bristol board and slip it under the unstuck area. Press lightly on the guard strip so that it will pick up the paste from the bristol; remove the bristol and rub the guard down in position.

Be sure that the guard strips are thoroughly dry before the signatures are stacked and put in the press. This usually takes several hours, although it depends to some extent on the amount of paste used, absorbency of the pages, and temperature and humidity.

FIGURE 6-11.

The first method of guarding described here attempts to keep the fore edge of the book pages in line, or even, if they have previously been cut even. This will not be accomplished if all pages within a signature require attention, unless they are completely separated. Then they can be lined up on the fore edge, and the guard strip will take care of the discrepancy on the spine edge. If the volume is a quarto, made up of 8 pages or 4 leaves, guard the 2 inner leaves on the inside and the 2 outer on the outside.

If the edges of the pages are deckled and uneven because of the deckle, either method of guarding will work satisfactorily. (A deckled edge is the untrimmed edge of a sheet of handmade paper.) If trimming is necessary to keep the fore edge even, trim the spine edge. The fore edge may be gilded, dyed, sprinkled, or just dirty, and to cut away any of these conditions would mar the fore edge of the book.

Hinging of Plates

Plates that were tipped in in the original binding (attached with a thin line of paste to the adjoining page) should be removed and hinged. This will allow them to open more freely and will remove any strain from the page to which they were attached. Before removing the plates, check to make sure that their proper position in the book is indicated on the plate, or that a list of the plates, giving their position, appears along with the table of contents. If this is not the case, mark lightly on the back of each plate the number of the page it faces.

Materials Needed

Japanese tissue Usugami or Sekishu for average-weight plates; Oka-wara for large plates on heavy paper
Mixture wheat paste and water-soluble PVA, equal parts
Wastepaper
Wax paper
Pulpboard
Brick
Pressboard

Cut the tissue hinges about 3/4 inch (1.9 cm) in width and 1 inch longer than the plate (grain direction running with the vertical measurement of the page). Attach the hinge to the back of the plate. Lay the plate facedown on a strip of clean paper; lay a second strip of paper 1/4 inch in from the spine edge of the plate and apply the adhesive to this area of the plate. Discard the waste strips; lay the pasted edge of the plate faceup on a strip of wax paper and place the hinge on the pasted area (Fig. 6-12); cover with wax paper and weight with a board and a brick. When dry, cut away the excess tissue at top and bottom. Put the plate in its proper position in the book and fold the hinge around the spine edge of the page next to it. If the plate falls in the center of a

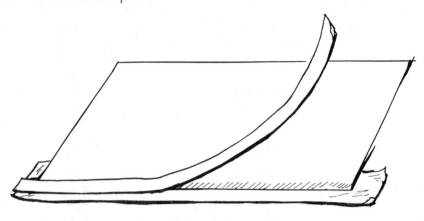

FIGURE 6-12.

signature, fold the hinge back on itself at the edge of the plate. This will mean that the entire hinge, both the portion attached to the plate and the portion that is free, will remain on the back side of the plate, and the plate will be sewn into the book through the fold in the hinge. The free portion of all hinges can be left free or they can be pasted down to the pages that they fold around or adjoin. Customarily they are left free; this, however, is a matter of personal preference.

When plates are located in such a position that they can be treated as a folded page (attached to the first and last pages of a signature, or to the last page of 2 adjoining signatures), attach the hinge to the back of 1 plate as described above. Lay both plates in their proper position in the book, lining them up evenly with the head, tail, and fore edge of the rest of the signature; fold the attached hinge around the signature and attach it to the back of the plate on the opposite side. Before applying the adhesive, check the width of the hinge on this plate. If it extends onto the plate more than 1/4 inch, mark its position at 1/4 inch and cut off the excess. Apply the adhesive to the side of the hinge that faces the back of the plate. This will depend on the orientation of the plate. If the back of the plate is exposed when it is in its proper position, the adhesive is applied to the inside of the folded hinge and the hinge is laid down on the plate. If, however, the face of the plate is uppermost, or exposed, fold the hinge flat, slip a strip of wax paper under it, apply the adhesive to it, and lay the plate in position on it—this would be the back side of the plate. Weight down in the customary way, and, when dry, cut away the surplus hinge at each end.

Single Pages

When a book consists entirely of single sheets, they can be made into signatures with guards, or they can be sewn along the gutter margin. For typescripts, articles cut from magazines, and the like, the time required to make them into signatures hardly seems justified. For books consisting chiefly of plates, the effort is worthwhile. It allows the book to open more freely and does little or no damage to the plates.

Materials Needed

See Hinging of Plates, preceding section.

The following directions are for making single sheets into signatures so that they can be saddle sewn (sewn through the center fold).

Check the number of pages in the book and decide on the number of pages for each signature. Factors governing this decision would be the number of pages and the thickness of the paper. It is generally advised to keep the number of signatures to a minimum. The guards will increase the thickness of the spine to some extent, and the more sewing thread introduced, the thicker the spine will get. A reasonable average would be 8 plates or sheets to the signature; so count the sheets out in groups of 8. If the number of pages is not equally divisible by 8, place the uneven number in the center of the book. In cases where the plates or sheets are not numbered, number them lightly in pencil on the back where the number can be easily seen while working with them and easily erased later.

The first group would carry the numbers 1,3,5,7,9,11,13, and 15; 7 and 9 make up the center of this signature of 8 leaves or 16 pages. Guard these 2 pages together, placing the guard strip on the back of each plate (see Hinging of Plates in preceding section). If the plates are so arranged as to require the adhesive to be applied to portions of both sides of the guard, apply the adhesive to the plate for attaching the first half of the guard and to the guard for the other half. In this case, attach the guard to 1 of the pages that make up the center fold of each signature throughout the entire book. When these are dry, add the other plate; this will complete the center fold of each signature.

To keep the fore edge of the pages even, particularly where there are a large number of pages, it speeds up the work to make a jig, or frame. This is done by laying the 2 plates flat on a piece of clean pulpboard larger by several inches than the 2 plates. Line up the plates at the top and allow a small space between the 2 in the center (approximately the combined thickness of the 2 sheets). This space will permit them to fold freely; if no space is allowed, they will bind when trying to fold them. Weight these in position, and with a straightedge placed along the top and both sides, draw the exact size of the 2 plates on the board. Remove the plates and attach along these lines narrow strips of board. The strips need not be entirely glued, but spot-tipped in several places. The strip across the top should be in 2 pieces, leaving space in the center to accommodate the portion of the guard that will extend beyond the top of the plates. This provides a frame into which 2 sheets can be laid, and when lined up against both the top and the fore edges of this frame, all center pages when folded should be the same size.

Place a strip of wax paper in the center of the jig to prevent the guard from sticking to the jig. As the plates are attached, remove them from the jig along with the strip of wax paper; lay them flat on a clean surface, cover the guarded area with an additional strip of wax paper, and weight down with a board and a brick. Continue in this manner until the center plates in all signatures have been hinged together.

When the guards are dry, cut away the excess tissue at both top and bottom and fold the plates in proper order.

The guards for the next series of plates should be cut slightly wider than those for the center plates. This will apply to the guards for each pair of plates as added. The added width should be the combined thickness of the plates and the guards; this thickness will increase with each pair of plates added to the signature. One-fourth of an inch is a suitable width for the guards to extend onto the plates. It is desirable that all guards be attached to the plates at the same distance from the spine edge.

The next plates to attach in the first signature are numbers 5 and 11. Attach the guard to the back of 5, and lay these 2 plates (5 and 11) in their proper position on 7 and 9, lining up the edges at top and fore edge. Then attach the free half of the guard to the back of 11. Again set this group, now consisting of 4 sheets, aside to dry as a unit, protecting the guarded area with wax paper, and weight down as previously described. When dry, remove and unfold 5 and 11, cut away the surplus tissue at top and bottom, and return to its proper position around 7 and 9. Proceed in this manner with 3 and 13, 1 and 15, and so on through the book.

When all plates have been guarded, are dry, and the excess tissue cut away, put them in proper numerical order. They should now be in the form of signatures. Press them in the usual way.

Repairing Torn Pages

Any necessary cleaning of the page should be done first.

Materials Needed

Silicone release paper
Japanese tissue
Starch paste wheat or rice
Pressboard
Brick

Most tears in paper result in a slight splitting of the paper, leaving irregular pulled fibers exposed on each edge of the tear. To repair this type of tear, lay the torn area on a piece of silicone release paper. Slip a strip of Japanese tissue, matching the page in color when possible, between the release paper and the page in the area of the tear. Apply a light coat of paste to both edges of the tear; pull the 2 edges of the page together, attempting to get the split areas back together in their proper position. This is usually not difficult to figure out, particularly if the tear is across a printed area. Place a strip of tissue on the top of the tear, cover with release paper and a pressboard, and weight down with a brick until dry, approximately 1 hour. When dry, carefully pull away the surplus tissue on both sides of the tear and on both sides of the page with a scalpel. This will leave some fibers of tissue along the tear. Lay a piece of clean paper over the area and rub gently with a bonefolder.

Next, reinforce the tear from the edge of the print out to the edge of the page. Take a strip of Japanese tissue—the same as used above—about 1/2 inch (1.2 cm) wide and long enough to cover this portion of the tear on both sides of the sheet. Apply paste to the tissue and lay it over the torn area on both sides. Place between release paper or pulpboards and weight down until dry. If the edges of the tissue are frayed, leaving a fibered edge, the repair is usually less noticeable. This, however, depends somewhat on the texture of the paper stock.

Fraying tissue This can be handled by paring the edges with a sharp scalpel; by folding, moistening the fold, and pulling apart along the fold while damp; or by tearing it along the edge of a straightedge held firmly on the tissue.

Re-edging Torn and Frayed Pages

First, clean and flatten the page. If badly wrinkled or creased, soak it in a pan of clean, lukewarm water until it is thoroughly wet (15 to 30 minutes should be sufficient).

Remove page and place between sheets of pulpboard and give it a light nip in the press. (This means screwing the press down lightly and immediately releasing the pressure.) Remove from the press, place between dry pulpboards and pressboards, and weight down until thoroughly dry—preferably overnight.

Materials Needed

Silicone release paper
Japanese tissue
Pulpboard
Pressboard
Water
Starch paste wheat or rice
Brick

Select a Japanese tissue that matches the page in color and a smooth starch paste thinned as for guarding. For each edge that needs attention, prepare 2 strips of tissue, with the grain direction in the tissue following that of the edge to which it will be attached. One edge of each strip should be frayed as described in the preceding section. The re-edging will be less conspicuous if the strips of tissue are cut wide enough to extend from the edge of the print to slightly beyond the edge of the page. The frayed edge of the tissue is placed next to the print, and the surplus is cut away from the outer edge when the repair is dry. Or if the page under repair is ruled off in any way, the re-edging should be attached just outside the ruled line.

The same techniques used in guarding (earlier in this chapter) are used in applying the tissue strips. The tissue is, however, placed on both sides of the page. As the pages are repaired, give them a quick nip in the press between silicone release paper and pulpboards. Remove from the press and take away the release paper, leaving the page between the pulpboards. Place this between pressboards and weight down until thoroughly dry. If more than 1 page requires attention, they can be piled up under the same weight after the repairs are made. Just be sure that a piece of pulpboard covers both sides of each page.

Missing fragments of the margin can be filled in with pieces of matching paper cut to the shape of the gap and laid in position after the tissue has been attached to 1 side of the page and before the second strip is laid on. If no matching paper is available, a heavy Japanese tissue (Okawara) should be adequate.

Replacing Missing Corners

Lay the page to be repaired on the matching paper in the same grain direction. If a laid paper, try to match up the chain lines. (These are the thin lines that are visible when the paper is held up to a light and are generally spaced about 1 inch apart; the spacing does vary, however.)

Materials Needed

Paper matching (if possible) color, texture, weight of page
Starch paste wheat or rice
Brick
Silicone release paper
Pulpboard
Pressboard

Trace lightly with a pencil onto the piece of paper to be added the shape of the missing area. Separate the sheets, and with a sharp scalpel, pare the edge of the piece of paper about 1/8 inch outside the line drawn; this will make it 1/8 inch bigger than the missing portion (Fig. 6-13). Erase all pencil marks.

Also pare the edge of the book page on 1 side the same 1/8 inch. Generally, this is done on the back, or verso, of the page. Do it, however, on the side where it will interfere least with the legibility of the page should some portion of the print be affected or missing. Do not pare away the print. If the overlapping of the piece to be added will obscure portions of the print, lay it carefully in position and lightly mark the areas where the print is covered, and cut the overlapping edge away at these points.

Both of these prepared edges should have a frayed or fibered edge, not clean-cut. If the paring is properly and carefully done, when the 2 pared edges are laid together—the pared surfaces facing each other— they should equal in thickness the rest of the page. Apply a light coat of paste to both edges, lay them together, give them a nip (short time) in the press, and set aside to dry under weights.

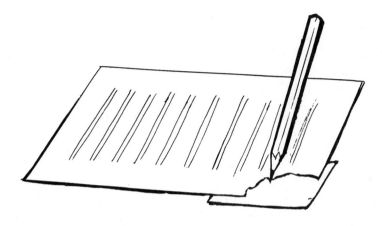

FIGURE 6-13.

Wormholes

The method of repairing wormholes depends on their size and the extent of the damage. Extremely small ones are perhaps best left untreated.

Materials Needed

Paper to match page
Water
Wheat paste
Wax paper
Spatula
Brick
Japanese tissue
Pulpboard
Pressboard

Small holes that do not fall on a fold or the very edge of a page can be filled or repaired by the pulping method. Find a piece of paper that matches the page in color. Tear into small pieces and put them to soak in a bowl of water; when thoroughly wet, mash or shred them into pulp. Drain off the water. Mix a small amount of the pulp with a thin wheat paste.

Lay the page to be treated on a piece of wax paper, which should be on a flat, firm surface. Using a small spatula, fill the hole or holes with the mixture, pressing it firmly into the hole. Try to keep it flush with the surface of the page. Cover with wax paper and put under weight.

Larger holes, especially those that have destroyed the folds in the spine area, are more satisfactorily repaired by tearing pieces of a matching paper the size and shape of the hole, leaving a frayed or fibered edge on the patch. Paste the edges of this and lay in position over the hole. Then cover the area on both sides with a thin Japanese tissue cut large enough to cover the patch and extend about 1/8 of an inch onto the page. Fray the edges of the tissue, paste, and lay in position. Put between wax paper, pulpboards, and pressboards, and weight down until thoroughly dry.

There are leaf-casting machines that fill wormholes, replace missing portions of a page, and the like by sucking pulp out of solution into the missing area by means of a vacuum pump. These machines are rather costly, however, and not considered a practical investment for the binder who runs into the problem of wormholes only occasionally.

Backing a Page

In cases where a plate or title page is damaged or fragile, it is preferable to reinforce it by backing with a Japanese tissue rather than laminating it (discussed later). A medium-weight tissue such as Usugami or Sekishu serves this purpose well.

Materials Needed

Tissue 1 sheet, larger in all dimensions by 1/2 inch (1.2 cm) than the page to be treated, cut the same grain direction as the page
Wheat paste
Silicone release papers
Pulpboards
Pressboards
Brick

To prevent one of the materials from pulling more than the other, causing the page to curl badly, apply paste to both the back of the page and to 1 side of the tissue. Lay the 2 pasted surfaces together; put between the silicone release paper, the pulpboards, and the pressboards. Give it a quick nip in the press. Remove, take away the release paper; leave the page between the pulpboard and pressboards and weight down. Check it in 10 or 15 minutes. If all is well, leave it for 1 hour or so; then change the pulpboards and weight down again until thoroughly dry. If, however, it has stuck to the pulpboards, free it carefully with a bonefolder, change the pulpboards immediately, and put back under weight.

Heat Set Tissue

This is a lens tissue coated with acrylic resins. It can be made up in quantity, allowed to dry, and stored until needed. It is applied to a page or sheet of paper by means of heat, which softens the resins and returns to them their adhesive qualities. So, it is a dry method of repairing or strengthening paper. It is useful in guarding and page repair, particularly when the conventional use of paste tends to water stain, and in backing pages that are too fragile to handle safely by other methods. Its preparation and application are described in detail by the

Library of Congress in its *Conservation Workshop Notes on Evolving Proce-dures*, Series 300, no. 1, Heat Set Tissue, May 1977 (see Bibliography under Conservation and Restoration).

Laminating a Page

When a page is damaged with multiple tears, frayed edges, missing portions, and the like, it can best be preserved by laminating. This means covering the page on both sides with a thin, transparent mate-rial. Lens tissue is frequently used for this purpose, and this is the method described here. Other methods of laminating are described in the rest of this section.

The lens tissue method is a wet process, so papers that will be dam-aged by water should not be treated in this way. Coated papers and certain types of imitation India paper, both of which contain some type of filler, are examples.

Materials Needed

Plate glass 1 piece larger by several inches than page to be treated, or porcelain or formica top table, lithographic stone, or smooth nonabsorb-ent surface that water will not damage

Wastepaper strip 2 inches (5 cm) wide and longer than width of page

Lens tissue 2 pieces larger by 1 inch in both dimensions than book page; cut same grain direction

Guard strip 1, Usugami

Paper matching page in color, texture, weight, cut to shape of missing portions of page

Flat pan roasting or baking type, larger than page, with clean water

Water

Wheat paste

Silicone release paper 2 pieces larger than book page

Pulpboards 8 pieces larger than book page

Polyester web 1 sheet larger than book page

Pressboards 2

Masking tape

Make a frame on the glass, or other surface chosen, with the masking tape. The inside of the frame should be larger by about 3 inches (7.6 cm) than the pieces of lens tissue. Place the page to be laminated in a pan of water. If the page is very fragile, or very thin, place it on the polyester web for support, so that it can be lifted out of the water without damag-ing it further.

Wet the surface within the masking tape frame by brushing with water. Lay the strip of wastepaper at 1 end of the wetted area, with an edge of it resting on the masking tape. Apply paste to the edge of this strip, which is on the wetted surface. Take a piece of the lens tissue, lay 1 end of it on the pasted area of the waste strip, while holding the remaining portion of the tissue up above the working surface (Fig. 6-14). The strip of paper serves as support for picking up the laminated sheet when the job is complete.

With the paste brush, lightly apply an even coat of paste to the surface of the tissue. Start at the edge that is resting on the wastepaper and lay the tissue down as the pasting progresses. Smooth the tissue with the brush; if the brush strokes are made across the grain direction of the tissue, wrinkling will be minimized. When the tissue is wet it is very fragile, so all brushing should be done lightly.

Immediately remove the page to be laminated from the pan of water. Hold it up by 1 edge and let the surplus water drain into the pan. Lay the page on the tissue with the fore edge of the page near the right-hand edge of the tissue. Paste the page and at the same time smooth it out with the brush (Fig. 6-15). Place the guard strip along the inner or gutter margin of the page, overlapping the edges about 1/8 inch. After wetting them, lay in their proper place any separated fragments of the page or any pieces prepared to fill in missing portions of the page (Fig. 6-16). Lightly paste the entire surface of the page, taking care not to move any of the added pieces out of position with the brush.

Lay the second piece of lens tissue on top of the page, brushing it lightly with water in the same manner as the first tissue was put down on the working surface.

Lift the laminated page carefully off the surface, starting with the edge of the waste strip that is resting on the masking tape. This is sort of a peeling motion for which both hands should be used. Lay the page on a piece of silicone release paper, which is supported by a pulpboard and a pressboard. Cut away the waste strip with scissors and discard it. Cover the page with the second piece of release paper, a pulpboard, and a pressboard. Place the whole in the press and give it a quick squeeze to get rid of the surplus moisture.

Remove from the press, transfer the page to dry pulpboards—without the release paper—1 on each side, and return to the press. With 3 such pressings and board changes, the page should be dry enough to eliminate any danger of its sticking to the pulpboards. Change the boards again, put between pressboards, and weight down with a lithographic stone or several bricks. Check it in about a half hour to be sure that it is not sticking to the pulpboard. If all is well, replace the pressboards and weight and leave overnight to dry thoroughly. If it is sticking to the pulpboard, free it at once, change the pulpboard, and weight down again.

To avoid the many pulpboard changes and the many pressings, the page can be hung up to dry by laying the strip of wastepaper, weighted down, on the edge of a piece of waste board that has been secured in position with 1 edge overhanging the edge of a table (Fig. 6-17). This will eliminate the possibility of the page inadvertently attaching itself to the edge of the table. Hang until almost dry and put to press between pulpboards. Leave in the press for a few minutes; remove and check. If all is well, turn the pulpboards over to their drier side and return to the press for several hours or overnight.

The first method produces the best results, but is more time consum-

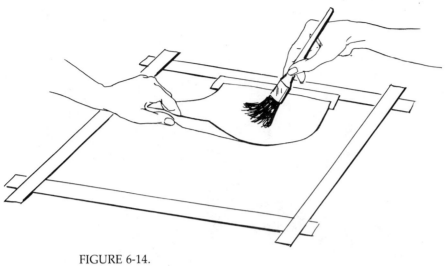

FIGURE 6-14.

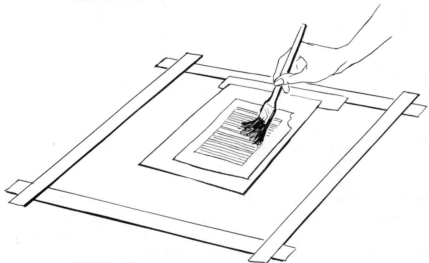

FIGURE 6-15.

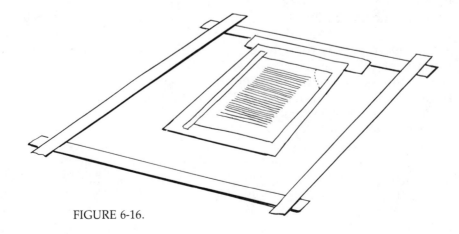

FIGURE 6-16.

FIGURE 6-17.

ing. The disadvantage in the second method is that the top portion of the sheet is likely to become too dry before the bottom portion is dry enough to press safely.

Other Methods of Laminating

Silk chiffon The procedures for laminating with silk chiffon are the same as for laminating with lens tissue (see above). It is generally believed by experienced binders today, however, that lens tissue is preferable to silk chiffon.

Cellulose acetate This method was developed by W. J. Barrow in Richmond, Virginia. It consists of sandwiching a damaged sheet between 2 sheets of cellulose acetate and 2 sheets of lens tissue, which is then put into a heated press where the heat softens the acetate and the pressure causes the whole to stick together. This method requires equipment not available in most hand binderies, so it is best left to those who specialize in this type of work. It changes the format of the page and thus the character of the book. The method has come into disfavor in some quarters in recent years chiefly because the process is not easily reversible.

Polyester film encapsulation This is a process much in use today, more perhaps for single documents than for book pages. Briefly, it consists of sandwiching a sheet of paper between 2 pieces of polyester film and closing the edges with a double-faced sticky tape. The sheet remains free in its encasement and can be removed at any time simply by cutting away one of the sealed edges. (The Preservation Office of the

Library of Congress has published a pamphlet describing this process in detail; see the Bibliography under Conservation and Restoration.)

Stay away from commercially prepared, pressure-sensitive cellulose laminating materials unless assurance can be obtained from the manufacturer (or a testing laboratory) that neither the type of cellulose nor the adhesive used is injurious to paper and that both have a long life expectancy.

Removing Water and Other Stains

Books that have been subjected to water damage frequently have unsightly water stains. These usually appear on the page or pages at the point where the water ceased to penetrate the book. They are believed to represent a concentration of the sizing that was used in the manufacture of the paper and can generally be removed by simply soaking the pages in warm water. It is always a good idea, however, to test 1 or 2 pages before taking a whole book apart to wash it.

Do not attempt to treat coated or clay-filled papers in this way.

In preparing pages for this treatment, clean off all adhesive and surface dirt before placing them in the water bath, and delay any guarding or page repair until after the pages are soaked and dried.

Materials Needed

Pan 2 or more inches deep (5 cm); larger in both dimensions than folded page when open
Paper towels
Pulpboards clean, larger than open page; 1 more than number of pages to be washed at 1 time
Wastepaper
Pressboards 2
Brick
Water warm

Fill the pan with water to a depth of about 1 1/2 inches (3.8 cm). Add the unfolded pages 1 at a time. Be sure that each page is thoroughly wet before the next page is added. Ten or 12 pages is a reasonable number to start with. Soak for about 1 hour. At the end of this time, if the water is very discolored, drain it off, add fresh water, and soak for another hour.

Remove the pages 1 at a time. Lay on the wastepaper and pat with a dry paper towel to remove some of the moisture. Transfer to a pulpboard, taking care that all wrinkles and folds have been flattened out. Cover with a pulpboard and proceed with the next page in the same fashion. When all of the pages are between pulpboards, put the "package" between pressboards and weight down. It is not advisable to put these pages in a press because pressure is likely to obscure the punch of the type in letterpress printing or the plate marks on an engraving.

Change the pulpboards after several hours and weight down again until thoroughly dry—overnight or longer. The pages are now ready for any necessary page repair or guarding.

It is virtually impossible to say with assurance that stains of unknown origin or indeterminate age can be removed with specific treatments. It is at best a matter of trial and error, and unless done with extreme caution, the treatment can do more damage to the page or the text than the initial stain did.

Solvents, in theory, remove grease stains, but which solvent for an unknown stain presents a problem. All solvents are something of a hazard both because of their flammability and toxic characteristics and because they are also solvents for some printer's inks. From the standpoint of safety, they should not be used for any sustained length of time unless a hood is available.

Fresh grease stains can sometimes be successfully removed by dusting the affected area heavily on both sides with French chalk and putting under weight overnight between blotting paper.

Most surface dirt can be removed with a pink pearl eraser (or an eraser that contains no abrasive) or an opaline bag. In using either of these, care should be taken to hold the area of the page being worked on firmly with 1 hand while putting pressure on the eraser or bag with the other.

Pressure sensitive tapes—so quick and easy to use—have over the years presented the binder with 1 of the most common problems. They invariably have a bad effect on both paper and other binding materials. Unfortunately, they can be completely removed—both tape and adhesive—only with a solvent; xylene or toluene generally works well. If a hood is not available and the job is small, work in a well-ventilated area away from other people. Always check the permanence of the ink before proceeding.

If the tape is on only 1 side and the other side is accessible, apply the solvent to the back side. Wait a few minutes until it has had time to soften the adhesive and then carefully and slowly lift the tape. Apply solvent to the surface and gently scrape away the remaining adhesive. If the tape is on both sides, flood the solvent along a small portion of 1 edge until it penetrates the adhesive. Lift the edge, add more solvent, and continue to lift the tape as the adhesive is softened.

Another method of removing these tapes is with heat, which, however, removes only the tape; the residue of adhesive must then be removed with a solvent. Heat a metal burnisher to the sizzling point when a drop of water is applied to it. Place the burnisher on one end of the tape. When the adhesive is soft, lift the tape off the page with the point of a scalpel and continue to lift it as the heat moves along it.

Deacidification and its various processes are not described here. Excessive acidity, inherent in the paper or absorbed from the atmosphere, or a combination of these 2 is perhaps the primary factor in the deterioration of paper. No agreement has been reached by research authorities as to which of a number of methods is the safest and which is practical economically. Deacidifying does not restore deteriorated paper to good health, but it does stop further deterioration in paper that has begun to show failing signs. Presently, it is a costly process, and the value of the material to be treated must be weighed against this cost.

Inner Hinges

These are hinges attached to the first and last signatures of a book and to which the endsheet sections are attached after the book is sewn. Several binders take credit for the development of this new technique. It seemingly, however, evolved at about the same time in widely separated geographic areas where the binders claiming the credit were working independently of each other. It replaces or is an alternative to the traditional, older technique of tipping (pasting or gluing a narrow area) the endsheet sections directly to the first and last pages of the book.

These hinges have several advantages over the older method. They permit the first few pages of the book, both back and front, to open more freely; the front hinge eliminates the riding up of the first (or last) page of the book when it is opened, which invariably happens when the earlier technique is used; and, most important, they remove all strain from the first and last pages of the book. Quite frequently, particularly in cases where new endsheets have been added in the rebinding of a book printed on somewhat fragile paper, the first page of the book is broken away at the point where the new and stronger paper was attached to it (following the older technique). It was doubtless this failing that pointed up the need for a new method.

Materials Needed

Japanese tissue strong and on the heavy side; Okawara (cream-colored) is good for many books; Hosho (white) is good for white book pages; 2 strips 3/4 inch (1.9 cm) wide, 1/2 inch (1.2 cm) longer than vertical measurement of the book (grain direction with length)

Wax paper 4 strips, 2 inches wide (5 cm), 1 inch (2.5 cm) longer than tissue hinges

Wastepaper 4 strips, 2 inches wide, 1 inch longer than tissue hinges

Mixture wheat paste and water-soluble PVA equal parts

Brick

Pressboard

One hinge is attached to the last page of the first signature of the book; the other to the first page of the last signature.

Lay the first signature facedown with the folded edge resting on a strip of the wastepaper; in other words, it is the first page of the book that will be in contact with the waste strip, and the last page of the first signature will be up, or exposed. Place a second strip of paper the entire length of the book page 1/8 inch in from the fold. Apply paste to this area. Remove the wastepaper and discard it; place the signature on a strip of wax paper and lay 1 edge of the hinge on the pasted area, placing it so that both ends of the tissue extend beyond the top and bottom of the page. Cover with a second strip of wax paper and weight down with the pressboard and brick. Repeat this process on the last signature. This time the last page of the book will be on the waste strip and the first page of the last signature will be faceup. Leave under the board and brick for about 15 minutes, or until dry. When dry, fold the hinges around the folds of the signatures and leave them free—meaning that this portion of the hinge is to have no adhesive applied to it at this time. When dry, cut the hinge even with the top and bottom of the signature and fold it flat onto the first or last page of the signature.

If properly done, the free portion of the hinge on the first signature in its folded position will be resting on the first page of the book; and on the last signature, this same portion of the hinge will be resting on the last page of the book. If this is not the case, moisten the pasted area of the hinge or hinges with a piece of damp cotton and try again.

These hinges remain folded against the first and last pages of the book, and nothing further is done to them until after the book is sewn.

Preparing Endsheet Sections

It has been the custom for a number of years for the hand binder to make up endsheet sections. These are composed of the flyleaves, endleaves, hinges, and protection sheets. The flyleaves should match as nearly as possible in both color and texture the paper on which the book is printed. The endleaves and board papers can be of the same paper, a solid color, or a decorated paper. The hinges are customarily made from the material used in covering the book, and, if two-tone, the material used on the spine.

The advantage of these sections is that they are incorporated in the sewing of the book, thus becoming a part of the book. It is a stronger form of construction than that routinely used in edition binding. Cloth or leather hinges also add strength to the binding. Since they have come into general use during this century, they are not recommended for older works or in conservation work, unless they were used in the original binding.

There are a number of ways of assembling these endsheet sections. The method described here is simply constructed, aesthetically pleasing, and proven to be both practical and durable.

Materials Needed
Pressboard
Brick
Mixture wheat paste and water-soluble PVA equal parts
Flyleaves 2, folded, matching book stock
Hinges 2, same cloth selected for cover
Wastepaper 2 clean sheets and 8 strips
Colored paper 4 single sheets that go well with cover material
Wax paper 4 strips
Right-angle triangle
Masking tape

These instructions are for endsheet sections for a cloth case binding using conventional book cloth, solid color (other than white) endleaves and board papers, and cloth hinges. Two such sections are required for each book, 1 for the front and 1 for the back. Following the directions are variations and some precautions. Read the entire section through before you start work.

Cutting the materials All materials should be cut so that the grain direction runs parallel with the vertical measurement of the book. Cut the folded flyleaves, colored paper, and protection sheets approximately 1/2 inch (1.2 cm) larger than the book page in both length and width; the hinges should be the same length as the other materials and 1 1/4 inches (3.1 cm) wide; the wax paper and the wastepaper strips, 1 inch (2.5 cm) or so longer than the other materials and 1 1/2 inches (3.8 cm) wide.

Assembling the sections Place the folded edges of the flyleaves—one at a time—on a strip of the wastepaper. Lay a second strip of paper on the flyleaf 1/8 inch in from the folded edge. Apply the prepared adhesive to this area. Remove the strip of paper from the top; transfer the flyleaf from the wastepaper to a strip of the wax paper; lay 1 edge of the colored paper, right side—if the sides differ, faceup—on the pasted area (Fig. 6-18). Cover the area where the 2 are attached with wax paper and weight down with the pressboard and brick until dry (about 15 minutes). Repeat this step with the second flyleaf. For drying, it can be placed on top of the first one, if the 2 are separated by wax paper, and weighted with the same board and brick. When dry, place the straightedge along the folded edge of the flyleaf, and with the bonefolder fold the colored sheet around the flyleaf (Fig. 6-19). The 2 additional colored sheets are put aside to be used as board papers when needed.

Hinges These are attached to the sections using the same pasting procedure as described above. The area to be pasted is the 1/8 inch of colored paper that is now the inside, or book side, of the section. One edge of the hinge should be laid on the pasted area with the right side of the material facing down. Weight down as previously described, and when dry, fold the hinge around the folded edge of the section. If done correctly, when folded, the right side of the material will be facing the right side of the colored endleaf (Fig. 6-20).

Protection sheets Insert 1 protection sheet between the colored endleaf and the hinge of each section (Fig. 6-21). Secure in position with 2 short strips of masking tape.

Pressing Place the prepared sections between pressboards and put in the press for a few minutes, screwing the press down firmly.

These sections are now ready to be cut to the size of the book page. There are several reasons why it is recommended that they be made larger to start with: The book may not be a true rectangle; some of the materials may have slipped a bit in the process of attaching them to each other; the measurements may not have been entirely accurate; and

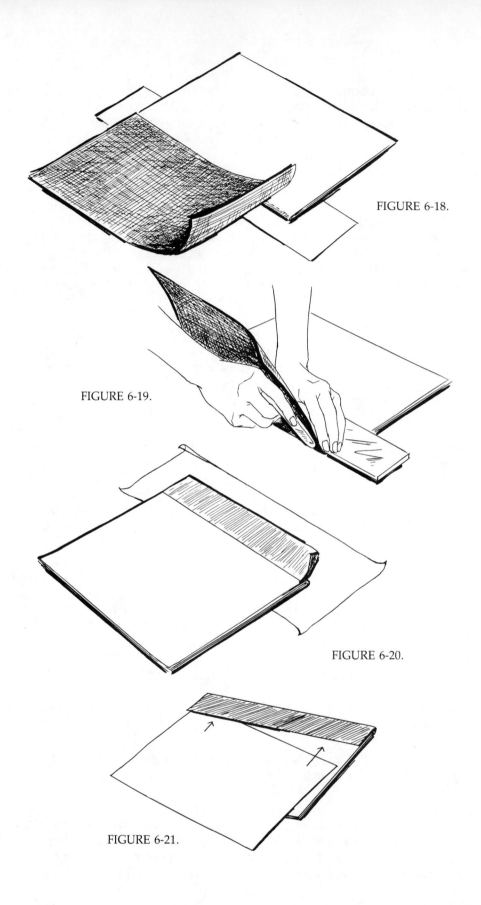

FIGURE 6-18.

FIGURE 6-19.

FIGURE 6-20.

FIGURE 6-21.

when trimmed to the exact size as a unit, it makes for neater work and ease in handling.

Cutting endsheet sections to size The cutting of these sections to size has a direct relationship with the planned treatment of the edges of the book (see Treatment of Edges following this section).

When the fore edge and tail are to be cut on the board shears a signature at a time, before sewing, cut the head of each endsheet section before setting the gauge on the board shears. Lay the folded edge of the sections—1 at a time—against the stop on the board shears and cut off only enough to ensure a clean, even edge on all of the pages that make up the section. After making the cut, check to be sure that it was correctly done. Place the 2 sections in their proper positions on the front and back of the book. The fore edge and tail of these sections can then be cut along with the rest of the book.

If all 3 edges of the book are to be cut after it is sewn and glued, cut the head of each endsheet section as described above. Lay 1 of the sections in position on the first signature of the book, lining up the 2 together at the spine and the head. Mark both the length and width of the signature on the section; then cut both sections to the size indicated by the marks. If a board shears with a gauge on the board is available, this can be set to the proper size for cutting these sections by using a signature of the book as a measure. Lay the folded edge of the signature against the stop; move the signature so that its head comes just to the edge of the blade attached to the board and bring the gauge in until it touches the tail; tighten it. Both sections can then be cut quickly to the proper size. Repeat this for the fore edge, laying the folded edge of the signature against the gauge and moving it so that the fore edge of the signature is flush with the edge of the blade attached to the table; tighten the gauge and cut both sections.

In the case of a book where the edges are not to be cut, the endsheet sections should be cut to conform in size with the first and last signatures of the book. First, check the book for squareness by placing a right-angle triangle along the edge of the spine at both head and tail of the first and last signatures. Make this same check against the fore edge. If the book is square, cut the endsheet sections to the exact size of the book pages.

The pages of many books are not true rectangles. This is frequently so in older books that have been cut with a plough and in books with gilt edges where the gilder has exerted more pressure in the scraping on 1 edge than the other, and in some modern books where 5 or 10 copies have been cut simultaneously with a power-driven guillotine.

If the edges are not square, or at right angles to each other, lay the endsheet section made for the front of the book facedown on the table, and place the first signature of the book on top of it, also facedown, lining the 2 up at the folded, or spine, edge. They should be laid together in the same relative position that they will occupy in the finished volume. Weight the signature down to prevent shifting; lay a straightedge across the head of the signature, lining it up exactly with the edge. Mark 2 cutting points, 1 on the spine edge and the other on the fore edge. Remove the signature, replace the straightedge on the marks, and make the cut. Check it with the signature for accuracy by lining them up as just described; if all is well, repeat this procedure for the cutting of the tail and fore edge. Mark this section in some way to show that it belongs on the front of the book. The back endsheet section should then be cut in the same way.

Endsheet Variations

Where solid color endleaves and board papers are not desired, simply eliminate them and attach the hinges directly to the folded edge of the flyleaves. Lay aside 2 pieces of the paper chosen for the flyleaves for the board papers. A third flyleaf can be added by using a single sheet of paper and attaching it to the folded sheet as described above for the colored paper.

Two additional flyleaves may be added by inserting another folded sheet inside the 1 already described. This would normally be the same type of paper. If done, this would provide 4 blank pages—flyleaves—both front and back. By most standards, however, this would be considered excessive, particularly for a book that is to be bound in cloth.

Traditionally, the endleaves and board papers are made from the same sheet of paper. If, however, it seems desirable to have a two-tone effect, do so. In cases where neither cloth nor leather hinges are appropriate or desirable, the hinges can be made of the same paper selected for the endleaves and board papers. The method of attaching them is the same as described earlier for cloth hinges. In addition, a hinge made from some closely woven fabric such as lawn or airplane linen should be attached as a reinforcement to the paper. The techniques used are the same.

This same effect can be obtained by making the endleaves and board papers a folded sheet instead of 2 single sheets. In this case, the folded edge is attached to the folded edge of the flyleaves and the whole folded around the flyleaves. The cloth reinforcement or lawn hinge and the protection sheet are attached as just described. Although this method is perhaps more conventional than the use of a hinge to cover the joint area and a single sheet as a board paper, it is not as easy to execute neatly. If the book is the least bit off-square, or crooked in its covers, the board papers will not be properly centered, and if the board papers stretch when they are pasted—and they are likely to—they will be too long on the fore edge and protrude beyond the book pages. These problems can be remedied by judicious and careful trimming. Unless, however, there is some specific reason why a folded sheet seems more desirable, it is recommended that beginners in particular stay away from it.

If a folded sheet is used in either a tight back or a German tube binding, the board papers should be made approximately 1/4-inch wider than the other sheets that make up the endsheet section. This must be taken into consideration in the cutting of these sections to size. This can be done by rolling them back free of the cutting action.

When either paper hinges or folded sheets are used, care should be taken in selecting a paper that is strong enough to stand the wear that it will receive in the opening and closing of the book.

For bindings to be covered with leather, it is customary to make the hinges of the same leather. These sections are made up in the same way as previously described, with 2 exceptions: The leather should be pared or thinned (see Leather Paring in Chapter 5), and the protection sheets are attached solidly to the 1/8-inch area of the materials that were pasted onto the flyleaves and are folded around the entire section. This 1/8-inch of the protection sheets remains permanently in the book. For this reason these sheets should be a good grade of medium-weight bond paper, preferably acid-free.

In a Bradel binding, the protection sheets are attached as for leather, regardless of the material used for hinges, and for the same reason they should be made of a durable paper. For a tight back and a German tube, when a leather hinge is used, the addition of 2 pieces of bristol board are required. One piece is cut the size of the endsheet section and inserted between the hinge and the endleaf. The hinge, which is already folded, is attached to the bristol with 2 or 3 tabs of masking tape. The second piece is cut the length of the first, and in width it is cut to cover the area from the edge of the hinge to the fore edge. Put a few spots of mixture on this piece of bristol and lay in position against the hinge and in line with the edges of the other bristol. These are added partly as an aid in the backing of the book and to give a bit more space between the book and the boards to accommodate for the thickness of the leather hinge.

If the covering material is to be a woven fabric other than book cloth, the hinges should be of the same material. Before making up the endsheet sections, the pieces cut for the hinges should first be mounted or attached solidly to a sturdy Japanese tissue such as Okawara or Hosho. This is done by applying mixture to the tissue, leaving it for a few seconds until the mixture becomes tacky, then lay the cloth on the tissue, smooth it out, place it between clean pulpboards, and weight down with a board and brick until dry. Do not put it in the press. This gives it the body or firmness that is desirable for a hinge and serves as a barrier against the adhesive oozing through the cloth in the covering operation. It is advisable to test an unfamiliar fabric before use. Mount a small piece as just described. If the adhesive comes through the material and stains it, try using a little less adhesive or let it set a little longer before attaching the cloth. If a satisfactory result cannot be attained, choose another material.

Leather and silk doublures The term *doublure*, broadly defined, means the lining on the inside of a book cover. Specifically in hand bookbinding, this lining is not referred to as a doublure unless it is made of leather or vellum that has been tooled or painted or of a silk fabric. The use of these materials can be confined to the board, in which case the endleaf would be paper and the hinge would be made of the material that had been selected for the covering material. The techniques in their construction are the same as those previously described. If the endleaves are to be of vellum, they can be treated in the same fashion as described for a colored paper.

Where leather is to be used as endleaves, it will require overall thinning and should not be incorporated in the endsheet sections until after the edges of the book have been cut—if they are to be cut—but before the edges are gilded. The edges of the leather should be pared very thin. First, cut the piece of leather slightly larger in both dimensions than the flyleaf (approximately 1/8 inch in length and 1/16 inch in width). Then pare the edges. Attach the leather solidly to the first flyleaf of the front endsheet section and to the last flyleaf of the back endsheet section by applying wheat paste to both the leather and the flyleaves. Place between clean pulpboards and weight down until dry. Then, using a sharp mat knife and a straightedge carefully, cut away any leather that overhangs the edges of the flyleaves. This should produce an even, clean edge.

In the case of silk endleaves, they, like leather, should not be incorporated in the endsheet sections until after all cutting of the edges is done and before gilding. The raw edges of silk are likely to fray in a short time, producing anything but an elegant appearance, which is the primary reason for its use. To eliminate any raw edges, they should all be turned in; this is done over a sheet of paper. Cut 2 pieces of paper (the same paper used for the flyleaves is good) the size of the flyleaves less the estimated thickness of the silk. In both length and width, 2 thicknesses of the silk have to be reckoned with. The best way to arrive at the proper amount by which these sheets should be reduced in size is to make up a small sample. It is contingent entirely on the thickness of the material selected.

These sheets should also be cut to conform in shape with the flyleaves and marked in some way so that when they are attached to the flyleaves, they will be put in the same position as when they were marked for cutting. This is not very important if all 4 corners of the book are true right angles, but this is not always the case. It is essential for a neat end result when the book is not a true right angle.

Once these sheets are cut to the proper size and the material has been ironed—if it was wrinkled or creased—cut the material 1 inch (2.5 cm) larger in both dimensions than the sheet of paper. Lay the material, right side facedown, on a smooth clean surface; place the sheet of paper on the material so that 1/2 inch (1.2 cm) of the material extends beyond the edges of the paper on all 4 sides. Weight the paper down so that it will not shift, and cut the corners (see Fig. 7-19) so when the material is folded around the paper, the cloth will come together as a mitered corner and there will be no surplus to make unsightly bumps.

Apply mixture to about 1/4 inch of each edge of the paper—top and bottom first, then the sides—and turn the cloth over the edge of the paper onto the pasted area. Care should be taken to keep the cloth smooth, while at the same time not pulling it to the extent that it buckles the paper. When all edges are turned, place between pulpboard and weight down until dry. These are then attached to the first and last flyleaves. First, check to be sure that they are exactly the size and shape of the flyleaves. If they are, slip a piece of wax paper under the first flyleaf—in the fold, in other words—and put a line of mixture about 1/8 inch wide on all 3 edges and in the spine area. Lay the silk doublure in position on the flyleaf, checking it carefully to be sure that all edges are properly lined up. Cover with pulpboard and weight down until dry.

If the cloth-covered sheets are too small, it is better to make them over than to try to remedy the error. If, however, they are too large, lift the material up on 2 edges—the bottom and fore edge or the edges that do not conform to the shape of the flyleaf—cut away the surplus paper, repaste the edges of the paper, and lay the material down again. In its finished state, the right side of the material is not attached to the paper, and all edges should be absolutely even with the edges of the flyleaf to which it is attached.

If the edges of the book are to be cut after it is rounded and backed, before proceeding with these steps add to both the front and the back of the book several sheets of paper estimated to be the thickness of silk and the paper on which it is mounted or the leather and paper. Since these will be added after the book is backed, it is necessary to provide space for them.

Precautions When a patterned paper is used that has an up-and-down design, take care in attaching this to the flyleaves so that the design will be properly oriented, or in the same direction on both the front and back sections. For the front endsheet section (Fig. 6-22a), the folded edge of the flyleaf, as it lies on the table, should be on the binder's left and the design in the paper running from bottom to top; for the back section (Fig. 6-22b), the folded edge of the flyleaf should be on the right, with the design running from bottom to top. It is advisable to make up 1 section, orient it correctly, check to see whether it fits the front or the back, and mark it accordingly; then proceed with the other.

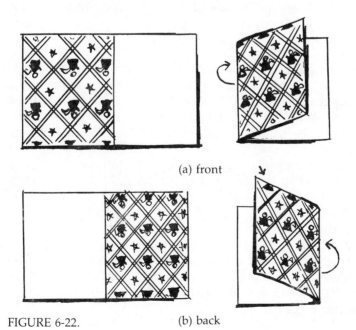

(a) front

FIGURE 6-22.   (b) back

Treatment of Edges

There are a number of possibilities in considering what treatment, if any, should be applied to the edges of a book. The first decision is whether the edges require alteration. There are many instances where the edges should be, and occasionally where they must be, left alone: according to the bibliographer and collector, the format of an old and/or rare book should not be altered, nor should first editions, books not cut when originally bound, and volumes with deckled edges. The edges should not be cut on volumes with marginal notes, folded maps, and charts, or the like, any of which might be endangered in the cutting process, or on ones with very narrow margins.

Materials Needed

Eraser
Pulpboard
Pressboards
Hammer
Sandpaper (specified in instructions)
Cloth
Beeswax
Wheat paste
Tissue paper (not Japanese tissue)
Agate burnisher

If the decision is not to alter the edges, but it seems desirable to clean them up a bit, this can be done with a pink pearl eraser or any eraser that is free of abrasive material. In cases where the edges are smooth, clean them before the book is taken apart or pulled. If the edges are irregular, cleaning is best done a page at a time either before it is taken apart or when it is in loose signatures.

For a smooth edge For the head and tail, place the book between clean pulpboards wide enough to cover it from the joint out to the fore edge and the length of the book. Place backing or pressboards on each side from the joint to the fore edge. Both the pulpboards and the pressboards should be flush with the edge of the book. This can be accomplished by putting the "package" in a finishing press or job backer and tightening the jaws enough to hold the material, but free enough so that the boards can be shifted by tapping lightly with a hammer. When the book and the boards are properly adjusted, and they are flush with the jaws of the press, screw the press up tightly. Go over the entire edge with the eraser. When it appears that all dirt has been removed— or all that it is possible to remove—repeat the process on the other end. The fore edge is treated the same way, although the boards used must be no wider than the book is from joint to fore edge and should cover the entire length of the book. Backing or gilding boards are useful for all work on fore edges.

Sanding the edges Sanding is another method of cleaning up the edges when cutting does not seem advisable. It is a method often used for the removal of unwanted colored edges. If the edges are reasonably even, sanding does not appreciably alter the size of the book. It is a safe compromise, although somewhat slow and tedious. Sanding can be done more quickly before the book is taken apart or pulled.

Place the book in a press as previously described. Start the sanding with a 2/0 garnet paper (or medium-grit sandpaper) and finish with a very fine paper such as a no. 4/0 garnet. Wrap a piece of the paper around a small, smooth block of wood and keep it flat or horizontal while in motion on the head and tail. Sand these 2 edges from spine to fore edge, not across the book from front to back. If the book is still in its rounded state and the fore edge concave, best results can be had by wrapping the sandpaper around a rounded object that can be handled easily and that is large or small enough to fit into the concavity of the fore edge. A short piece of dowelling, the spool from an adding machine tape, or a small round bottle are possibilities.

After the edges are sanded, they can be polished, if desired, by rubbing with a soft cloth to which beeswax has been applied. Rub the wax on the cloth and the cloth on the edge; then burnish with an agate burnisher. Another polishing method is to apply a coat of thin wheat paste to the edge, let it dry for a few minutes, then rub with a wad of soft tissue paper. (Do not waste Japanese tissue for this.)

If the decision is to cut the edges, this can be done in 1 of several ways, with the board shears, a guillotine, a plough, or even with a mat knife and straightedge (not recommended except possibly in the case of a book with very few signatures). The desired appearance of the finished edge determines the method and also the proper stage in the binding process when it should be done. It is generally considered preferable to cut the head smooth, for the practical reason that a smooth, even surface picks up less dirt than does a rough edge.

If you want a slightly rough or sheared edge, sometimes referred to as a "simulated deckle," the tail and fore edge are cut 1 signature at a time on the board shears at the stage when the endsheet sections are in position and the book is otherwise ready for sewing. The head is then cut on a plough or guillotine. If a guillotine is used, it is cut after the book is sewn and glued and while the spine is still straight or squared-up; if a plough is used, the head is cut after the book is rounded and backed.

Cutting on the board shears If earlier instructions were followed in making the endsheet sections, the head or top edges of both front and back sections have been cut clean and even. If not, first cut the top edge of both sections at a right angle to the spine edge. Be sure to get a clean and even edge on all of the leaves that make up these sections.

The object is to clean up the edges and make the signatures all the same size. No more should be cut away than the minimum required to accomplish this. If there are a few short pages—in either length or width—ignore these rather than reduce the size of the book appreciably. Cut the tail first. Select a signature that seems to conform in size to most of them. Lay the folded edge of the signature against the stop or ruler on the board shears; push it under the pressure bar, allowing the amount to be cut off to protrude beyond the cutting point; hold the signature in this position with the pressure bar; adjust the gauge on the board so that it makes contact with the head of the signature. The head of the signature may not be at a true right angle with the spine, so the gauge might not touch it along its entire edge. The important thing is to have the cut that is being made on the tail at right angles with the spine. Once the machine is set, start at the back of the book and cut the tail of every signature, including the endsheet sections. When completed, repeat the procedure on the fore edge, placing the tail against the stop and the folded, or spine, edge of the signature against the gauge. When all signatures have been cut, the book is ready for sewing.

For smooth even edges, the book should be cut with a plough or on a guillotine. In this case all 3 edges—head, tail, and fore edge—are cut. If a guillotine is used, the edges are cut after the book is sewn, the spine glued, squared-up, and the glue is dry. In using a plough, the fore edge can be cut at this same stage, but the head and tail should be cut after the book is rounded and backed. (See plough and press in Chapter 3.)

Cutting on a guillotine If the book has been lined up at the head in the sewing, as recommended, cut the tail first, then the head, and last the fore edge. In cutting the head and tail, always place the spine of the book so that the cutting action starts at the spine. The knife on many guillotines moves in a slicing motion from left to right. If this is true with the one you are using, the spine of the book should always be on your left as you face the machine.

Check the knife to be sure that it is held firmly in its safety position before beginning work with a guillotine.

Inspect the book and estimate the minimum needed to be cut off to produce a clean, smooth edge. Mark the cutting point with a pencil. Short signatures will cause the pages immediately above them to have a ragged edge, due to their lack of support. When the knife strikes these unsupported pages, the pressure tends to bend them and tear them off rather than cutting them cleanly. So the book should be cut to the size of its smallest signature. A few isolated short pages, however, will cause no trouble and can be ignored.

To get even pressure in the area to be cut, build the book up on both front and back to compensate for the swell in the spine area. If this is not done, the spine will be forced into a rounded position when the pressure bar is tightened, leaving the upper corners on the fore edge unsupported and subject to breaking off when the knife strikes them.

Place several pulpboards on both sides of the book, offsetting them approximately 1/4 inch in from the spine. Press down on the fore edge and check to see if its height is equal to that of the spine. The number of boards (or packing) required will depend on the extent of the swell that is being compensated for. When this is accomplished, remove the boards from the top of the book, place an additional piece of pulpboard under the entire book on the bottom, and put it into the guillotine, head against the gauge. Adjust the gauge to bring the book into the position where the cutting point previously marked is just visible when the pressure bar is lowered. When properly positioned, raise the pressure bar and add the packing to the upper side of the book and cover the entire book with an additional piece of pulpboard. Hold the book firmly in position with 1 hand and tighten the pressure bar with the other. If the pressure pulls the head of the book away from the gauge, raise the pressure bar, add more packing, and try again (Fig. 6-23).

There is 1 other precautionary note: Check the head of the book to be sure that it is at a right angle with the spine. If the head is off-square and is placed solidly against the gauge, the whole book will end up with uneven margins on the tail. If such is the case, place a right-angle triangle or square against the gauge and line the spine of the book up against the square. This would mean that the head of the book would be touching the gauge only partially or possibly at only 1 point. When everything seems in order, make the cut on the tail. Remove the book and check the margin on the tail on a number of pages to be sure that the space between the last line of type and the bottom of the page is the same from spine to fore edge. If the tail is satisfactory, the head can be cut following the same procedure; this time, however, the tail can rest solidly against the gauge.

On the fore edge cut, the packing need not be so carefully positioned. Just be sure that each piece of board is as long as the book, wider than the pressure bar from front to back, and that the spine of the book is resting squarely against the gauge.

Do not use for packing binder's board or any type of board that may contain grit or other abrasive material. The knife on a guillotine is ground to a very fine edge and the smallest piece of grit can nick it; a nicked blade will make a ragged mark diagonally across the book. If this should happen, sand the edges to remove the blemish. Follow the procedures given under sanding of edges described earlier in this section. The edges may also be polished as described in the same section. If the cut, however, is clean and smooth, the time expended in sanding and polishing is not justified by the difference in appearance.

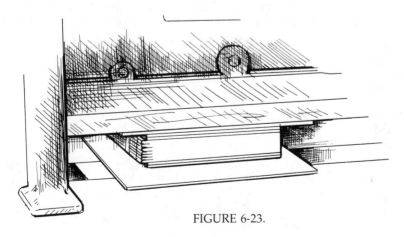

FIGURE 6-23.

Colored edges Over the years this has been a popular treatment for the edges of books. It has taken the form of solid colors, sprinkled or spattered, and marbled—usually matching the endleaves or the covering paper in a half-leather binding.

Due to the great variety in quality and texture of book papers, no one type of color will be successful on all papers. So only general instructions are given here, along with several possible coloring materials, and the recommendation that the 1 selected be tried out on a small area of the tail before proceeding.

The coloring of edges is done after the book has been sewn, glued, edges cut, rounded, and backed.

Screw the book up in a press as described earlier in this section under sanding of the edges. First, however, place a piece of wax paper on the inside of both boards, protruding sufficiently to fold down over the edges of the boards. This is to protect the boards from the colors. If there are slight irregularities on the edges, sand them lightly. Do not attempt, however, to get them smooth to the point of looking polished, for the color will not stick.

Some possible coloring materials are dye that is sprayed or painted on; show card or tempera colors, diluted enough to be evenly and smoothly applied; tube watercolors mixed with a little Chinese white and diluted; dry pigments dissolved in a little water and mixed with a thin wheat paste.

One edge at a time is treated and allowed to dry before shifting the position of the book. On the head and tail, spray, sponge, or brush on the selected color, working from spine to fore edge, and on the fore edge, from the center out toward both ends. When dry, rub with a soft cloth to which beeswax has been applied. They can then be polished with a small wad of crumpled tissue paper or an agate burnisher.

Other edge treatments See Cockerell and Town in the Bibliography under Instructional Manuals for edge gilding. The binder might also be interested in gauffering, the process of tooling or embossing the edges after they have been gilded. This is decorative, but damages the edges of the pages to some extent. Fore edge painting is done by fanning the leaves slightly, holding them firmly in a fixed position, and painting a watercolor picture or scene on the edges of the pages in this fanned position. When the book is closed, the picture is not visible. Usually the edges are gilded after the painting is added.

Sewing

Sewing plays a very important role in holding a book together, and it should be done with care. All threads should be pulled firmly, trying to keep the tension even. In a book made up of signatures, the sewing is done in the center fold of each signature with what, in effect, is a continuous thread. The signatures are held together by sewing around the tapes or cords and at the head and tail by the kettle stitches. These are chain stitches, and their name is derived from a corrupted use of the German word for chain—*kette*.

Materials Needed

Sewing thread
Needle
Sewing frame
Keys 3-pronged for stringing sewing frame
Pressboard larger than book
Small weight
Triangle
Linen tape unbleached
Paper strip the length of the book

Additional materials are indicated in the appropriate section for particular sewing problems.

Threads are tied on with the weaver's knot or sheet bend. Make a loop at 1 end of the thread that is to be tied on by crossing the end of the thread over the longer portion; while holding the end of the thread firmly, pull it back through the loop with the thumb and forefinger of the other hand (Fig. 6-24a). Place the end of the thread that is attached to the book in the second loop made, slide the loop up close to the spine, and tighten the new thread; this should bring the thread attached to the book into the first loop made (Fig. 6-24b). If properly done, the knot made at the joining will remain close to the spine.

It is difficult to say precisely what weight thread should be used, as evidenced by the fact that authors in the field vary widely in their recommendations. The thickness of the signatures and of the paper, along with the size of the book and its anticipated use, all enter into the picture. In general, books made up of signatures containing up to 8 leaves can safely be sewn with a medium-weight thread such as no. 30/2 cord, and signatures of 12 leaves or over with a heavier thread, no. 18/2 cord. An unnecessarily heavy thread can produce excessive swell in the spine, which creates problems in the backing of the book.

If the fore edge and tail are to be trimmed on the board shears, 1 signature at a time, do so before the sewing is started. The book should be collated—paged through to be sure that the pages are in proper order—before sewing is begun.

Sewing on tapes This type of sewing is suitable for case and Bradel bindings and for tight back and German tube bindings when a smooth spine is desired. Three tapes are adequate for most octavo volumes, and 2 for books 4 inches (10.1 cm) or less in height. For larger books, a good rule of thumb is to space the tapes approximately 1 1/2–2 inches (3.8–5 cm) apart. These directions are for sewing on 3 tapes.

Jog (tapping the material as a unit lightly against a clean, flat surface to get the pages or signatures lined up evenly) the book to the head and then the spine. Place it flat on the pressboard with the head to the left. Put the weight on the fore edge and square the head and spine up against the triangle. Fold the strip of paper in half twice, lengthwise.

Lay the strip of paper against the spine of the book and mark on the

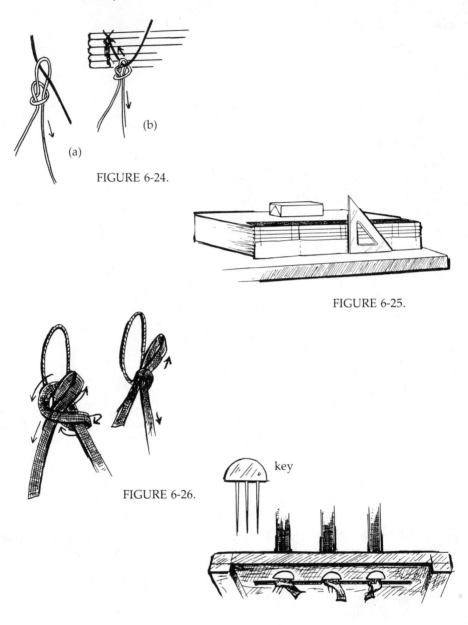

FIGURE 6-24.

(a)

(b)

FIGURE 6-25.

FIGURE 6-26.

key

FIGURE 6-27.

spine the position of the folds. The middle tape is centered on the center mark and the other 2 tapes are positioned from the mark toward the head and tail, respectively. Mark the position of the tapes, making the spaces slightly wider than the width of the tape used. Draw lines across the spine at the marks, using the triangle to keep them straight and neat. Mark the kettle stitches at both head and tail in the same manner. These are generally marked about 1/4 inch in from the head and tail (Fig. 6-25).

If the edges of the book are to be trimmed after it is sewn, the kettle stitches should be placed far enough away from the head and tail so that they will not be endangered in the trimming.

Stringing up the sewing frame For 1 book, lower the crossbar all the way down. Tie the tapes to the lay cords (these cords are only a means of conserving tape) using a half bow knot (Fig. 6-26) and cut them long enough to go through the slot in the board with enough to spare so that the 3-pronged keys will hold them securely. Pull the tapes tight and stick the keys through them (Fig. 6-27). If these keys are not available, 2 large pins or needles will serve the purpose. It is an advantage to fasten the tapes so that they can be moved.

Put the pressboard on the frame against the tapes. Place the book, head to the left, on the board and move or adjust the tapes so that they rest within the spaces marked for them. Leave the pressboard in position; remove the book and place it face, or front, down where it is easily accessible, but not in the way of the sewing operation.

These directions provide for the sewing to begin at the back of the book, but it could as well start with the front of the book. Choose the way that seems most natural and comfortable, and stick with it. The object is, of course, to have the pages in proper order when the sewing is completed.

Sewing the book Start the sewing with the back endsheet section. The thread should show inside the folded flyleaf, about 1/32 to 1/16 inch away from the fold on the sheet next to the last page of the book (Fig. 6-28). It is a good idea to prepunch the holes for sewing on both of the endsheet sections. Trial and error tends to leave unsightly holes. It is important that the thread does not go through the outside pages or the hinges of these sections.

After the holes are punched in the back endsheet section, lay this in position against the tapes, opened at the folded flyleaf. Place a weight on the fore edge (Fig. 6-29). Start sewing with a piece of thread estimated, or measured, long enough to sew 4 or 5 signatures. If there are many signatures, it saves some time to cut a number of lengths of thread, and hang them around 1 of the upright posts on the frame.

Begin the sewing by going from the outside into the section at 1 of the kettle stitches. Leave a tail of thread about 3 inches (7.6 cm) long at this point; come out on the near side of the first tape; go back into the inside on the far side of the tape; out at the near side of the middle tape; in on the far side and so on; and out at the kettle stitch. Hold the tail of thread left at the beginning with 1 hand and pull the other end of the thread tight with the other hand. When tightening the thread, always pull it gently but firmly in a direct line with the spine.

Remove the weight. Take the next signature (which will be the last signature of the book itself), jog it to the head, and lay it in position, lining it up at the head and spine with the 1 just sewn. Open it at the center fold; place the weight on it and sew through the center of the fold, starting at the kettle stitch, and proceed in and out around the tapes. When the thread is brought out at the kettle stitch mark, tie the

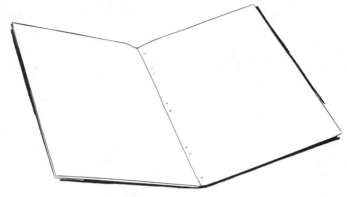

FIGURE 6-28.

FIGURE 6-29.

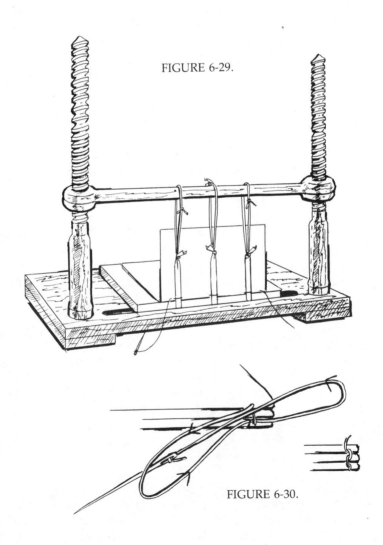

FIGURE 6-30.

thread with which you are sewing and the free tail of thread together with a square knot. Add the next signature and sew it on in the same manner. When the kettle stitch is reached, insert the needle between the endsheet section and the signature adjoining it. Bring the sewing thread around the existing thread, make a loop, stick the needle through the loop, and tighten the thread (Fig. 6-30). This is the first kettle stitch, and this procedure is repeated at each end of the book with each added signature. Do not, however, go back to the endsheet section each time; drop back to the signature below the 1 just sewn on.

Continue in this fashion. When additional thread is needed, tie it on to the existing thread with the weaver's knot, as previously described, at 1 of the kettle stitches. The front endsheet section should be treated in the same way as the back section. This time, however, the holes should be punched on the underside—the side next to the book. When the sewing is completed, secure the thread by making several kettle stitches downward. Cut all tail ends of thread, leaving them about 3/4 to 1 inch (1.9 to 2.5 cm) in length. These ends will be caught and secured in the gluing.

When the sewing is completed, remove the keys, untie the tapes from the lay cords, and remove the book from the sewing frame. Again, collate the book.

If 4 or more tapes are to be used, measure the length of the spine and mark it so that the tapes are equidistant apart. The kettle stitches would be marked as previously described.

The next step is attaching the endsheet sections to the book.

Remedying possible troubles If the thread breaks, remove the sewing back to the nearest tape or kettle stitch and tie on a new thread.

If kettle stitches have been missed and you discover this before the sewing has progressed more than a few signatures from the missed point, work the thread downward along the kettle stitch to the spot and add the missing kettle stitch. If the missing stitch is not detected until the sewing is finished, tie a piece of thread onto the nearest existing tail and catch the signatures together; then secure the thread by making a couple of additional kettle stitches.

When collating the book after sewing, if you discover that a signature is out of order or upside down, cut the threads in the center of the affected signatures, pull the threads out at the kettle stitches, freeing the signatures, and correct the error. Tie a new thread to 1 of the pieces that was pulled out, resew the signature or signatures, and secure all loose threads on the spine by making additional kettle stitches or tying them to an existing thread.

If the center of a signature was missed and there are loose pages, tie a thread on at one of the kettle stitches and resew the signature.

Sometimes the thread gets caught on the edge of the sewing frame or the book and a long loop of thread is found later on. Pull this out at 1 of the tapes on the spine, cut it in 2, and tie the 2 pieces together.

Check the sewing in the endsheet sections. If any thread is visible between the hinge and the endleaf or between the endleaf and the first flyleaf, the section has been sewn on incorrectly. Remove the section by cutting the thread at the center tape and pulling it out of the section at the kettle stitches. Tie on a new thread and resew the section correctly through the folded flyleaves, just off the fold on the flyleaf next to the book.

Sewing on cords This method of sewing is used for tight back and German tube bindings when raised bands are desired. It is frequently referred to as "flexible" sewing. There seems no logical reason, however, that it is any more flexible than the tape method just described.

Five cords or bands are the traditional number for large books— quartos and larger, 4 bands for octavos and smaller books. Five bands will divide the spine into 6 panels, and 4 bands will produce 5 panels. Before deciding on the number of bands, check the length of the title and the author's name to be sure that the size of the planned panels will accommodate them. If title and/or name are too long to fit comfortably into the planned panels, reduce the number of raised bands or sew the book on tapes.

To mark up for 5 cords, cut a strip of paper the width of the spine and 1/4 inch longer than the book. Trimming the edges should be considered here and any measurements adjusted accordingly. Mark 1/8 inch off at each end of the strip of paper; the space between these marks indicates the length of the book. The overall length of the strip represents the height of the finished volume—the book plus the square on the boards, or that portion of the board that protrudes beyond the head and tail of the book. Measure the length of this strip and divide the measurement by 6. For example, if the strip is 12 inches long (30.5 cm), the space between the bands will be approximately 2 inches (5 cm). The space between the last band and the tail of the book is, however, usually slightly larger than the space between the other bands. There is no set rule as to how much larger, but 1/4 inch is average. Set the dividers a fraction of an inch less in width than the figure arrived at in the division—a scant 1/16 inch to start with. Try them out on the strip of paper, adjusting until you have the desired spacing.

Jog the book to the head and spine; square it up against a triangle and place a weight on the fore edge to prevent shifting. It is especially important in this type of sewing that the head is evenly lined up and straight.

Lay the strip of paper against the spine of the book, allowing it to extend 1/8 inch beyond the book at each end. Lightly mark the position of the cords and the kettle stitches, as previously described. Using a triangle, draw 1 line across the spine at each mark (Fig. 6-31).

Stringing up the sewing frame The diameter of the cord used will depend on the size of the book and the effect desired. One-sixteenth to 1/8 inch in diameter is average. First, secure the cords around the keys (Fig. 6-32), and while holding these firmly, insert the cords from the underside of the frame through the slot. Pull them up tight and tie them to the lay cords. Lay the pressboard and the book on the frame with the spine close to the cords and move the cords into position over the lines. Check all cords with a triangle to be sure that they are vertical

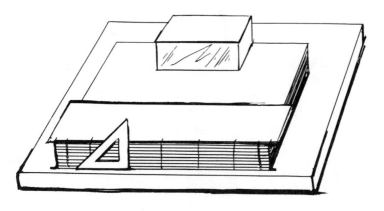

FIGURE 6-31.

FIGURE 6-32.

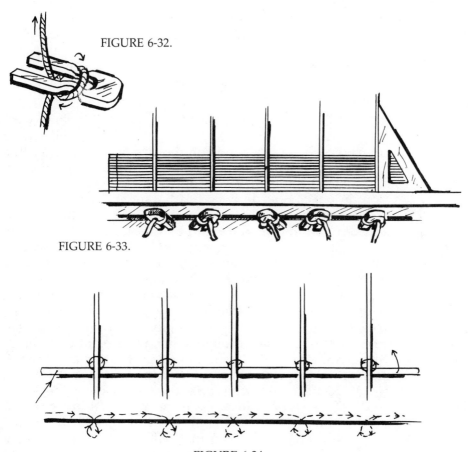

FIGURE 6-33.

FIGURE 6-34.

(Fig. 6-33). If the cords do not remain vertical, the bands will be crooked on the spine.

Prepunch the endsheet sections as described earlier for sewing on tapes. In this type of sewing, only 1 hole is made at each mark. The sewing is started on the outside at one of the kettle stitches; the thread is carried into the endsheet section between the folded flyleaves and brought out on the far side of the first cord. The thread circles the cord by bringing it back toward the kettle stitch, and the needle is inserted in the same hole on the near side. The sewing continues in this way; treatment of the kettle stitches is the same as for sewing on tapes (Fig. 6-34). This permits the cord to stand out, whereas if the thread were brought across it, as in the sewing on tapes, it would tend to flatten the cord. Tighten the thread with each stitch around a cord. It is easy to catch the cord in the sewing (try to avoid this), which makes it impossible to tighten the thread further along. As the sewing progresses, check the head and the cords at frequent intervals to be sure that they are remaining straight and vertical. After 2 or 3 signatures have been sewn on, press them down tightly along the entire length of the spine to keep the swell at a minimum; repeat regularly. When the sewing is completed, remove the book from the frame and collate it.

Sewing on double cords or split thongs This type of sewing is suitable for either a tight back or a German tube binding. It is customarily used on rather large volumes—quarto or larger—that will be bound with a tight back. The choice of cord depends on the size of the book and the effect desired. The sizes mentioned above are average. In stringing up the sewing frame, the 2 cords are placed side by side, wrapped around the key, and put in position as described earlier for single cords.

Thongs are customarily made from strips of vellum or leather pasted together. The width and thickness depend on the effect desired. Three-eighths inch wide is average, and 3 strips of vellum or 2 of leather should serve most needs. If uncertain, experiment. Cut the strips, paste them on a practice tooling block—or any rounded surface similar in shape to the spine of a book—and work a scrap of leather over it. When the desired width and thickness have been determined, cut the necessary number of strips about 4 inches (10.1 cm) longer than the estimated thickness of the book. Paste the strips together and weight down until dry. To slit them, find the center of the thong in width; mark this at 2 points. Using a straightedge and mat knife, cut or slit it in the center lengthwise for a distance that represents the thickness of the book. Leave both ends of the thong unslit. Use the keys that are used for sewing on tapes to hold the thongs to the base of the sewing frame. With an awl, punch a hole in the end that will be attached to the lay cords on the crossbar. Slip a string through the hole in the thong and attach it to the lay cord. These should be attached to the lay cord first, and the height adjusted so that the opposite end of the slit will be even with the level at which the sewing will begin. Pull the thongs tight and secure on the bottom of the frame with the keys.

The same general procedure for marking up the spine is followed as for sewing on single cords. The sewing, however, differs. The center of the 2 cords and the slit in the thongs are positioned on the lines drawn on the spine. The width of these materials should be taken into account in laying out their desired positions. Again, take care that they remain vertical throughout the sewing; the signatures as added should be pressed down firmly along the fold. Treatment of the endsheet sections and the kettle stitches remain the same.

Start the sewing at 1 of the kettle stitches. Bring the needle out between the 2 cords (the same technique is followed for thongs); circle the near cord by bringing the thread back toward the kettle stitch; carry the thread between the cords and the outside of the signature to the far side of the second cord; circle this and take the thread back into the center of the signature through the same hole between the cords (Fig. 6-35). Continue in this manner around the other cords; add the next signature and so on. When the sewing is complete, remove the book from the frame and collate it.

Sewing two-on In cases where a book is made up of thin signatures—2 or 4 leaves—or when the repair or guarding of the folds has been extensive, it is often desirable to reduce the amount of thread by using this method of sewing, thus keeping the swell in the spine to a minimum. It is not as strong as "all-along" sewing, but in most cases it is preferable to excessive swell. This method of sewing can be done on either tapes or raised cords. The same sewing technique is used in both cases. This means that the sewing thread will be brought across the cords, flattening them to some extent. The circling of the cord in the conventional manner cannot be done with this method.

The first and last 5 or so signatures should be sewn "all along"; the number depends on the thickness of the book and the number of signa-

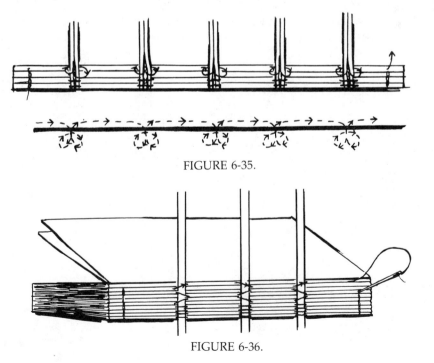

FIGURE 6-35.

FIGURE 6-36.

tures. In a book of 70 signatures, the first and last 10 signatures can be sewn in the conventional way.

In two-on, the first signatures to be treated in this way are laid in position. The needle goes through at the kettle stitch, out on the near side of the first tape; the next signature is added, opened at the center, and the needle inserted on the far side of the first tape; brought out on the near side of the second tape; carried down to the first of the 2 signatures and inserted on the far side of the second tape; brought out on the near side of the third tape, carried up to the second signature, and inserted on the far side of the third tape, and out at the kettle stitch (Fig. 6-36). The thread comes out at the kettle stitch mark on only 1 of these signatures, so the kettle stitch is made by going down to the last 1 made at each end. Since the sewing is alternating between 2 signatures and the center of each has to be found several times, it is helpful to cut a piece of lightweight bristol board about 4 inches (10.1 cm) wide and 6 inches (15.2 cm) long, fold the length in half, and insert one half in the center of the first signature and the other half in the center of the second (Fig. 6-37). Half of each signature is then enclosed in the folded bristol.

Sewing a single signature book Two methods are given: 1 for a leaflet of a few pages and the other for a heavier signature. A piece of thread approximately 3 times the length of the book is required; no. 18/2 cord is a good weight.

In this case, endsheet sections are not made up. The flyleaves and endpapers are made of folded sheets and wrapped around the book. Needed for a hard-cover cloth binding are 1 folded flyleaf, 1 folded endpaper, 1 folded cloth hinge, and 2 protection sheets. Cut the flyleaf and the endpaper the length of the book and about 1/2 inch (1.2 cm) wider; the cloth hinge the length of the book and 2 1/2 inches (6.3 cm) wide; and the protection sheets the size of the book in both dimensions. Paper matching the endleaves should be reserved for the board papers.

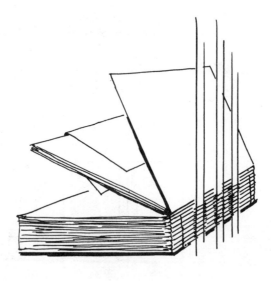

FIGURE 6-37.

The protection sheets are attached after the book is sewn, so lay them aside for later use. Place the other materials in position on the book and jog it to the head and spine. Open the book at the center, lay a folded strip of paper over the edges of one-half the book at both head and tail, and secure with paper clips or small spring clamps. The paper strips are to prevent the clips from marring the pages, and the clips are to hold the pages in position while sewing. It is advisable to prepunch the holes for sewing from the inside of the center fold. Determine the position of the holes and, with the book only partially open, punch the holes through the center fold of the entire book. Check to be sure that the needle comes out exactly in the fold. This is especially important in a thicker book as it is rather easy to get the needle off-center. If the edges are to be trimmed after the book is sewn, bring the last stitch at both head and tail in far enough so that it will not be endangered in the trimming.

The first method, suitable for a few pages, is commonly referred to as butterfly sewing. To find the position at which the holes should be punched, cut a strip of paper the length of the book, fold it in half lengthwise, and make a mark on it at both ends 1/2 inch (1.9 cm) in from the end. Lay this strip against the inside center fold and punch 3 holes, 1 at the center and 1 at each end at the point where the strip was marked off. Start the sewing on the outside at the center hole (Fig. 6-38). Bring the thread through to the inside center fold, leaving a free tail of thread about 3 inches (7.6 cm) long at this point. Carry the thread on the inside to the head of the book and take it out through the hole; carry it on the outside from the head to the tail. Go back into the inside of the book at the tail; back to the middle and out at the center hole where the sewing was started. Tie the tail left at the beginning and the remaining thread together with a square knot, after checking to be sure that the thread is pulled tight all along. Cut the surplus threads back to about 1 inch (2.5 cm) in length. Trim the fore edges of the flyleaves and endleaves even with the book pages.

Insert the protection sheets between the cloth hinge and the endleaf on both front and back of the book, and secure in position with tabs of masking tape.

For a book that is to have only a paper cover, the selected paper is cut and folded as described for the flyleaf, wrapped around the book, and sewn on along with the book. In this case, start and end the sewing on the inside of the book. This will prevent the knot from showing on the outside and also protect it from being chafed and possibly coming un-tied. The position of the knot in either case is more a matter of prefer-ence than importance. The significant thing is that the 2 threads be securely tied together.

The second method, for a heavier book, differs from the above only in that more holes are punched and used in the sewing. Cut a strip of paper the length of the book, mark it at both ends 1/2 inch in; mark off the space between these 2 points in segments of about 1 inch (2.5 cm). Lay the strip against the inside center fold and punch the holes as indicated by the marks. Start the sewing on the outside at the hole nearest the center of the spine in length; bring the thread into the

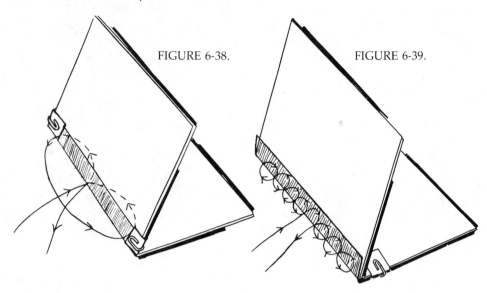

FIGURE 6-38.   FIGURE 6-39.

inside, leaving a 3-inch (7.6 cm) tail; take it out at the next hole, moving in the direction of the head of the book, and back in at the next hole, and so on until the head of the book is reached (Fig. 6-39). Retrace the stitches, using the same holes; proceed to the tail of the book and return to the center in the same manner. The last stitch made from the inside out probably will not come out on the spine at the point where the sewing was started, but 1 space away. Tie the 2 threads together and cut off the surplus as described above.

Sewing of single pages Make the endsheet sections as described earlier. These directions are for a book or pages with sufficient margins so that they can be trimmed on the head, tail, and fore edges after the book is sewn. Variations follow.

Lay the endsheet sections aside. Cut 2 pieces of clean wasteboard the size of the book pages. Put 1 on the front of the book and 1 on the back. Jog the pages to the head and spine, and weight down. Glue the spine lightly and set aside until the glue is dry.

If the book is no more than 1/2 inch thick, it can be sewn as a whole. If thicker, it is advisable to sew it into sections and then sew these onto tapes as described earlier.

For a thin book, after the glue is dry, draw a line 1/8 inch in from the spine edge from head to tail on both the first and last pages of the book. Clamp the edges with spring clamps so that the pages will not creep in carrying out the next step. With an awl or a hand drill, using a bit no larger in diameter than the needle to be used, punch or drill holes about 1 inch (2.5 cm) apart along the line. Make the last hole at both head and tail 1/2 inch (1.2 cm) in from the edge. Be sure to hold the tool vertically so that it comes out on the opposite side on the line drawn. To protect the surface of the table, lay the area where the holes are to be made on several thicknesses of heavy wasteboard. If neither of these tools mentioned is available, a small nail and a hammer can be used satisfactorily.

Use a no. 18/2 cord thread; cut a piece about 3 times the length of the

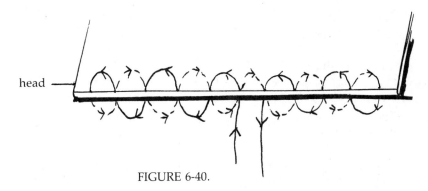

head

FIGURE 6-40.

book. Start the sewing in the center, lengthwise, and leave a 3-inch (7.6 cm) tail of thread. Carry the thread in a running stitch, using the pre-punched holes, to the head of the book. Retrace the stitches, proceed to the tail, and back to the center (Fig. 6-40). Tie the 2 threads together and cut off the surplus as described earlier.

Sewing on endsheet sections Cut 3 tapes 2 inches (5 cm) longer than the thickness of the book. Attach to the spine with glue or mixture, putting the adhesive on the spine of the book and not on the tapes, spaced as described earlier under Sewing on Tapes. Prepunch the holes in the endsheet sections to conform to the position of the tapes, and make the position of the kettle stitches fall in line with the outermost thread at both head and tail. Open the book 6 or 8 pages from the back; sew through this in and out around the tapes as if it were a folded signature. Lay the endsheet section in position and sew it on in the usual manner. Leave the usual 3-inch (7.6 cm) tail of thread at the starting point, and when the endsheet section has been sewn on, tie the 2 threads together as already described. Turn the book over and repeat this step with the front endsheet section. Do not sew these 2 sections on with the same piece of thread. If done so, it would necessitate carrying the thread across the spine of the book from back to front, and the thread would in all probability be broken in the process of backing.

The endsheet sections are now tipped or attached directly to the first and last pages of the book. Open the back endsheet section; lay a strip of wastepaper on the fore edge side of the sewing; apply mixture to this area, covering the threads. Remove the strip and in closing the book, be careful to line up the endsheet section with the spine and head of the book. Repeat on the front endsheet section; then weight the book down until dry. This is a variation from the routine way of handling these sections, and it is done to prevent the stitches from showing when the book is opened. The book is now ready to have edges cut either on a guillotine or with a plough.

For a thicker book, the procedures are the same as described above, up to the point of sewing. After the glue is dry, measure the thickness of the book and separate it into sections of equal thickness—3/8 to 1/2 inch. Each section is then sewn as described above for a thin book.

These sections, along with the endsheet sections, are now sewn onto tapes. The general procedures for sewing on tapes are followed with these exceptions: Sew each section onto the tapes about 3 or 4 times by roughly dividing the sections into equal parts. The sections are attached to each other as the sewing progresses. Several wastepaper strips and mixture will be needed. Lay a strip of wastepaper on the fore edge side of the original sewing; apply mixture to this area covering the threads. Remove the wastepaper and lay the next section in place, lining it up properly with the edges of the one just sewn. The endsheet sections are attached with mixture directly to the first and last pages of the book as described earlier for a thin book. Weight down and when dry, reglue the spine. When this is dry, the book is ready to have the edges cut.

In a case where the pages are not to be trimmed after sewing, line them up or jog them to the fore edge and the head. Let any unevenness fall at the spine edge and the tail. If pages have been carelessly cut or torn from magazines, check carefully to be sure that they are wide enough to be caught in the sewing. On pages that are not wide enough, extend them with a guard strip cut from paper that matches as nearly as possible the book stock. Attach these to the pages with about a 1/4-inch tip-on, using mixture.

Attaching Endsheets

Books sewn in the center fold of each signature should have an inner hinge attached to the first and last signatures of the book (see the section on Inner Hinges earlier in this chapter). After the sewing is completed and the book removed from the sewing frame, open it at the location of the back inner hinge—between the last page of the book and the endsheet section.

Check the width of the hinge against the width of the material that was attached to the flyleaves in the preparation of the endsheet sections. This hinge should be wide enough to completely cover these materials, plus about 1/16 inch. If excessively wide, mark the desired width, slip a piece of protective board under it, and, using a straightedge to indicate the cutting line, cut away the excess. If, on the other hand, it is too narrow, cut a strip of the hinge paper—Okawara—the proper width and attach to the inside of the hinge, the side that faces the book, at the point where it folds around the signature.

Slip a strip of paper under the hinge. Apply mixture to the hinge in its folded position, replace the paper with a strip of wax paper, and close the endsheet section onto it. In closing, take care to keep the endsheet section properly aligned at the spine and the head. If these 2 edges are lined up, the others will fall into place. It is especially important that the endsheet section be lined up exactly even and flush with the folded edge of the last signature of the book.

Since the endsheet section was sewn slightly off center, it has a tendency to stick out beyond the signature next to it. After the adhesive has been applied to the hinge, hold the section up and gently pull it toward the fore edge until it is properly lined up. Then lay it down and rub the edge for a minute or two.

Turn the book over and repeat this step with the front endsheet section. When both hinges are in place, weight the book with a board and brick until they are dry—about 15 minutes.

The treatment of the endsheet sections on books made up of single pages has been described earlier in this chapter.

Reducing the Swell

The "swell" is the difference in the thickness of the fore edge and the spine after the book has been sewn. This is produced by guarding, if any; by the thickness of the sewing thread; and by the air that gets into the pages in the process of sewing. A small amount of swell is desirable, for it is needed to round the spine; excessive swell, however, can cause trouble in the backing of the book. On a book that is 1 1/2 inches (3.8 cm) thick at the fore edge, a suitable amount of swell would be for the spine to measure 1 3/4 inches (4.4 cm) in thickness.

Materials Needed

Pressboards 2 (1 should be 3/4 inch, 1.9 cm, plywood, larger by several inches than both dimensions of book; the other same size as book)
Pulpboard same size as book
Binder's board narrow strip
Triangle
Hammer

Jog the book to the head and spine and place it on the larger pressboard, leaving the ends of the tapes exposed. Square up the head and spine against the triangle. Lay the pulpboard on the book about 1 1/2 inches (3.8 cm) in from the edge of the spine. Then place the other pressboard on top of the pulpboard so that it covers approximately half the width of the book, from the center out toward the fore edge.

Place this "package" in a press, leaving the spine area exposed and not covered by the platen of the press. Tighten the press.

Hold the strip of binder's board on the edge of the spine, and with the hammer pound on it the entire length of the spine, moving the strip of board if necessary (Fig. 6-41). This board serves as a protection to the book pages. Remove the binder's board and tighten up the tapes or cords by holding the end that is resting on the bottom pressboard firmly and pulling up on the other end. Repeat this process until the tapes cease to wrinkle.

If the book paper is brittle or fragile, use a moderate amount of force behind the hammer blow. It is easier to cope with excessive swell at this point than with damaged pages.

It is essential in this operation that the tapes or cords be free to move. If they have been inadvertently caught by the sewing thread in 1 point, they can be pulled in both directions from this point. If caught in more than 1 place, it will be almost impossible to straighten them up. A little wrinkling in a tape will cause no particular problem, but it is necessary that all cords be pulled tight and straight. If a cord is so affected, use a

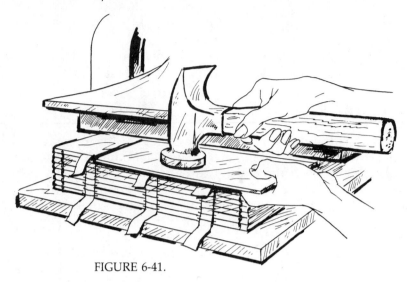

FIGURE 6-41.

needle to pull away a few of the fibers from the cord until the thread is free. This step should not be attempted when the book has been sewn on double cords or split thongs. This method of sewing makes it very difficult or virtually impossible to shift the cords.

If the book paper is soft and spongy and the swell persists or pops up as soon as the hammering ceases, glue the spine while the book is still in the press. First release the pressure and slip a piece of wastepaper under the edge of the spine that rests on the larger board. This will prevent the book from sticking to the board, and it also protects the board. Glue the spine with a light coat of thin glue (see next section) after the press has again been tightened. As soon as the glue is applied, repeat the hammering process while the glue is drying, pulling up on the tapes as the swelling is reduced. Leave the book in the press until the glue is thoroughly dry, 1 hour or more.

Gluing the Spine

The spine of a book is glued to hold the signatures together, or rather to keep them from shifting, during the rounding and backing of the book. The glue should be thin and applied lightly. A thick glue, heavily applied, tends in time to crystallize and break away from the spine.

Materials Needed

Pressboard several inches larger than book
Binder's board 2 strips as long as book
Wastepaper strip as long as book
Glue
Hammer small with flat end, such as tack hammer
Brick
Triangle

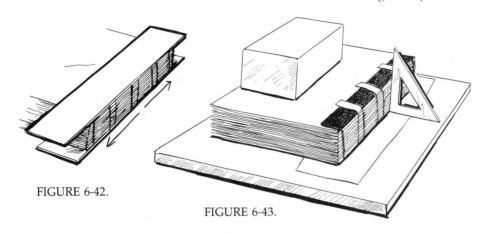

FIGURE 6-42.

FIGURE 6-43.

Jog the book to the head and to the spine. Place the strips of binder's board on the front and back edges of the spine, with the tapes or cords under them, thus protected by the strips. Lay this on a flat surface near the glue pot, with the spine slightly overhanging the edge of the surface. Hold 1 hand firmly on the top strip of binder's board.

Start in the center of the spine with the glue brush—after having dipped it into the glue and squeezed it out on the edge of the pot—and apply a light coat of glue first toward 1 end then the other (Fig. 6-42). Glue the entire spine with the brush up to the kettle stitches, working the glue between the signatures with a wriggly motion of the brush. Carry the glue out to the ends using a finger or the flat end of the hammer.

Lay the strip of wastepaper on the pressboard. Remove the strips of binder's board from both sides of the book. Place the fore edge of the book close to 1 edge of the board; adjust the wastepaper so that the spine edge of the book is resting on it, and put the brick on the fore edge of the book. Square up the head and spine against the triangle and set aside to dry (Fig. 6-43)—1 hour or more.

If all or any of the 3 edges are to be trimmed on the guillotine, this is the next step; if to be trimmed with a plough, the fore edge is cut at this time. The cutting is done, of course, after the glue is thoroughly dry.

Rounding the Spine

The rounding or shaping of the spine is done to distribute evenly the swell caused by the sewing thread or the guards. If the spine is not rounded, the book in time and use will round itself in reverse, causing a convex fore edge and a concave spine.

This step is more a matter of encouraging the book to take its proper shape rather than forcing it to do so. A book rounded against its will will not stay rounded. The extent to which a book should be rounded is not entirely under the control of the binder. Thick books of many signatures with extensive guarding will tend to round themselves more than is desirable with no help; and thin books of few signatures often do not have sufficient swell to permit any rounding. The ideal rounding, if

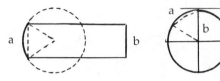

(a) 60° arc

(b) thickness of fore edge
    and radius of circle

FIGURE 6-44.

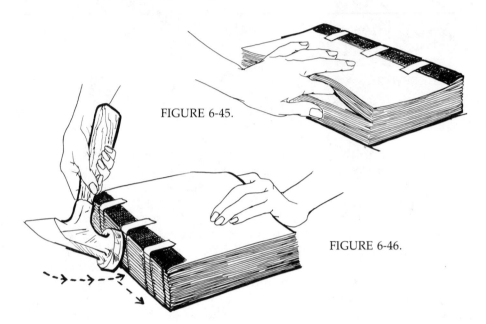

FIGURE 6-45.

FIGURE 6-46.

possible, is approximately 1/6 of a circle, the radius of which is the thickness of the book measured on the fore edge (Fig. 6-44a and b).

Some binders advocate rounding as soon as the glue ceases to be tacky. There is, however, some danger in knocking the signatures apart if done at this stage. It is recommended here that the glue be allowed to dry thoroughly before proceeding with this step.

Materials Needed

Cotton moistened
Hammer
Pressboard
Brick

Moisten the spine with the cotton. Lay the book on a flat surface with the fore edge facing the binder. Open the book near the center. Place the index finger of the left hand on the book page, the thumb on the fore edge of the portion of the book next to the table, and the other fingers on the outside of the uppermost page. Grasp the portion of the book between the index finger and the other fingers by exerting a bit of pressure (Fig. 6-45). Pull these signatures forward while pushing with the thumb to hold the other half of the book steady. While holding the book in this manner, hit the spine with the hammer near the center along the entire length (Fig. 6-46). Turn the book over and repeat this step. It should then be possible to complete the shaping with the book closed. If not, repeat this step. With the book closed, pick it up and place the index finger of the left hand on the fore edge, the thumb on 1 side, and the other fingers on the other side of the book, at the fore edge. Keep the book tightly closed by exerting pressure with the thumb and fingers on the outside. Press the index finger against the fore edge in the center, while with the right hand work the first few and the last few signatures forward from the spine edge.

After the desired round is attained, place the book on the pressboard and weight with the brick until ready to proceed with the next step, which is the backing (Chapter 7). The work can continue immediately or the book can remain in its present state until a later time.

7 Specific Techniques

When you reach the point in binding a book where specific techniques are required, the techniques will vary appreciably for different binding styles. The specific techniques covered in this chapter include backing, making headbands, headbanding and lining up the spine, cutting and attaching tapes and cutting hinges, cutting and paring leather, making a case binding, a Bradel, a tight back, and a German tube binding.

Backing

If you have not already determined the style of binding, you must do so now, before proceeding with the backing.

A book is backed, in a sense, to set the rounding and to distribute the remainder of the swell, and at the same time providing shoulders to accommodate the thickness of the boards to be used in making the cover. The backing is done by fanning the signatures out from the center, first toward 1 edge and then toward the other, with the backing hammer.

The proper weight binder's board should also be selected before starting the backing. The extent of the backing has a direct relationship to the thickness of the boards to be used. Small, lightweight books with little swell in the spine area need only a lightweight board—.059, for example. The greater the swell and the thicker and larger the book, the heavier the board should be. Large octavos and quartos could appropriately use a .082 or heavier. The proper backing will produce a spine that is the same width as the thickness of the book at the fore edge plus the thickness of 2 binder's boards (those selected for the book).

The backing for a book that will have a visible joint or French groove—case and Bradel bindings fall into this category—is described first.

Materials Needed

Job backer
Backing hammer
Wheat paste
Binder's board scrap similar to that used for covers
Wastepaper
Band nippers for raised bands
Masking tape

Draw a pencil line on both front and back of the book, 3/16 to 1/4 inch from the spine edge. Place the book in the job backer, tapes out, in its rounded state. Tighten the backer enough to hold the book, leaving it loose enough so that the book can be shifted. Adjust the book so that the pencil lines are just visible above the jaws of the backer. Check the head and tail of the book to make sure that they have retained their roundness and that the rounding is symmetrical. If adjustment is necessary, catch the book on the fore edge, hold it shut with the thumb and last 3 fingers on opposite sides of the book, and with the index finger push it up in the center, while holding it firmly in position on the lines with the other hand. When it appears to be properly positioned, tighten the backer. Check it again to be sure that the edges of the jaws are on the lines, and check the evenness of the rounding by placing a small piece of board on 1 end and drawing the shape of the end of the book on it. Place this drawing against the other end of the book and repeat (Fig. 7-1). With the shape of the 2 ends drawn 1 on top of the other, any difference in shape can readily be seen. If there is a marked difference in shape, try to get them uniform before proceeding.

When the book is properly positioned, apply a light coat of wheat paste to the spine and spread it evenly with a finger. In this type of backing, very few strokes of the hammer are required; the pressure of the jaws alone tends to fan the spine. The strokes of the hammer should be light, glancing blows (Fig. 7-2). Downward blows will crush the signatures and create a condition that is difficult to remedy.

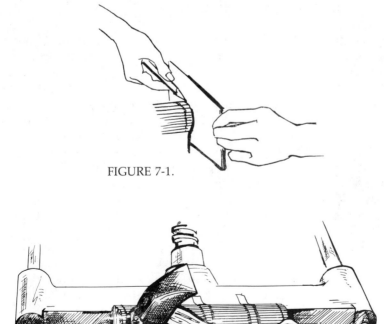

FIGURE 7-1.

FIGURE 7-2.

As the backing progresses, check it from time to time for the proper amount of fanning. Hold the scrap of binder's board vertically along the inside of the jaw of the backer. The fanned area should exceed slightly (1/16 inch) the thickness of the board. The book will expand when the pressure is removed. This fanned-out area should be roughly at a 45° angle to the sides of the book; however, this will vary some in accordance with the thickness of the board used. When the backing is complete, lay a strip of paper across the spine at head or tail and mark its exact width. Check against the other end. If they do not agree, fan the smaller end a bit more.

Apply a coat of paste to the spine and rub it in well with the fingers. If possible, leave the book in the backer until the spine is dry. If further treatment of the edges is planned, do so at this stage. If not, the next steps of headbanding and lining up the spine (described later) can be done while the book is still in the backer.

After the book is removed from the backer, keep it resting on a pressboard with the edge of the board at the base of the joint or along the line drawn earlier. If it is necessary to transfer the book from the backer before it is dry, do so with care. Place the book between pressboards, lining up the edges of the boards with the lines previously drawn, and put it in a finishing or lying press. Before tightening the press, reshape the spine if necessary.

Backing for a smooth joint This joint is not visible in the finished binding; tight back and German tube bindings are backed in this manner. The same general procedures are used as described above, with some variations.

The lines drawn indicating the depth of the joint should be placed so that the space from the edge of the spine to the line is the exact width of the thickness of the binder's board to be used. Hold a scrap of the board vertically along the edge of the spine, first at 1 end and then the other end of the book; mark it, and with a ruler draw a line between the 2 points. It is easier and more accurate to mark it at 2 points than to hold a piece of board along the entire length and mark along it.

No paste should be applied to the spine. More hammering is required in this operation, and if the paper is softened from the moisture in the paste, there is danger of "chewing it up" a bit.

If the work is started in a job backer, as it nears completion, remove the book, place it between pressboards, return it to the backer, and complete the work. The signatures are backed over, starting at the edges and working back toward the center. The work should be started with the same glancing blows and finished off with downward blows along the edges to bring these snug against the wooden boards. The covering boards sit in these right-angle joints, bringing them closer to the spine than in the other type of backing.

When the book is sewn on raised cords, use a hammer with a head small enough to get between the cords. In other words, try to avoid hitting the cords. An old-fashioned tack hammer serves the purpose very well. After the backing is complete, apply paste to the spine; using a pair of band nippers, straighten the cords while the spine is still moist

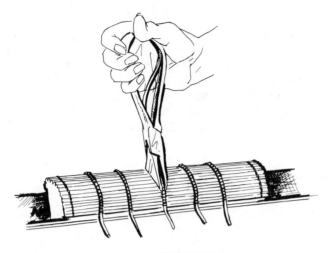

FIGURE 7-3.

(Fig. 7-3). Check the cords to be sure that they are parallel with the head and tail of the book and with each other. If any further treatment of the edges is planned, this is the point at which it should be done. If not, the next step is the attaching of the covering boards (see Tight Back and German Tube Bindings later in this chapter).

All backing can be done satisfactorily in either a lying press or a wooden backing press, using wooden pressboards on each side of the book.

The problem most commonly encountered in the backing process is the book riding up out of the backer when the backer is tightened firmly. This is generally due to unavoidable excessive swell, which can be remedied by placing a piece of scrap board on each side of the book from the fore edge to the drawn line. Sometimes all that is needed is a piece of bristol; start with something thin and increase it until you have the desired result. This packing can be held in position on the book with strips of masking tape attached to the boards and the spine. When the book is properly positioned and the backer tightened, remove the masking tape from the spine before fanning. If appreciable packing has been added, check for the proper amount of fanning from the inside of the packing, not the jaw of the backer.

If you discover in the course of backing that the book has slipped and that the jaws of the backer are no longer on the drawn lines, the backer was not tight enough. Release the pressure, make the necessary adjustments, and start over. If signatures are inadvertently crushed or fanned in the wrong direction from the center, remove the book from the backer, apply wheat paste to the spine, and follow the procedures described in Chapter 6 under Reducing the Swell. It is not necessary to reglue the spine. Let the spine dry thoroughly, then try backing it again.

Headbands

Headbands, sometimes referred to as head and tail bands—which in truth they are—can be made from leather or cloth, or can be sewn directly on the book. (It is a good idea to read through this section and the next, Headbanding and Lining Up the Spine, before proceeding to make any headband.) Made headbands are suitable for case and Bradel bindings and sewn ones for tight back and German tube bindings. The use of leather should probably be limited to twentieth-century volumes, whereas cloth headbands were in general use from the early nineteenth century on. Book cloth is not suitable for headbands because of its stiffness, and commercially woven ones, which can be bought by the yard, are not considered in good taste by most hand bookbinders.

Leather Headbands

Before beginning work on any leather headband, read over the section on Leather Paring in Chapter 5. Then assemble materials as noted below.

Materials Needed

Leather strip 1 1/2 inches (3.8 cm) wide, slightly longer than twice width of spine
Polished cotton string 1/16-inch diameter, 1 inch (2.5 cm) longer than leather
Mixture wheat paste and water-soluble PVA equal parts
Wastepaper

Pare the leather until it is thin and pliable, and feather both edges in its entire length. Lay the leather strip facedown on the wastepaper and apply mixture to the entire surface; place the string on the leather about 1/2 inch (1.2 cm) from 1 edge (Fig. 7-4); turn the 1/2 inch of leather over the string and with a bonefolder, push the leather firmly against the string.

Cloth Headbands

These are made in the same fashion as leather headbands. Any medium-weight woven material can be used. Traditionally, striped shirting was used. The material for both leather and cloth headbands should be selected along with the other binding materials for a particular book so that the overall effect in the finished product will be aesthetically pleasing.

Sewn Headbands

These are worked directly on the head and tail of the book, customarily done after the boards are attached to the book. There are a number of ways to work these bands. Four styles or types are described here. They are all usually sewn with a twisted silk thread, frequently using 2 colors, or on older volumes with unbleached linen sewing thread either in its natural color or dyed. The color or colors chosen should go well with the leather and the endleaves, if colored or decorated. If 2 colors are used, choose 1 light and 1 dark one; if they are the same intensity in tone they tend to blend together.

The thickness of the thread and the diameter of the core on which the

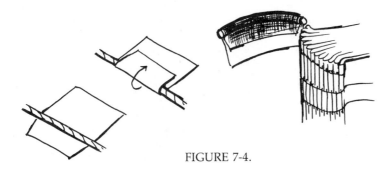

FIGURE 7-4.

band is worked should be chosen with some regard to both the size of the book and the square on the boards. A small volume, for instance, should have a smaller, more delicate-looking headband than a larger volume. Headband straws that are sold as core material are made of twisted paper, which in the past was very poor quality with a relatively short life expectancy. Unless the quality of the paper used in their manufacture has improved in recent years, they are not recommended. Suggested materials for the core are hemp cords of varying diameters or thin strips of vellum pasted together to get the desired thickness. Sand the edges to remove any irregularities or sharpness that might cut the thread.

The 2 headbands that have been traditionally used for centuries, and are probably the ones most frequently used today, will be described first. These consist chiefly of wrapping the thread around the core. The core is not attached to the spine beforehand, but is attached as the work progresses by frequent tie-downs.

Single-Core Headbands

The instructions and materials listed in this section are for a two-tone silk headband with hemp core for a 1 inch thick (2.5 cm) book.

Materials Needed

Hemp cord, 4 inches (10.1 cm) 1/16 in diameter
Needles 2
Silk 10 inches (25.4 cm) of 1 color; 18 inches (45.7 cm) of the other
Wasteboard 2 clean pieces as large as book covers
Usugami 1 strip twice as wide as spine
Wheat paste

Rub the cord with paste and lay aside to dry. Place the book, protected by the scrap boards, in the finishing press fore edge facing out (or facing the binder) and tail up (Fig. 7-5). Tie the 2 silks together at 1 end and thread 1 needle with the longer piece. Secure the needle by sewing through the thread about 2 inches (5 cm) from the end just put through the needle. This is done simply by sticking the point of the needle through the thread and pulling the thread tight.

Start the work from the side that seems most natural or comfortable.

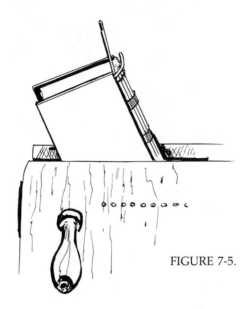

FIGURE 7-5.

The sewing can start from either the outside or the inside of the book. If the knot made by joining the 2 threads will be unsightly on the inside of the book, start on the outside. Some people, however, believe that unless these silk threads are showing inside the book, it is not hand-bound. It would seem to be purely a matter of personal preference.

Cut the core material in half; shape 1 piece with the fingers to conform to the rounding of the spine. Fix in position by sticking the second needle through it and sticking the needle in the edge of the wasteboard.

For this example, let us say the colors are red and white, the needle is threaded with red (the longer of the 2 threads), and the sewing will begin on the outside of the book. Starting at 1 edge of the spine, just below the kettle stitch, take the red thread up through the endsheet section, bring it down across the core, and take it up again in the same hole. This will make a loop or circle and secure the core at its first point (Fig. 7-6a). Now red is up and white down. Bring white up, wrap it completely around the core once, then bring it up over the core; hold firmly and cross it with red. Wrap red completely around the core once, bring it up over the core, hold firmly, and cross it with white; continue in this sequence (Fig. 7-6b). As the work progresses, the crossing of the threads on the tail of the book produces the desired bead (Figs. 7-6c and d). About every 1/4 inch, or third time in handling red, take it down into the book and bring the needle and thread out below the kettle stitch.

When the other side has been reached, take red down through the book and out, bring white down on the outside of the spine, and tie the 2 threads together with a square knot. Paste a narrow strip of Usugami over the threads on the spine—after cutting the surplus silk back to about 3/4 inch (1.9 cm)—letting it extend just enough above the tail of the book to catch the edge of the headband. Shape the headband against the tissue and cut off the extra core material on both sides. Turn the book around and repeat at the head.

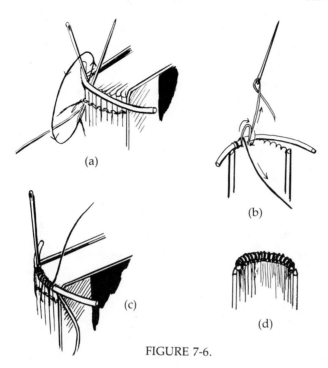

(a)

(b)

(c)

(d)

FIGURE 7-6.

This method produces a headband that has 2 red, 2 white, 2 red, and so on threads alternating. If the desired effect is single threads alternating, eliminate the step calling for a complete wrap around the core. After crossing white with red at the starting point, take red under the core, bring it over the top across the core, hold it firmly, and cross it with white.

Double-Core Headbands

This type of headband is usually reserved for rather large books, where the square-on-the-board is wider than the usual 1/8 inch.

Materials Needed (in addition to materials for single-core headbands)

Hemp cord 1 large, 1 small
Silk threads 2: 15 and 27 inches (38.1 and 68.5 cm) long

Follow the instructions for a single-core headband to the point where the large core is in position. The needle is threaded with red; red is up and white is down on the spine. Lay the smaller cord on top of the larger and hold it in position with the same needle. Bring white up, take it between the 2 cords; wrap it around the smaller or top cord (Fig. 7-7a); bring it back between the 2, hold it firmly on the tail of the book, and cross it with red (Fig. 7-7b). Take red under the bottom cord, bring it out between the 2 cords, wrap it around the top or smaller cord, bring it down across the bottom cord, and cross it with white. Proceed in this sequence until you reach the other side (Fig. 7-7c), taking red down into the book every 1/4 inch, and finishing off as described for a single-core headband.

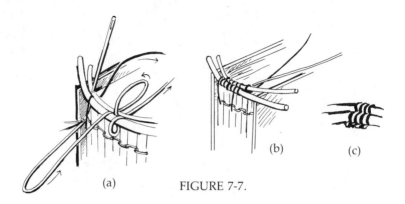

FIGURE 7-7.

If 2 threads of each color are desired, repeat the wrapping each time before crossing with the other color.

German Style Headbands

The type of headband where every stitch is carried into the book—usually referred to as German style—is probably the strongest and most durable, but it takes longer to work. Reputedly it was not introduced until the early twentieth century, so it probably should not be used on older books. The materials listed below are for a volume 1 inch (2.5 cm) thick with 1/8 inch square on the boards and worked in 2 colors.

Materials Needed

Needles 2, slender, fairly long, with large eyes
Hemp cord 1/16 inch diameter, twice as long as spine width
Lawn 1 1/2 inches wide (3.8 cm), twice as long as spine width
Silk 2 colors, each 12 inches (30.5 cm) long
Mixture wheat paste and water-soluble PVA equal parts
Wastepaper
Hammer
Usugami strip

Place the book in the finishing press with the spine exposed. Make a headband using the cord and lawn as described earlier under Leather Headbands. Cut from this 2 pieces exactly the width of the spine; attach 1 piece to the head and 1 to the tail of the spine, applying the mixture to the spine. The string should rest on the head and tail, not on the spine. The cord fills up some of the space between the ends of the book and the edges of the boards. Set aside for about 30 minutes or so until thoroughly dry. If you try to start sewing before this is dry, it will probably pull away from the spine.

Thread the needles and secure them by sewing through the thread 2 inches (5 cm) or so from the end and tighten the thread. This is done simply by sticking the needles through the threads; otherwise, the needles tend to drop off. Tie the other ends of the 2 threads together.

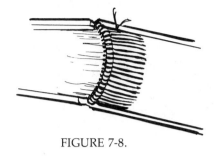

FIGURE 7-8.

Shift the position of the book in the finishing press so that 1 end of the spine is facing out and extending beyond the end of the press. If you are a beginner, start with the tail of the book.

The sewing is started from the outside, just below the kettle stitch, and at 1 edge of the spine. Choose the side that seems most natural (Fig. 7-8). Push 1 needle up through the endsheet section, and pull the thread up until the knot—where the 2 threads are joined—is resting against the spine. One thread will then be up at the tail of the book and the other down in the spine area. Continuing in our example, the threads are red and white, and red is up, white down. For the colors to alternate with each thread, bring white up on the outside of the spine across the cord, hold it firmly down on the tail of the book; cross it with red and take the needle with the red thread down into the book, bringing it out below the kettle stitch. Now, white is up and red is down. Bring red up as just described for white, cross it with white, and carry white down. The crossing of the threads produces a bead; to keep this bead even, the threads should be pulled tight with each stitch, and the stitches should be close enough together so that the cord is completely covered.

Repeat until you reach the other edge of the book. Then carry the needle that is up, down through the endsheet section and bring it out on the spine. The threads are now both down; tie them together. Leaving about 3/4 inch (1.9 cm) of thread beyond the knot, cut off the surplus. Turn the book around and repeat the process at the head.

To alternate the colors in pairs, 2 red, 2 white, 2 red, and so on, go back to the starting point above where red is up and white down. Bring white up and carry it into the book, circling or looping the cord. Then bring white up again across the cord, hold it, cross it with red, and take red down. Red is then treated in this same fashion, followed by white, and so on. If you want 2 red and 1 white, white is treated according to the single-thread technique and red according to the double-thread technique.

When both headbands are worked, secure the book in the press with the spine exposed. Apply a light coat of wheat paste on the threads showing on the spine and gently hammer them flat, especially in the area where the needles have come out and tended to push the paper outward. While the paste is still moist, cover the threads with a strip of Usugami.

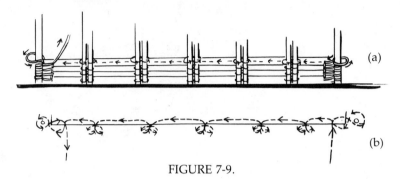

FIGURE 7-9.

Headbands Worked with Sewing of Book

For headbands that are worked along with sewing the book, string up on the sewing frame, in addition to the usual or desired number of cords, a single cord at both head and tail. Start the sewing as usual on the outside at the tail kettle stitch; go into the center of the signature, but instead of proceeding to the first cord, bring the thread out at the tail of the book. Carry it under and around the cord and back to the kettle stitch on the outside of the book (Fig. 7-9). Proceed with the sewing in the usual fashion until you reach the kettle stitch at the head. Come out of the book at the head kettle stitch; carry the thread on the outside of the spine to the head of the book, under and around the cord, back into the book at the head, and out at the kettle stitch. Add the next signature, go in at the kettle stitch, out at the head of the book, under and around the cord, back to the kettle stitch on the outside, and back into the book. This is repeated at both ends with each thread until the book is completely sewn. The headband cores should be completely covered with thread. If the signatures of the book are thicker than the thread being used, it may be necessary to wrap the thread around the cores once or twice before going back into the book and proceeding with the sewing of the next signature. This type of sewing produces no bead. When the book is removed from the sewing frame, the cords that serve as cores for the headbands should be left at least 1 inch (2.5 cm) longer on each edge of the spine. These are cut to the width of the spine after the book is backed.

Headbanding and Lining Up the Spine

These instructions are for the spine of a book that is to have either a case or Bradel binding. (A tight back and German tube are discussed later.) The book should now be sewn, glued, rounded, backed, and the edges treated. If it has been removed from the backer, return it to the backer or put it in a finishing press, protecting the backing with pulpboards.

Materials Needed

Headbands 2

Hosho, lawn and acid-free paper all cut to width of spine and length of book pages

Wastepaper
Wheat paste
Mixture wheat paste and water-soluble PVA equal parts
Glue

Attach the headbands first (instructions for making headbands are found in the preceding section). Cut them to the exact width of the spine. Apply mixture to the ends of the book, lay the headbands in position with the string area resting on the head and tail, not on the spine. Rub firmly and shape with the fingers. These take shape more easily if attached immediately after being made and not left to dry in a straight or flattened condition.

Next, the Hosho is attached with wheat paste. Hosho, a heavy, soft, Japanese tissue, is used to fill in the areas on the spine between the headband and the first tape, between the first and second tape, and so on (Fig. 7-10). The strip should be the width of the spine; cut this into pieces to fit the spaces, apply paste to the spine, and lay the pieces in position. The paste should be fairly thick. Rub firmly with the bonefolder. Let dry thoroughly before proceeding. The drying time depends on the amount of paste used, its consistency, and general atmospheric conditions. An hour would be the minimum.

The lawn is added next by applying paste to the entire spine and laying it in position, centering from head to tail. If properly cut, it should cover the area between the strings in the 2 headbands and the entire width of the spine (Fig. 7-11). Rub this down firmly, and again leave to dry thoroughly.

Next, moisten the paper with water, apply a coat of thin glue, and lay it in position on top of the lawn. Rub with the bonefolder to remove any air bubbles or wrinkles.

If a mistake has been made in cutting any of these materials, recut them.

Adequate drying time is important in these steps, for if the paper is added before the lawn is dry, the paper will dry first because of its

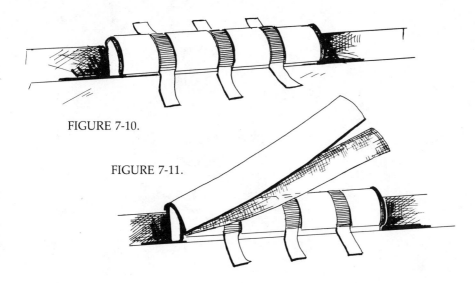

FIGURE 7-10.

FIGURE 7-11.

exposure to the air and will tend to pull the lawn away from the spine of the book. The paper is moistened because it is easier to handle if relaxed before gluing. This prevents curling up when it is glued. And in drying, it contracts a bit, making for a firmer spine. After about 30 minutes, the book can be removed from the backer or the press to proceed with the next step. It should not, however, be opened until the paper is thoroughly dry.

The next step is to attach the tapes to the hinges.

Cutting and Attaching Tapes, Cutting Hinges

Case binding Cut the ends of all tapes at a 45° angle and short enough so that they do not extend beyond the edge of the hinge (Fig. 7-12). Apply mixture to the tapes and lay in position on the hinge, first 1 side of the book, then the other. Rub these down firmly and smoothly with a bonefolder, particularly in the joint area. When 1 side is done, turn the book over onto a strip of wax paper to prevent the tapes from sticking to the pressboard.

Cut the hinges on a diagonal from the fore edge to the base of the joint. If the hinges are leather, tear away the protection sheets before attaching the tapes. Insert them between the endleaves and the hinges, as the endleaves will need protection in the casing-in process. If the hinges are paper reinforced with lawn, insert a strip of wax paper between the 2 when attaching the tapes; otherwise the adhesive is likely to ooze through the lawn and cause it to adhere to the paper hinge at these points.

Bradel binding Cut the tapes as described above and attach them in the same fashion directly to the protection sheets.

The book is now ready for its covers. The covers for case and Bradel bindings as well as tight back and German tube are described later in this chapter.

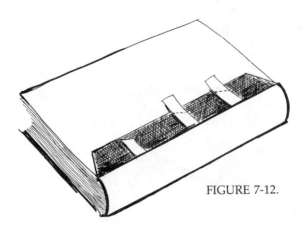

FIGURE 7-12.

Cutting Leather to Size and Paring

The principles involved and the variety of tools used in the paring of leather were discussed in Chapter 5 under Leather Paring. This section considers the details of selecting, cutting to size, and paring leather for specific types of bindings and other uses.

Leather is 1 of the few materials used by the binder that has no grain direction, so a given piece can be cut from what seems the most desirable area of the skin both from the standpoints of appearance and economy. It is wise to be as economical as possible; for fine work, however, quality should come first.

The areas nearest the spine of the animal are the stronger and more durable portions of the skin, so it is advisable to use these when cutting for a full leather binding. Try to center the spine of the animal on the spine of the book. There are occasions, however, when the graining of the skin in this area—particularly near the neck—is too coarse and heavy to title satisfactorily. In such instances, it should not be used. When a skin is large enough to get a whole cover out of 1 side of it, in covering the book orient the leather so that the area nearest the spine is at the tail of the book. The tail is subject to more wear in taking the book in and out of a shelf than is the head. If the book, however, is to have a protective case other than a slipcase (see Chapter 10), this is relatively unimportant. There are other times when it is necessary, because of the largeness of the book or the smallness of the skin, to orient the spine of the skin horizontally on the volume. If so, try to place the spine on the book covers so that it will fit into the planned decoration and not interfere with it.

Reserve the flank area, or softer part of the skin, for headbands and labels, neither of which is subject to heavy wear. The legs of a skin are of little use because of their stretchy characteristic.

Before cutting into a skin, make a paper pattern. This will aid in selecting a piece of leather that is free of flaws or discolorations, or as nearly so as the condition of the skin permits, and it serves as a check against the possibility of underestimating the amount of leather needed. It is distressing to cut the "heart" out of a skin only to discover later that the measurements were inaccurate and the piece is too small for the job. So cut a pattern and lay the book on it to check for size.

Full leather cover, tight back, German tube, Bradel bindings On a large piece of paper, square 1 corner and draw lines on the 2 edges 3/4 inch (1.9 cm) toward the center. This represents the needed amount for turning the edges in most cases. Lay the head and fore edge of the book on the 2 lines. Draw a line along the tail of the book and mark the joint area at both head and tail. Turn the book over, keeping the spine on the paper, and lay it flat on the opposite cover or side (Fig. 7-13). Mark the joint area again and draw a line along the fore edge of the book. Remove the book; add about 3/4 inch (1.9 cm) to the pattern on the tail and the fore edge just marked off, and cut to this size. For volumes with unusually heavy boards, allow 1 inch (2.5 cm) for the turn-ins. This should provide the necessary material for an even turn on all 4 edges. If correct, cut the leather to this size.

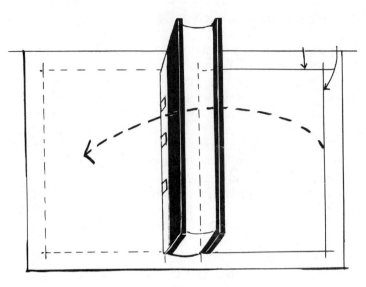

FIGURE 7-13.

Full leather cover, case binding Make the paper pattern by laying the component parts of the case—2 boards, 1 spine, and 2 joint spacers—on the paper instead of the book. Otherwise follow the directions above.

Lay the skin face or right side up on a flat surface. Place the pattern on the skin and move it around until you find an appropriate area. If the spine of the skin is selected, fold the pattern in half lengthwise and center the fold on the center of the spine. Slip a piece of smooth waste-board under the skin in the area of the pattern and weight down the pattern to keep it from shifting. Place a metal straightedge on the edges of the pattern—1 at a time—and with a sharp knife cut the leather around all 4 edges of the pattern.

Turn the just-cut piece of leather over on the flesh side and draw off the amount allowed for the turns. Lay the book in position and mark the width of the spine at both head and tail. Make all marks on the leather with a pencil. Do not use a ball point or other ink-filled pen, for in pasting the leather, there is danger that the ink will bleed through and stain it. These marks or lines will serve as a guide in the paring of the edges. If it is desirable or necessary to thin the entire piece, do so before the margins are drawn off.

Paring For a tight back or German tube binding, all 4 edges should be bevelled from the lines drawn out to the edges, and the edges should be thinned to approximately the thickness or thinness of a piece of bristol board, which will be used to fill in the space between the turned edges. At the head and tail, the edges in the spine area, plus about 3/4 inch (1.9 cm) on either side should be pared to a feather edge. (A feathered edge is pared as thin as possible.) This is done to prevent the turned edge from making a slight ridge or step down on the spine at the point where it stops and to reduce the thickness in the area where the leather hinge will overlap the turned edge.

The areas that will cover the joints should be sanded lightly to make

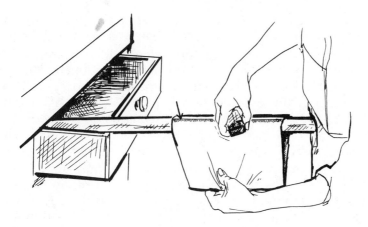

FIGURE 7-14.

them more pliable. These areas, however, are the portions of the cover that will be subjected to the hardest use, so strength and durability should not be sacrificed for neatness. Draw pencil lines between the points previously marked, indicating the width of the spine, and sand on the outside of these marks—between the spine and the fore edge of the leather. Hang the leather over a piece of dowelling or some small round object so that the area to be sanded is supported by it. If a dowel, place 1 end of it against the edge of a partially opened drawer and support the other end with the body (Fig. 7-14). Pull the 2 sides of the leather downward, holding it tight across the dowel, and sand lightly with fine sandpaper as indicated above.

For a case or Bradel binding, the margins are bevelled, the joints sanded as just described, and all 4 edges of the leather are feathered. This difference is due to the fact that bristol board is not customarily used on the inside of the covering boards in these 2 styles of bindings.

Half-leather binding These instructions are also applicable to 1/4 and 3/4 bindings (see Designing a Binding in Chapter 2). First, decide how much leather you want on the sides. Add twice this width to the width of the spine and an additional 1/4–1/8 inch for each side—this will be covered by the material used on the rest of the sides, and allow the usual 3/4 inch (1.9 cm) at head and tail for turning in. Cut a pattern this size. Choose the area of the skin to be used, lay the pattern on it, and cut around it as described earlier.

In paring, mark off 3/4 inch (1.9 cm) at both ends, bevel this and feather the edges. On the sides, bevel only 1/8 inch and again feather the edges. If, however, the skin is unusually heavy, the sides should be bevelled back about 1 inch (2.5 cm). This will prevent a marked step-down from the thickness of the leather to the thinness of the other covering material at the point where they come together.

Corners The size of corners is discussed later in this chapter under Case Binding (Corner Size). When the size is determined, cut a pattern, allowing the usual 3/4 inch (1.9 cm) turn on the 2 edges and 1/8 inch more on the diagonal than will be exposed when the covering material is added to the sides. Remember that 4 corners are needed for each volume.

The edges to be turned are pared as described earlier for the head and tail of half leather, and the diagonal is treated as described for the sides.

Fore edge strips These are strips of leather added to the fore edge of both boards in lieu of corners, or as a decorative touch. These 2 strips should be cut the width of the desired exposed leather, plus 1/8 inch for the overlapping of the other material, plus 3/4 inch (1.9 cm) turn-ins, and 1 1/2 inches (3.8 cm) longer than the boards on the book. The ends should be bevelled 3/4 inch and the edges feathered. Both sides should be bevelled 1/8 inch and the edges feathered.

Hinges Two important factors enter into the preparation of leather hinges. They should be thin enough to go down nicely without wrinkling and without impeding the ease with which the covers open and close, and at the same time the leather should not be thinned to the point where its strength is appreciably jeopardized. The problem is, of course, at what stage in the paring both of these requirements are met.

Hinges cut from small skins often need little, if any, overall thinning. For thicker skins, a general rule is not to reduce the thickness of the leather by more than half. The overall thinning is applicable to all leather hinges, and this should be even and uniform. Both ends of all hinges should be pared to a feather edge after they are attached to the endsheet sections and these have been cut to size.

For case and Bradel bindings, both edges should be feathered. For tight back and German tube, the edge to be attached to the endsheet section should be feathered, and the edge that will go back on the board should be thinned to the approximate thickness of a bristol board.

Headbands The leather should be uniformly thinned to the approximate thickness of a piece of bristol and both edges in its width feathered.

Labels The same instructions for headbands apply to leather for labels, except that the edges do not need to be feathered at this time. This is done after the label is cut to its exact size. It is particularly important here that the leather be uniformly thinned, for if there are thick and thin areas, there will be difficulty in the titling.

If, in paring, the leather is inadvertently cut through, this can usually be remedied by pasting the edges of the cut and carefully pulling them together to their original position. After making the repair, put it between boards and weight with a brick until dry. Then complete the paring.

Lay the book on the flesh side of the skin in its planned position, and if the repair falls where it would have to be turned over the edge of a board, shift the position of the leather so that the damaged spot will be on the inside of the board, where it will not be conspicuous or subject to wear. Shifting might necessitate some additional paring, but this is preferable to losing the piece of leather.

Case Binding

These instructions are for a cloth case bound book using conventional book cloth in one color, cloth hinges, and an indented patch leather label.

Materials Needed

Binder's board 2 pieces (weight determined at time of backing the book; see Backing earlier in this chapter), larger by 1 inch (2.5 cm) in both dimensions than book page, grain direction vertical with book length

Binder's board strip any width, 12–15 inches (30.5–38.1 cm) long

Bristol board 1 piece, 220M weight, length of binder's board, 1/2 inch (1.2 cm) wider than twice spine width, grain direction same as boards

Acid-free bond paper width of spine, length of boards

Book cloth 1 piece, larger by about 3 inches (7.6 cm) in both dimensions than amount needed to cover entire book (cut from roll with scissors, vertical measurement of book parallel to selvage on cloth)

Strips 2 cut from binder's board, 1/4 inch wide, long as the boards

Paper narrow strip, 4–5 inches (10.1–12.7 cm) long

Newsprint several sheets unprinted, larger than book cloth (do not use newspaper)

Wastepaper 2 strips slightly longer than book

Wax paper 2 strips slightly longer than book

Leather and lens tissue for title label (can be selected after label size is determined)

Glue

Other possibilities and variations in techniques with different materials are also discussed in this section, along with suggestions for remedying problems.

Cutting Materials to Size

On the binder's board, bristol, bond paper, and cloth, cut a straight edge, then a second edge at a right angle to the first. This should produce a square or right-angle corner and provide a point of departure in measuring the materials to their proper size. (See detailed cutting instructions under Cutting, Chapter 5.) Mark this corner on all materials with a little penciled cross or check mark. The boards should be 1/8 inch longer at both head and tail of the book—or 1/4 inch longer than the vertical measurement of the book. This overhang protects the edges of the book and is commonly referred to as the "square on the boards."

Lay the squared corner of 1 board at the head of the book, with the vertical straight edge of the board resting along the joint; extend the board 1/8 inch beyond the top edge of the book; and at the tail, mark the board at the point where it extends 1/8 inch beyond the edge. Cut both boards to the size indicated by the mark and at a right angle to the previously cut straight edge.

If using a board shears, while the gauge is set, cut the strip of bristol the same length as the boards.

In width, the boards are measured from the base of the joint and should extend 3/16 inch beyond the fore edge of the book. Lay 1 of the joint strips along the edge of the spine on the joint, or backed area of the book (Fig. 7-15). Place 1 of the boards against this strip in such a

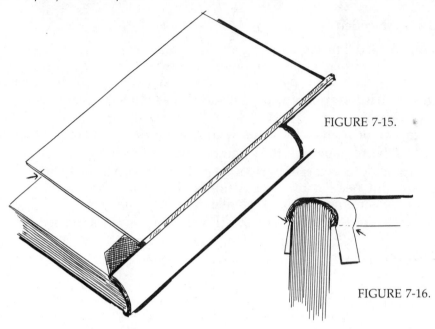

FIGURE 7-15.

FIGURE 7-16.

position that the fore edge of the book will be partially exposed. Mark it at the point where it extends 3/16 inch beyond the fore edge; cut both boards as indicated by this mark at right angles with the top and bottom of the boards.

Spine Strip

Lay the narrow strip of paper across the spine, over 1 of the head-bands (Fig. 7-16); pull it taut and mark it on both sides at the points where it crosses the edges of the spine. Check this over the other headband to be sure that the spine is the same width at both head and tail. Lay the outside of 1 of the pencil marks on the straight edge of the bristol, and mark on the bristol the position of the other pencil mark— also its outside. Cut 2 strips of bristol and 1 of bond paper this width. One strip of bristol serves as the spine of the case; the other is used to create the depression for the indented leather title label.

Cloth

Be sure to determine the right side of the cloth from the wrong side— the right side being the side that will be exposed in the finished case; the wrong, the one to which the glue will be applied. Make all pencil marks on the wrong side.

Starting at the right-angle corner previously cut, draw a line on both edges 3/4 inch (1.9 cm) in toward the center of the cloth. Lay 1 of the boards in this right-angle corner and weight it down; place 1 of the joint strips next to the inside edge of the board, then the bristol spine strip, the second joint strip, and finally the second board (Fig. 7-17). Mark the position of the boards on the cloth at top, bottom, and both outside edges. The cloth extends 3/4 inch (1.9 cm) beyond the 2 edges of the

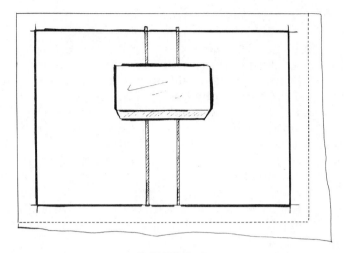

FIGURE 7-17.

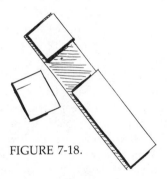

FIGURE 7-18.

board laid down in the right-angle corner. On the 2 other edges of the cloth, make a mark 3/4 inch outward from the edges of the board, and cut the cloth at these points. This should give a margin of 3/4 inch on all 4 edges of the cloth, with all 4 corners right angles.

All materials are now cut to proper size. Lay them aside and prepare the spine strip. Write on 1 of the pieces of bristol the author's name, the title of the book, and other information that might be needed or wanted on the label, such as volume number and date. To determine the space for the label, see Titling in Chapter 8.

When you know the amount of space required for the label, cut this amount or length off 1 of the strips of bristol. Lay this on the other strip of bristol, about 1 inch (2.5 cm) from the top, and move it up or down until you locate a position that is aesthetically pleasing. There is no set rule as to the positioning of the title on the spine. It varies with the length of the title, the length of the spine, and personal taste. Generally speaking, 3/4–1 inch (1.9–2.5 cm) from the top looks good.

When you have the desired position, mark it on the bristol, and mark on the piece of bristol from which the size of the label was cut the length of the space between the top of the label and the top end of the bristol; cut it at this point (Fig. 7-18). Glue the piece just cut and lay it in position on the uncut piece of bristol, lining it up precisely at both top and edges; lay the piece representing the size of the label in position against this; glue the remaining piece and lay it on the bottom of the strip, again lining it up evenly with all edges. Remove the unglued piece, lay it aside to serve as a pattern for the size of the leather, and weight down the prepared spine strip with a brick.

Place the cloth right side facedown on the sheets of unprinted newspaper. Glue the entire piece of cloth—the glue should be thin—starting in the center and working out in all directions with short, light strokes, while holding the cloth firmly in position with the fingertips. As soon as the gluing is completed, place 1 board in the right-angle corner as indicated by the lines previously drawn; rub it down firmly with the fist. Quickly pick up the cloth and the board attached to it, remove the top piece of wastepaper, and lay the whole thing down again on a fresh sheet of paper.

Lay the strip of binder's board across the top edge of the attached board and weight in position. This serves only as a guide in lining the materials evenly at the top. Add one of the joint strips, placing it exactly against the inside edge of the board. Do not rub this; it serves only as a measure for the proper joint space and will be removed; the less it sticks the better. Place the prepared spine strip against the spacer, the indention facedown, and the top lined up against the strip of binder's board across the top edge. Rub firmly. Add the second spacer, then the second board, rubbing it firmly. If done properly, all pieces will fit closely together, all lined up against the strip of binder's board at the top, and there will be a 3/4 inch (1.9 cm) margin of cloth on all 4 sides.

Remove the strip of board across the top and the 2 joint strips or spacers. Turn the case over and check to be sure that the cloth is well stuck to the boards and free of wrinkles. Draw the point of a small bonefolder along both top and bottom edges of the indention made for the title. Turn the case over again onto a clean piece of paper.

As an alternative to gluing the cloth in its entirety, you can glue it in stages and add the boards and other parts as the cloth is glued. Or the boards and spine strip can be glued and laid on the cloth.

Cutting the Corners

To make neat corners, some of the material at these points is cut away (Fig. 7-19). The cut is slightly curved, and it is important to leave at the right angle of the board slightly more cloth than the thickness of the board. When all 4 corners are cut, reglue the edges lightly with a small brush. Do 1 edge at a time in this sequence: bottom, top, and then the sides. To avoid getting glue on the work surface, slip a narrow strip of paper under the edge to be glued, glue the edge, and immediately remove the strip, or pull the edge to be glued just off the edge of the table and apply the glue.

Turn the 3/4 inch (1.9 cm) of glued cloth onto the board, pulling it tight and firm against the edge of the board. This can best be accomplished by running a bonefolder on the outside of the cloth and pushing it up against the board before laying the cloth onto the board. Quite

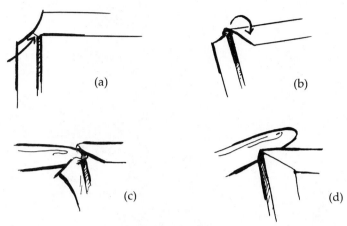

FIGURE 7-19.

a bit of thumb pressure is required to get the cloth to fit snugly against the edge and to lie wrinkle-free on the board. When the bottom is turned, tuck the surplus material at the corners against the edges of the board with a bonefolder or thumbnail. Turn the top edge in the same way, then the sides.

The case is now complete and ready to be attached to the book. Before proceeding, line the inside of the spine strip with the piece of bond paper. This was cut to the proper width; in length it should fit in the area between the turned edges of the cloth. Apply glue to the paper and lay in position.

Place a strip of paper in the book with 1 inch or so protruding at the head. This will serve as a marker or flag so that the head of the book can quickly and easily be ascertained. Write lightly in pencil the word *front* on the inside of the front cover, and *front* and *top* on the front protection sheet. These are precautionary measures and may seem unnecessary, but it is surprisingly easy to inadvertently case a book upside down.

Casing-In

The inside of the spine strip has been lined with bond paper, and now you are ready for casing-in, or attaching the completed case to the book.

Materials Needed

Boards pair, brass-bound, larger than case
Pressboards pair small enough to fit inside brass edges
Wastepaper strips longer than book
Bristol board 2 pieces slightly larger than book
Glue
Wheat paste

First, check the fit of the case by folding it around the book, centering the book in it from head to tail, and pushing the book firmly against the

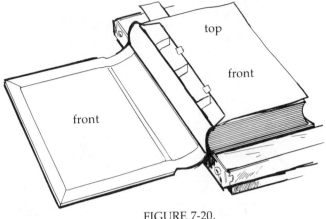

FIGURE 7-20.

spine of the case. While holding it firmly in this position, pinch the case in at the joints. If the square on the boards seems to be 1/8 inch at head and tail and slightly more on the fore edge, proceed with the casing-in.

The book is first "hung-in" to prevent slipping during the process of permanently attaching the case to the book.

Lay one of the brass-bound boards on a pressboard—the pressboard serves as protection to the brass edge that is not in use when the book is put in the press (Fig. 7–20). Glue the joints of the case up to the turn of the cloth at both ends. The joints are the 1/4-inch areas of cloth exposed on both sides of the spine strip. Lay the joint of the back cover of the case along the brass edge and press in place. Be sure that the brass edge is resting in the joint and that the inside edge of the cover board is next to the brass edge in its entire length. Place the book on the case, oriented properly, centering it from head to tail and offsetting it 1/8 to 3/16 inch from the fore edge of the case.

Hold the book firmly in position with 1 hand, and with the other bring the case snugly around the spine of the book and into the joint, putting pressure on it at this point. Remove hand from the book and let the front cover (the other half of the case) fall into place. Hold the front cover in position and place the brass edge on the second board in the joint area; add the second pressboard. Keep a firm grip on both ends of the pressboards and put the whole "package" in the press so that the center of the book is approximately under the spindle of the press, and with the spine of the book exposed at the front of the press (Fig. 7–21). Tighten the press. Check to make sure that the spine of the case is firmly against the spine of the book; this is done by pressing on it at the ends over the headbands. The headbands increase the width of the spine slightly in these areas, so if the spine of the case is fitting firmly at these points, it should be all right. Also check to see if the square on the boards is even on all 3 edges. If all is well, leave in the press for 10 or more minutes. If the book has slipped in the case, remove it from the press, free the joints, reglue them, and try again.

After the book has been hung-in successfully and pressed, remove from the press, take the 2 boards off the top, and open the cover to an upright position, pressing it down in the joint area (Fig. 7–22). Do not

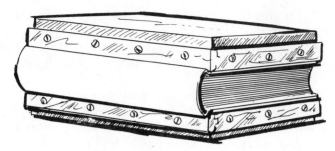

FIGURE 7-21.

let the cover fall all the way open; if it does, it will likely free the case from the book. Remove the tabs of masking tape from the cloth hinge and protection sheet, but leave the protection sheet in position.

Place 1 of the strips of paper—the wastepaper previously cut—under the hinge. Glue the hinge, remove the paper, slip a strip of wax paper under the hinge, and close the cover. Turn the book over, placing the joint of the case on the brass edge, and repeat this step. Add the brass-bound board and the pressboard and return it to the press under medium pressure for 15 minutes or more. After gluing the hinges and closing the covers, do not open them until the book has been pressed. Binders often have a desire to peek to see if all is well. Curiosity, however, can result in wrinkled hinges.

The binding is now ready for the board papers. If earlier instructions were followed, these were rough cut and laid aside in a safe place. They should now be located and cut to size. First, get a square corner on each. In length they should be cut slightly shorter (1/16 inch) than the flyleaves to allow for possible stretching. In width they should be 3/16 inch from the fore edge of the board and about 1/8 inch from the spine; again make allowance for stretching. Generally speaking, they will

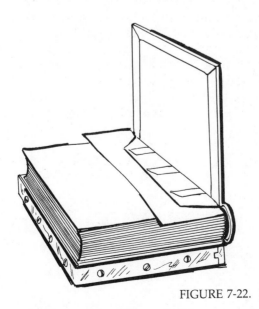

FIGURE 7-22.

stretch more in width than in length, although the amount of stretching depends on the type of paper, the size of the sheet, and the amount of moisture absorbed from the paste. No portion of the board papers should show on the edges or squares on the boards when the covers are closed.

Open the back cover all the way and support it with pressboards equivalent in height to the thickness of the book (Fig. 7–23).

Paste the wrong side of the board paper (the paste should be thin enough to spread easily, but not soupy); hold it firmly and continue to brush it—without adding more paste—until the paper ceases to curl. Pick it up, position evenly on the fore edge, and center it from head to tail. Lay it down, gradually smoothing it out at the same time. When in position, lay a clean piece of paper over it and rub gently but firmly. Insert a piece of bristol board between the board paper and the endleaf, and close the cover. Repeat on the front cover. Return to the press between the brass-bound boards as previously described. Screw the press down firmly. In about 2 minutes, remove it from the press and check to be sure that no paste has oozed beyond the edges of the board papers. If all is well, with the bristols in place, return to the press; this time screw the press down just enough to hold the covers flat. Leave several hours or overnight. If paste has oozed, wipe the surplus away; free any stuck areas with a small bonefolder; replace the bristols with fresh ones; and return to the press following the steps just described.

When the board papers are attached, the boards are very likely to warp outward. This is a normal reaction and nothing to be alarmed about. When the board papers have dried in a flattened state under light pressure, they will balance the pull set up by the cloth on the outside of the boards and the covers should remain flat.

For instructions regarding the making and attaching of a leather or paper patch title label, see Patch Labels or Titles in Chapter 8.

If the endleaves are a colored or decorated paper, it is usually considered desirable to attach them to the first flyleaf in both front and back. This is done only on the fore edge. Place a strip of paper under the flyleaf at the fore edge. Lay a second strip of paper 1/8 inch from the fore edge on the top of the flyleaf (the side next to the colored paper) and apply mixture to this 1/8 inch. Remove the strip of paper; slip a strip of wax paper under the flyleaf; lay the endleaf down, letting its fore edge fall on the pasted area; put a strip of wax paper over it and

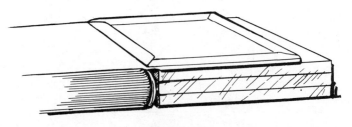

FIGURE 7-23.

close the book. Repeat on other endleaf; then weight the book down until dry.

Variations

As stated earlier, a case binding can be executed in a variety of materials or combinations. As in the decoration of a full leather binding, there is almost no limit to the number of pleasing and attractive possibilities. A few are full leather; half leather with cloth or paper sides, with or without leather corners; two-toned cloth; cloth spine, paper sides with or without corners; cloth spine and fore edge with a panel of another color cloth or decorated paper; woven fabric other than book cloth; all paper (not recommended because of possible lack of durability); and the use of the original covers of a paperback, for instance, or some portion of them.

The cutting of the materials for any of these variations differs little from that previously described. What follows are some differences in techniques.

The hinges that are attached to the endsheet sections are made from the same material that covers the spine.

If a paper label is preferable to leather, an indention on the spine strip is not necessary, so only 1 strip of bristol is needed.

When the endleaves and board papers are folded sheets, reinforced with lawn, the book is hung in the case in the manner already described. Then place a piece of clean wastepaper, larger than the page size, between the board paper and the endleaf. With the covering board (1 side of the case) in an upright position, paste the area of the board paper to be covered by the lawn and lay the lawn in position on it. The tapes should have been attached to the lawn earlier; if not, attach them at this time. Then paste the entire board paper, including the lawn; remove the wastepaper and close the cover; press on the cover for 1 minute or so; open it just enough to slip a piece of bristol, larger than the book, between the board paper and the endleaf. Repeat on the other side and put the book in the press between brass-bound boards. Follow the procedure previously described for pressing and checking. Do not open the covers all the way until the book has been pressed.

When the case is to be either full or half leather, the leather is first pared. The spine is made from 2 pieces of acid-free paper, not from bristol board. One layer or piece of this paper is mounted in the center of the leather. This is done by gluing the paper, laying it in position, and weighting it down until dry. The spine is then titled before the boards are added (see Titling in Chapter 8). If the titling is to be done on a stamping press, see Stamping Presses in Chapter 8, before cutting the paper for the spine.

The boards are attached by using the same joint strips and strip of binder's board described earlier. Work from the spine strip, first 1 side and then the other, taking care to get all materials lined up properly across the top and fitted closely together. When the boards are in position and before the edges are turned, glue the second spine strip and lay it on top of the first, lining it up exactly on all 4 edges.

In two-tone bindings where the materials are of different weights or textures, it is customary to let the material covering the sides overlap, by about 1/8 inch, that which covers the spine. Where book cloth of the same texture and weight is used, the 2 pieces can be abutted. These differences should be taken into account when cutting the materials to proper size.

There is no set rule regarding the amount of 1 material in proportion to the other. This is a matter of personal preference. If, however, for instance, the sides are to be covered with a decorated paper and you want to use as much of the pattern as possible—or the whole board covered with the paper—the material covering the spine must be brought over onto the boards about 1/2 inch (1.2 cm). This means that the overlap of the 2 materials would be greater than the above-mentioned 1/8 inch. This is required for strength in construction; if only 1/8 inch of material is attached to the boards, the edges will be difficult to turn and might pull away in the process of casing-in.

In any two-tone binding, the spine strip is attached first to the material selected for this part of the case. Then the boards are attached, and, finally, the material to be used on the sides. In this instance, the boards can be left slightly wider, the case partially made, the book cased-in, and the hinges attached; the fore edge of the boards cut to the desired square; and the covering material added to the sides. If the board paper and endleaf are a folded sheet, the book could only be hung-in the case by following this sequence of steps.

The spine material is cut, allowing the usual 3/4-inch (1.9 cm) turn at head and tail; and in width it should be the width of the spine plus 1/2 inch (1.2 cm) for the 2 joints, twice the amount of material that is to be attached to the boards, and 1/4 inch or more for possible overlapping of the 2 materials mentioned earlier.

After cutting the material to size, find its center and draw a line on the wrong side from head to tail at this point. Do the same on the spine strip, on the side that will be visible after it is attached to the material. Apply adhesive to the material. Lay the spine strip in position, lining up the center lines drawn on the material and the spine and centering it from head to tail. Add a joint strip on 1 side, then the binder's board. Lay the strip of binder's board across the top of this board and the spine and add the other board in the same manner, taking care to keep them all lined up evenly and squarely.

If the material was carefully and accurately cut and the spine strip and boards attached properly, the space from the edge of the material to the fore edge of each board should be the same.

It is desirable, of course, that the material covering the sides—both front and back—be uniform in size and parallel with both spine and fore edge of the boards. Check the distance from the fore edge to the edge of the material on front and back, at both head and tail, measuring from the fore edge of the boards. This can be done easily with a strip of scrap board. Mark on this board the distance at 1 of the points mentioned and compare it at the other 3 points. If these distances are the same or nearly so and the material on the sides will overlap the spine material, mark off an additional 1/8 inch on the strip of board with which the measuring was done. Using this as a gauge, mark at the 4 points (head and tail of both boards) this exact width; this mark can be just a dot made with a pencil point. Lay a straightedge between these marks—both front and back—and draw a line with a small bonefolder. This will provide a guide for laying on the covering material.

When the same material that covers the spine is to be used in a strip on the fore edge of the boards, the above guideline should be established before the material is attached to the fore edge, and measurements to arrive at the proper position on this strip of the additional covering material should be made from this guideline.

Where the 2 covering materials are to abut, make the measurements as just described, but instead of making a guide with a bonefolder, the surplus and irregular material is cut away with a mat knife against the straightedge. To get a clean-cut edge on the entire length of the material, slip a scrap of binder's board, the thickness used in constructing the case, under the overhanging material at both ends. This should give it proper support so that the cut can be made with 1 stroke of a sharp knife. Lift up the surplus and pull it away in the direction of the cut. If a bit of the surface of the board is pulled off in the process, sand the roughened area with fine sandpaper, then burnish it by rubbing with a bonefolder.

The edge of the second material that is to abut this cut should, of course, be a clean-cut, straight edge; and great care should be exercised in bringing the 2 together. Any overlapping or gapping of or between the 2 materials will produce a far from pleasing result.

Corner size Where corners are desired, they are customarily made from the same material used on the spine. They are attached to the boards before the material is added to the sides, and the material covering the sides should overlap both the spine and corner material by about 1/8 inch. In size, corners traditionally are in proportion to the width of the spine material showing on the boards. If, for example, 1 1/2 inches (3.8 cm) of this material is to show, 1 1/2 inches plus allowance for overlapping should be marked off on both edges of the board at each corner and a diagonal line drawn between the 2 points. Possibly an easier and more accurate way to get all 4 corners the same size is to make a pattern of some material stiff enough to draw against. Lay the pattern in position on each corner and draw a line along the diagonal. There is also an adjustable gadget, known as a traçoir d'angles, made expressly for this purpose. The traditional proportions are mentioned here only as a guideline. There would seem to be no logical reason why corners could not be any size that is aesthetically pleasing to the binder. In cutting the material for the corners, the usual 3/4-inch (1.9 cm) turn-in must, of course, be allowed for.

Materials For the material that will cover the sides of the boards, cut 2 pieces 1 1/2 inches (3.8 cm) longer than the boards and 3/4 inch (1.9 cm) wider than the board measured from the point on the leather in the area of the spine where the material will be placed. The leather should be marked with a bonefolder line as just described, and a similar line should be drawn on all four corners.

For fabric other than book cloth, choose a medium-weight, closely woven material—cotton such as gingham or chintz, dress linen, or silk shantung are suitable. Burlap, monk's cloth, or other heavy, loosely woven materials produce rather unattractive, bulky corners that are very subject to fraying.

Some materials will stain when they come in contact with adhesives no matter how carefully they are handled. Before attempting to cover a book in an unfamiliar material, take the time to test a sample following the techniques described below. If the results are good, proceed; if bad, choose another material or try again.

It is very difficult to keep the lines in a striped or plaid material absolutely straight. Stay away from symmetrical or geometrical patterns unless there is some special reason why they seem particularly desirable. If used, much care must be taken in keeping the pattern straight so the end result will be pleasing. Again, try a sample.

The procedures or techniques for stripes or plaids are somewhat different from those previously described. After the cloth is cut to size, mark off an area in the center equivalent in width to the width of the spine, the 2 joints or 1/2 inch (1.9 cm), plus an additional inch. Cut a piece of Japanese tissue—Hosho or Okawara—this width and the length of the material from head to tail. Apply a coat of mixture to the tissue; let it dry for 1 minute or so, then lay it in position in the marked-off area. Weight down with a board and brick until dry. The tissue serves a two-fold purpose: It gives body to the cloth, thus preventing the joints from being wobbly, and it serves as a barrier against the adhesive used in the casing-in from oozing through the material. (The sizing in conventional book cloth serves these same purposes.) The hinges attached to the endsheets should be similarly lined for the same reasons.

In making the case, the spine strip is added first in the center of the tissue; the joint strips are laid in position; then the boards are added after the adhesive is applied to them and permitted to dry for 1 minute or so. The adhesive should be tacky but not runny. When the boards are attached, turn the case over, lay a clean piece of wastepaper on the material, and rub it down gently. If the material is not sticking properly, weight the case down with a board and bricks for a few minutes; do not put in the press.

The corners are cut in the usual manner, but the edges of the material are turned onto the boards after mixture (the estimated width of the turn) has been applied to the boards and allowed to dry for the usual minute or so. The cloth is not stuck to the actual edge of the boards, just pulled tight over them. The casing-in and other steps follow as described earlier, using mixture. The board papers should be put down with mixture instead of wheat paste.

If an all-paper cover is desired, attempt to choose a good quality paper, preferably with rag content, that folds smoothly and nicely with the grain direction. The paper will be folding in the joint every time the covers are opened.

The case would be constructed following the same general procedures as described earlier for full cloth, with these exceptions: Only 1 spine strip is needed; the spine and joint area should be reinforced with a piece of lawn cut wide enough to cover this area and attached to both boards and the length of the paper from head to tail. The adhesive should be paste-applied to the paper.

Attach the strip of lawn first in the center of the paper; weight down with a board and brick until dry. Then make the case by pasting the entire piece of covering paper and laying the component parts of the case on it as described for full cloth. When casing-in between the brass-bound boards, the pressure should be very light. If the paper is very soft and absorbent, it is advisable to bypass the press and weight the brass-bound boards with several bricks or a lithographic stone. A brass edge can very easily break a soft paper in a moistened state.

The other steps in carrying the book to completion follow the usual procedures.

Setting in original covers When it is desirable to use the original covers or any portion of them in the construction of a new binding, a better job will result if they are set into a frame rather than just attached to the surface of the case. These directions are applicable to both front and back boards of the case when both the front and back original covers are to be used. If only the front cover is to be saved and set in, the back board of the case is handled in the usual fashion.

Estimate the size of the portion that is to be saved and cut a pattern this size. Do not cut the cover until ready to put it in position. Lay the pattern on the binder's board and move it around until the most pleasing position is found. Customarily, the space at the head and at the fore edge are the same; the space at the tail slightly wider—1/16 inch or so—and the cover even with the spine edge of the board. This is assuming that the entire original cover, or most of it, will be used. Small portions will be discussed later.

Mark the position of the pattern and cut strips of bristol (grain going in the grain direction of the board; for head and tail, the grain direction should be with the width of the strip, and for the fore edge, with its length). No strip is added to the spine edge of the board, so it is, in effect, a 3-sided frame. Cut these strips the length and width of the board. Apply glue to them and lay in position on the edges of the board. Attach the fore edge strip first; abut the head and tail strips to this, and cut the surplus away at the spine edge of the board, flush with the edge.

The work with the case can proceed after the frame is added. The frame goes facedown on the glued cloth. Since the width of the frame at head and tail differ, care should be exercised in positioning the boards properly.

After the book is cased-in and the hinges attached, and before the board paper is put in, line the inside of the board with bond paper. Cut the paper to fit inside the turned edges of the cloth and the hinge; glue the paper and lay in position, rubbing it down smoothly. This paper serves to balance the pull that will be set up by the addition of the original cover. Then complete the binding.

Check the pattern against the frame and cut it, if necessary, until it fits exactly within the frame. Then cut the cover to the size of the pattern by positioning it on the cover and marking the cutting points. After cutting the cover, lay it in position in the frame to make sure that it fits properly. If not, make the necessary adjustments. When it is the proper size, apply mixture to it and lay it in position within the frame. Put a piece of wax paper over it and put the book in the press between pressboards. Check after a few minutes to be sure that the adhesive has not oozed. If all is well, return it to the press under light pressure for several hours or overnight. If there is surplus adhesive, wipe it away, replace the wax paper with a clean piece, and return the book to the press.

When only a small part of the original cover is to be used, cut a pattern to size. Cut 2 pieces of bristol the size of the covering boards. Lay the pattern in the desired position on 1 of the bristols—it can be attached with a spot of glue to keep it in position. Then, using a straight-edge and a mat knife, cut the size of the pattern out of the bristol. Glue the bristol and lay it in position on the binder's board. The second piece of bristol is then glued and attached to the other side of the binder's board to balance the pull of the first piece. The 2 pieces of bristol will increase the thickness of the binder's board, so if only the front board is to be so treated, it can be thinner than that used for the back cover. If an .082 board is used for the back cover, use an .059 plus the bristols for the front cover.

Library corners These are corners that are turned in without cutting away any of the material. They are rather unattractive and bulky, but they do eliminate any possibility of the material fraying. They are made as follows: Fold the glued edge of the cloth at the corners onto the board (this is the portion of the cloth that forms a right angle) and work it down against both edges of the board (Fig. 7–24). Glue the surface of the turned material lightly, and turn this onto the board along with the rest of the edges as previously described.

Common Problems

Following are a few of the problems most frequently encountered or created, with suggested remedies.

One of the most common mistakes is getting glue on the right side of book cloth. If the material is pyroxilin-coated or -sized, glue can be removed by rubbing the area lightly with moist cotton. If the material is

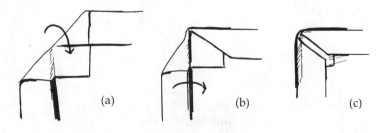

(a)   (b)   (c)

FIGURE 7-24.

starch-sized—as many of the better book cloths are—moisture will dissolve the sizing and remove the color or some of it, so it should be used only as a last resort.

If the layer of glue is thin, it can sometimes be flaked off after it is dry with a fingernail or the point of a knife using very little pressure. A piece of paper laid over the affected area and rubbed with a heated burnisher will sometimes pick up surplus glue.

If neither of these works, moisten the area by patting or daubing it with a wad of damp cotton—do not rub. Lay a piece of paper over the moistened area and rub it with a bonefolder. If it seems to work, repeat. If some color comes off with the glue, moisten a scrap of the same cloth, lay it facedown on the spot, and rub with a bonefolder. Or the faded spot or spots can be touched up with watercolors or crayons. When the glue is removed and the color restored, rub the whole surface with a lightly greased rag.

It is always advisable to start with the simplest remedy first, and wise to simulate the trouble on a scrap of the same material and experiment with it until a satisfactory result is obtained.

If the glue is unevenly applied and dries in spots before the material adheres to the board, this can generally be made to stick by softening the glue with heat. Heat a metal burnisher to the point where a drop of water placed on it will sizzle. Place a clean piece of paper over the area to be treated and iron it slowly with a fair amount of pressure on the burnisher. The burnisher should stay in 1 spot long enough to soften the glue. If a burnisher is not available, an ordinary iron set at a low temperature will serve the purpose. This treatment is effective only on cloth that has been glued with hot glue.

If you experience the same difficulty with paper that has been pasted, dampen the area and rub gently through a piece of paper. If a board paper, after moistening, return the book to the press with a bristol between the dampened sheet and the book.

When the cloth wrinkles slightly or the surface seems bumpy, this is probably due to excess glue or glue that was too thick. Press the cover immediately between zinc sheets or smooth pressboards as tight as possible. This should be done before the edges are turned so that any surplus glue will be squeezed out and can be removed from around the edges of the boards. In this operation, protect the pressboard on which the inside of the case rests with a piece of wax paper. The heated burnisher is also effective.

In cases where not enough care was taken in making the case and 1 board is unevenly lined up across the top or the joints are not even, remove the board and the spine strip as soon as you detect the error. Some of the board will probably remain on the cloth; remove as much of this as possible by lifting up an edge with a dull knife and pulling it off. When this no longer works, apply a light coat of thin glue to a small area at a time and then scrape it with a bonefolder. When the cloth is clean, sand the board smooth and try again. Both the cloth and the board can generally be saved, but it is a tedious and time-consuming process. Except as a warning to exercise more care in the future, it probably is more practical to start over—unless it happens to be the only piece of cloth of the desired color available. Even then, the cutting of a new board and spine would be advisable.

Where the boards have not been placed in the proper position on the cloth and the material to be turned in against the inside of the board is uneven, it makes for a neater job if this inside turn is trimmed to an even and uniform width. This is best done before the edges are turned. Set the dividers to the width of the narrowest edge—if there is sufficient material at this point to make the turn adequately—and transfer this measurement to all edges. Cut them against a straightedge. If one area is dangerously narrow, but will make the turn, even the other edges, allowing a 3/4 inch (1.9 cm) turn, and after all edges are turned in, glue a strip of material going in the same direction and butt it carefully along the narrow edge. When dry, cut it even with the rest of the edges.

If you cut a corner too close, leaving the board exposed after the edges are turned, find the piece that was cut away, fit it into the exposed gap, and cut off the surplus. Then glue and lay in position. If the piece cannot be found, lay a piece of material larger than the area over it and cut through both this and the material on the board. This should produce a patch the exact size and shape needed; remove the surplus from the board (the cut edges), glue the patch, and put it in place.

If after the case is completed, you see that the boards are too narrow and the square on the fore edge is insufficient, there is little to do but make a new case, or live with the mistake, which is not recommended. On the other hand, if the boards are too wide and the square is larger than desired, lift the turned edge of the material on the fore edge and a short distance at head and tail; turn the material back, freeing the edge of the board and cut off the excess. Reglue the cloth and press the boards immediately, screwing the press as tight as possible, first 1 side, then the other. Recut the corners and turn the edges again. This repair is less likely to show if you can avoid creasing the cloth.

The square on the fore edge is controlled by several factors other than the width of the boards. If either the spine or the joints are too narrow, the boards will be pulled back, thus reducing the size of the square. If either of these is too wide, the boards will be pushed forward, producing more square than intended.

If in checking the fit of the case, you discover that the headbands extend beyond the head and tail, they should be replaced with smaller headbands. This error could be caused by using a cord or a piece of leather that was too heavy or by having cut the boards too short. Moisten with paste the paper and lawn used to line up the spine in the area of the headbands; life these up just enough to free the headbands. Remove them, make new and smaller ones, attach in the usual manner, and replace the lawn and paper.

Bradel Binding

A general description of this binding style can be found in Chapter 2, Types of Hand Bindings. If earlier steps have been followed, the book is now sewn, glued, rounded, backed, edges treated, headbanded, spine lined up, and tapes attached to the protection sheets. It is now ready for the covers. Read the instructions in the preceding section for making the case for a case binding before undertaking the Bradel binding. Where there is similarity in techniques, they are given in detail for the case binding and are not repeated here in entirety.

The following instructions are for a 1-color book cloth cover, with cloth hinges and indented leather label. Many of the variations and remedies for problems discussed in the preceding section on case bindings apply here as well.

Materials Needed

Dividers
Boards pair, brass-bound
Pressboards pair small enough to fit inside brass edges
Binder's board 2 pieces, weight determined at time book was backed, 1 inch (2.5 cm) larger in both dimensions than book
Bristol board 1 piece, width of spine plus 4 inches (10.1 cm), length of boards; 1 piece slightly wider than spine, length of boards; 1 narrow strip
Bond paper 1 piece slightly wider than spine, length of boards
Book cloth 1 piece larger by 3 inches (7.6 cm) in both dimensions than amount needed to cover entire book (grain direction running with vertical measurement of book)
Leather
Lens tissue
Paper few strips
Newsprint several sheets, unprinted
Glue

Get 1 square corner on all of the materials that make up the binding and mark it. Flag the book at the head with a strip of paper.

First, make the bristol board spine, or bonnet. Find the center of the largest piece of bristol, mark it at both ends, and draw a line at this point from top to bottom. Measure with a strip of paper, over a headband, the exact width of the spine of the book; check this against the other end to be sure that they are the same width. Mark the width of the spine, half on 1 side and half on the other of the line just drawn at both ends of the bristol; this can be done with dividers or a folded strip of paper (Fig. 7–25). Place a straightedge on the marks on 1 side, and with a bonefolder fold the bristol; repeat on other side. Sharpen the folds by running a bonefolder along the folded edge. Mark the depth of the joints—which should be 1/4 inch—on the outside of the bristol, measuring from the folds just made. In the manner just described, fold both sides of the bristol again. The first fold will be inward; the second outward. In other words, they are reverse folds.

Measure and mark off 1 1/2 inches (3.8 cm) from the second fold toward the edge of the bristol on both sides and cut away any excess. Lay the folded bristol, or bonnet, in position over the spine and check it

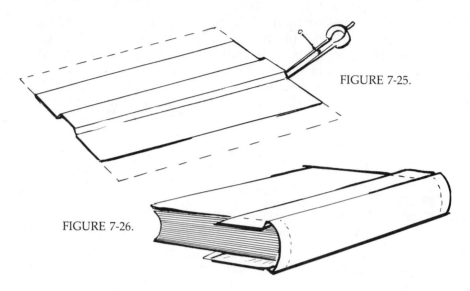

FIGURE 7-25.

FIGURE 7-26.

for size: it should fit firmly against the spine of the book, and the joint areas—the spaces created by the second folds—should rest on the backed area of the book (Fig. 7–26). If it seems to fit properly, proceed. If it is either too large or too small, it is easier and faster to start over than attempt to refold the bristol. Sand or pare to a feather edge both outside edges of the bristol. This is the side to which the boards will be attached, and it is desirable that the joining of the 2 materials be as smooth as possible, not an abrupt stepdown.

Cut the second piece of bristol the exact width of the spine of the piece just prepared, measuring it on the outside. This piece is used to make the indention for the label; instructions for this are given in detail in the preceding section on Case Bindings.

When you arrive at the space for the title and its position is determined, glue the pieces of bristol that will create the indention to the outside of the bonnet. Cut the bond paper to the exact width of the inside spine area of the bonnet; glue this and lay in position, rubbing firmly. The bonnet is now ready to be attached to the book.

Glue 1 side of the bonnet on the inside from the base of the joint (the second fold made) to its fore edge in its entire length. Put the bonnet in position on the spine of the book; be sure that the book is centered in its length and that the indention for the label is at the head. Lay the side just glued down onto the protection sheet and rub firmly. Glue the other side in the same way, pull the bonnet firmly around the spine of the book and attach the second glued side to the other protection sheet. Place between pressboards, leaving the spine and the joint exposed, and weight with a brick until dry.

Cutting the boards Measure and cut the boards as described earlier under case binding, with this exception. The point from which to measure their width is a board thickness from the base of the joint, or the second fold on the bonnet. Measure this off and draw a line at this point on both sides of the bristol; this will provide a guideline for

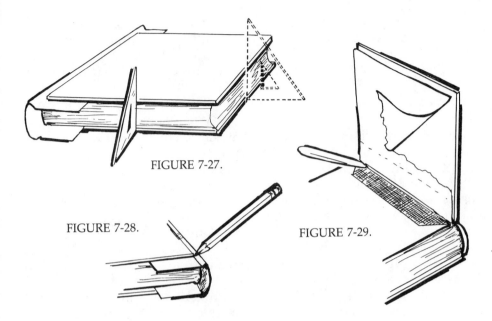

FIGURE 7-27.

FIGURE 7-28.

FIGURE 7-29.

attaching the boards. This additional space is desirable so that the boards will open freely. After cutting the boards, check them against the book to be sure that they are the proper size and that 1/8 inch square has been provided for on all 3 edges—head, tail, and fore edge. If they are correct, continue; if not, remedy the trouble.

Attaching the boards Apply glue to approximately 2 inches (5 cm) of 1 board, from 1 edge in toward the center and along its entire length; lay this in position along the line just drawn on the bristol at the base of the joint, taking care that the square on the board is even at head, tail, and fore edge. The position of the board from head to tail can be marked on the bonnet before gluing the board, if this seems helpful. The glued area of the board should cover the bristol and extend slightly onto the protection sheet.

Turn the book over and place it on a level surface; glue the second board and place it in position in the same way. With a triangle (Fig. 7–27), check all 3 edges to be sure that they are lined up evenly with the edges of the first board. When both boards are attached, put the book between pressboards, with 1 edge of each pressboard lined up with the spine edge of the binder's board. Put in the press, under firm pressure, for 30 minutes or more.

Take the book out of the press after the specified time and cut the bonnet at both head and tail flush with the edges of the boards. Do this by laying a narrow strip of bristol along the edge of 1 board, carry it across the spine, and line it up with the edge of the other board. Draw a line along the edge of the bristol and cut with scissors along this line; repeat at the other end (Fig. 7–28).

Open the book, 1 side and then the other, and tear away the portion of the protection sheets that is free—that is, not glued to either the bristol bonnet or the binder's board (Fig. 7–29). At both head and tail, front and back, slit the protection sheets with a small bonefolder at the point that they wrap around the endsheet sections, or along the edge of the spine. These slits should be about 1 inch (2.5 cm) long, or enough to permit the covering material to be turned into the bristol bonnet.

Insert new protection sheets between the hinges and the endleaves. These should be cut the exact size of the book pages.

Covering At the right-angle corner previously cut on the cloth, mark off a right-angle corner 3/4 inches (1.9 cm) in from both edges and carry the lines the width and length of the material. Lay the cloth face, or right side, down on a smooth clean surface; place the book in this right-angle corner so that the fore edge of 1 board and the head are resting on the lines just drawn. Mark a cutting point at the tail, allowing a 3/4-inch (1.9 cm) turn-in; turn the book over carefully on its spine along the line at the top of the cloth so that the second board is resting on the cloth, and mark the cutting point for the other edge, again allowing the usual 3/4-inch margin, or turn-in.

Transfer the cloth to a sheet of unprinted news and glue it in its entirety. Place the book in position in the marked-off corner. Pick up both the book and the cloth, turn them over, and lay the book down on the edge of the table with the spine extending beyond the table's edge, permitting the cloth to hang free (Fig. 7–30). Rub the cloth down firmly onto the board to which it is attached; with a bonefolder rub the cloth into the joint; then pull the cloth firmly over the spine and rub it down well. Turn the book over again and while holding the cloth free of the book, rub it into the other joint (Fig. 7–31). Then lay the cloth down gradually on the other board, rubbing it down smooth and evenly in the process. With a small bonefolder, mark the edges of the indention on the spine provided for the label.

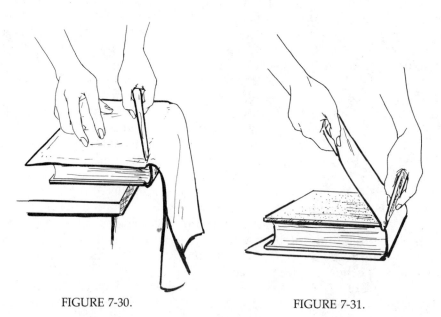

FIGURE 7-30.   FIGURE 7-31.

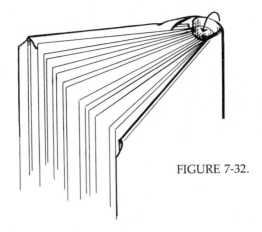

FIGURE 7-32.

Cut all corners as previously described; reglue the edges 1 at a time and turn them in the following order: tail, head, and fore edges. On the tail and head, the cloth must be turned into the bonnet, or hollow spine area. Turn the edges on both boards from fore edge to spine, then work the material into the bonnet. This is best, or more easily, done with the book standing up and open (Fig. 7–32). More space for turning the material into the bonnet is provided if the book is open, for it arches away from the spine of the covers. If the book is thick and heavy, support its fore edge during this process. A few scraps of binder's board or something about 1/8 inch thick—equivalent to the square on the board—can be slipped under it.

After the material is turned into the bonnet, lay the book open on the table and rub the turned area with a bonefolder to ensure its sticking and to smooth out any small wrinkles; give special attention to the joint areas. Repeat at the head, then turn the fore edges in the usual manner.

Place the book between brass-bound boards—the edge of the brass resting in the joints. Put in the press under medium pressure for 30 minutes or longer. Remember to protect the brass edges on the other sides of the boards with pressboards. Brass-bound boards make for a sharper joint, but they are not essential in this step. If not available, lay a clean piece of wastepaper over the joint areas—the point where the binder's board is attached to the bonnet—and rub with the side of a bonefolder. Put the book to press between pressboards, taking care to line up the edges of the boards with the spine edges of the binder's boards.

Remove from the press; open 1 cover to an upright position, slip a piece of waste paper under the cloth hinge, and glue it in its entirety. Replace the wastepaper with a strip of wax paper and close the cover. Repeat on the other side, and return the book to the press for 15 minutes or so.

Cut the board papers to size and attach as described earlier under Case Binding.

For the title, make the label and attach as described in Chapter 8 under Patch Labels or Titles.

Tight Back and German Tube Bindings

Many of the steps and techniques used in producing these 2 styles of bindings are identical. The basic difference is that 1 has a tight back, as its name implies, and the other has a hollow back (see Chapter 2 under Types of Hand Bindings). Where techniques differ, they will be discussed separately; otherwise, assume that these instructions apply to both styles of binding.

At this point the book is sewn, glued, rounded, backed, and the edges treated, unless they are to be ploughed "in boards."

Materials Needed

Binder's board 2 pieces previously selected, 1 inch (2.5 cm) larger in both dimensions than book

Bond paper 2 strips, acid-free, 3 inches wide (7.6 cm), length of boards

Bristol heavy, 2 strips, or other board the thickness of leather to be used on binding, same width and length as boards

Sandpaper fine

Glue

Triangle

Hand drill

Pressboards

Hammer

Wax paper

Wheat paste

The first 2 steps are to prepare and attach the boards. The thickness or weight of the board to be used was—or should have been—determined at the time the book was backed.

Preparing the boards For measuring and cutting of the boards, see earlier under Case Binding. Leave 1/8 inch square on all 3 edges, except that the boards fit into the right-angle joints produced in the backing and are not offset. If uncertain about width, make them slightly wider; they can easily be cut to the proper width after they are attached.

Draw a line on both boards about 1 1/2 inches (3.8 cm) from 1 edge; fold the strips of paper in half lengthwise and attach 1 strip to each board. Glue the paper; lay the fold along 1 edge of the board and attach half of the paper to 1 side of the board. Pull it tight around the edge of the board and lay the other half on the other side of the board, rubbing it down firmly on the edge and both sides of the board (Fig. 7–33). This prevents possible splitting of the board by the "pull" created when the covering leather and the leather hinge are in position. The edge thus treated is the spine edge of the board. When the paper is dry, pare or

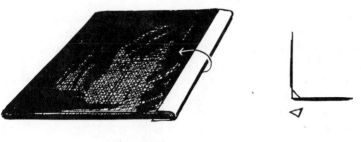

FIGURE 7-33.   FIGURE 7-34.

sand the edges to a feather edge, and sand away any surplus paper at head and tail.

Back cornering Both corners on the spine edge of each board are now back-cornered on 1 side—the side that will be the outside when attached to the book. This is sometimes referred to as nicking or careting the corners. It is done by cutting the corners of the boards off at a bevel, starting about 1/4 inch from the corner (Fig. 7-34). The thinning of the corners at these points gives a bit more space for the opening of the boards at the turns of the leather in the spine area where it is double thickness and aids in shaping the headcaps.

Glue the narrow strips of bristol and attach them to the edges of the boards on top of the bond paper. They may be slightly narrower than the thickness of the board, but should not be wider. These prevent the boards from being pulled too close in the joints in the contraction of the leather when drying. The boards are now ready to be attached to the book.

Attaching the boards There are several methods of attaching the boards. The traditional way, and the 1 still thought by some binders to be the strongest, is the technique of lacing the cords into the boards. The point of wear on the cords, however, is in the joint and not where they are attached to the board. Many boards securely laced on have broken away from the book, leaving the cord intact on the board but severed in the joint.

One plausible theory for the development of this early technique is that it saved boards and time when they were scarce and tedious to make and cut. Boards were—and still are—needed to protect the joints when the book was screwed up in a press preparatory to ploughing the edges, and if 1 pair could be cut to the proper size for the covers, and loosely attached so they could be shifted up or down, this eliminated the necessity of additional boards for this purpose.

The picture has changed somewhat, and it is questionable whether there is any virtue in religiously following this traditional technique, particularly in cases where the thinness of the boards used necessitates the fraying of the cords in the joint area. However, the 2 most common methods used today for attaching cords and 1 for attaching tapes to the boards will be given here.

Lacing in the cords These directions are for a book that was sewn on raised cords and the cords are intact, in other words, not frayed. Draw a line on both boards 3/8 inch from the spine edge—the line will be on the bond paper attached earlier. Lay 1 board in position on the book; check the evenness of the squares; and mark the diameter of each cord from the edge of the board to the line, pulling them tight and straight across the board. Turn the book over with this board still in position. Put the other board on the book and with a triangle line up the edges of it with those of the first board, and mark the location of the cords in the same way. It is safer to mark off the position of the cords on both boards and not mark the second board by the first. The cords do not always fall in exactly the same position on front and back boards, although ideally they should. Mark the boards by simply putting an "F" on the front board.

Remove the boards from the book and at the points where the cords crossed the drawn lines, bore a hole. Use a gimlet or a hand drill with a bit the approximate diameter of the cord. Draw a second line on both boards about 1/4 inch from the first and parallel to it toward the fore edge (Fig. 7-35). Bore another series of holes along the second line about 1/4 inch below the holes already made, in the direction of the tail of the book. Notch the boards at the edges where the cords cross it, and cut a V-shaped groove between the notches and the first series of holes. It is assumed that the boards are heavy enough to permit the cutting of these grooves sufficiently deep to accommodate the cord without fraying it. This should be just deep enough for the cords to fit snugly into it. If too deep, a depression will be evident after the book is covered, and if not deep enough, a bump will show. Work on 1 until the cord seems to lie flat, then proceed with the others. Then turn the boards over and cut similar grooves from the first holes to the second. Put a bit of paste on the end of each cord and twist it to a point; let dry for a few minutes. Lace all cords into the first series of holes from the outside; on the inside of the board, carry them from the first holes to the second ones and bring them out to the outside surface of the board.

If the edges of the book are to be cut "in boards" with a plough, the cutting is done at this point before the cords are permanently attached to the boards.

Setting the boards and securing the cords Loosen the cords on the boards—first 1, then the other; apply paste to all of the cords beginning at the point where they fit into the notched edges. Hold the board in a slightly upright position and pull the cords tight (Fig. 7-36). Lay the board down on the book; if it seems to ride up on the fore edge, loosen

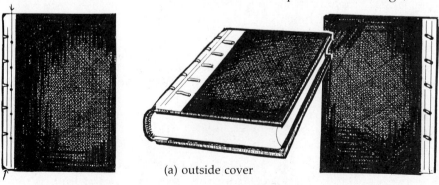

(a) outside cover

FIGURE 7-35.   FIGURE 7-36.   (b) inside cover

the cords a bit until the board lies flat. After both boards have been so attached, check the evenness of the squares with a triangle and make any necessary adjustment while the paste is still moist.

Cut off the surplus ends of the cords flush with the surface of the board. Lay wax paper over the pasted areas, and put the book between pressboards and weight down until dry. When dry, if the cords are higher than the surface of the boards, moisten the exposed part both inside and out with paste. Open the cover and lay it on a firm surface. Put a scrap of binder's board over the cords and hammer them flat. If the cords are depressed as a result of the grooves having been cut too deep, fill them in with strands of cord to which paste has been applied.

The second method of attaching the cords is to cut them approximately 1 inch (2.5 cm) long. Lay the boards in their proper position and mark the location of the cords on the edge of the boards. Notch the edge of the boards at these points to accommodate the thickness of the cord in its unfrayed state; lay the cord in the notch and fray the remainder of it. Untwist it and separate the strands or fibers by combing with a needle. Apply mixture to the cords, lay them on the positioned boards in a fanlike fashion (Fig. 7-37), combing out the fibers to make them lie as flat as possible. Attach 1 board, lay a strip of wax paper over the frayed cords, turn the book over, and repeat. Take care to check the evenness of the squares; adjust if necessary and weight the book down between pressboards until dry. For additional flattening of the cords, the same procedure described above under Lacing-In can be used.

Attaching the boards to a book that has been sewn on tapes Cut all tapes about 1 inch (2.5 cm) long with a straight or square end. Lay the boards in position and check the squares. When properly positioned, pull the tapes, 1 at a time, tight and straight onto the board; mark the exact width and length of each on the boards. Using a small metal edge as a guide, cut along the marks as deep as the estimated thickness of the tapes. This is very little more than the thickness of the bond paper. Try 1 before cutting the others. Lift out the piece cut, lay the tape in the indented area, and see if it feels flush with the board (Fig. 7-38). If all right, apply mixture to both the cut-out area and to the tapes, and lay the tapes in position. Cover with wax paper; turn the book over and repeat the process on the other board. When both boards are attached, check the evenness of the squares and weight down as described above.

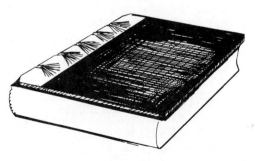

FIGURE 7-37.

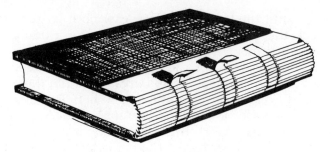

FIGURE 7-38.

Tight Back Variations

First, line the spine between the cords or tapes with Hosho as described earlier under Case Binding. Techniques for lining up the spine, as well as the following steps, differ for tight back and German tube bindings (German tube is discussed in the next section).

Materials Needed

Sandpaper file (made by gluing narrow strips of binder's board together and covering part of it with fine sandpaper) or an emery board
Leather fairly thin piece, free of injurious acids; length can be made of scraps butted together, preferably of even thickness
Acid-free paper strip slightly wider than spine, about 1/2 inch (1.2 cm) longer than boards
Glue
Wheat paste
Finishing press

The next step is the working or sewing of the headbands. As stated earlier, headbands worked with either silk or linen thread are preferable to prefabricated ones in these 2 styles of binding. Detailed instructions for their construction are in the section on Headbands earlier in this chapter.

For a smooth spine Put the book in the finishing press, spine exposed. Feather the edges of the leather at both head and tail where it will come in contact with the headbands, and cut it to the exact width of the spine and the length of the book pages. Apply a coat of paste to the spine of the book; lay the leather on the pasted area, taking care not to cover the headbands. Rub firmly with a bonefolder; apply a second coat of paste to the exposed surface of the leather (on top); rub again and set aside to dry. When thoroughly dry (at least several hours or overnight), with the sandpaper file sand the leather, using a circular motion, until the spine is smooth and free of any irregularities.

Cut the strip of paper the exact width of the spine; leave the excess length. One inch (2.5 cm) of each end of this strip is not attached to the spine, but is left free so that the covering leather can be turned into the space between the spine and this paper. Mark off 1 1/4 inches (3.1 cm)

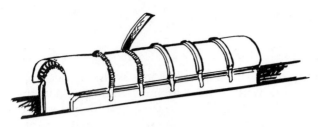

FIGURE 7-39.

at each end of the strip and glue it between these marks. Lay it in position on the spine. Approximately 1/4 inch should protrude beyond the edges of the boards at both head and tail; and the sides should be even with the edges of the spine. Rub down with a bonefolder. When thoroughly dry, if the spine is not even and smooth, sand the paper lightly.

Cut the ends of the paper flush with the edges of the boards at both head and tail. For the recommended technique, see Bradel Binding in the preceding section. Before covering, insert a strip of wax paper between the unattached ends of the paper and the spine. Let this extend beyond the ends so that it can be easily removed. This is added to eliminate the danger of the paper adhering to the spine at these points.

If the spine is unusually rough and, in the attempt to get rid of the irregularities, holes are made in the leather, fill them with thin scraps cut to the shape of the holes. Apply paste to the hole or holes, set the patch in, and when dry sand again. If the paper is sanded away in any area for the same reason, cut a second strip the same size as the first. Glue it and lay it in position on the spine; rub down firmly.

For raised bands Follow the same procedure as just described except that both the leather and the paper are cut in pieces that are fitted between the raised bands. The edges of the pieces of leather that come in contact with the headbands are feathered, and the pieces of paper at head and tail are cut longer and left unattached for 1 inch (2.5 cm) at both ends.

In cases where the cords are not as pronounced or as high as wanted, build them up with strips of leather cut slightly narrower than the cords and slightly longer than the width of the spine (Fig. 7-39). Attach with glue; care should be taken to keep these straight and parallel with the head and tail and with each other. When dry, cut these off on both sides of the spine at a bevel to the exact spine width. Lightly sand the surface smooth. Usually 1 strip on each band is sufficient, if needed at all. The size and height of raised bands, however, depend on the effect desired.

German Tube Variations

This is sometimes referred to in the United States as the Wiemeler tube.

Materials Needed

Metal burnisher
Sandpaper file
Acid-free paper (Permalife text works well), 1 piece slightly wider than 3 times the spine width and 1 inch or so longer than the boards; 6 strips 1 inch or so longer than the boards, 1/4 inch wider than spine (grain direction for all should run with vertical measurement of spine)
Glue
Sewing thread
Bristol board strips
Finishing press, nails on the side preferred

For a smooth spine Square one corner on the larger piece of paper. Mark the width of the spine at both ends, measuring from the edge just cut. Lay a straightedge along the marks and fold the paper against it. Move the straightedge and fold the paper flat; place the straightedge evenly along the edge of the paper in its folded state and fold the remaining paper against it; again fold it flat (Fig. 7-40). Cut away the paper that extends beyond the edge of the first fold. Apply hot glue to the inside of the section produced by the second fold and lay it down on the section produced by the first fold. Rub it smooth with a bone-folder. This will produce a hollow tube, one side of which—in its flat-tened state—is a single thickness of paper, the other side 2 thicknesses.

Put the book in the finishing press with the spine exposed. Check the width of the tube against the width of the spine. It is important that the tube be the exact width of the spine. If this is not accomplished in the first attempt, it is easier and faster to start over with a fresh piece of paper. Lay the single side of the tube next to one edge of the spine in

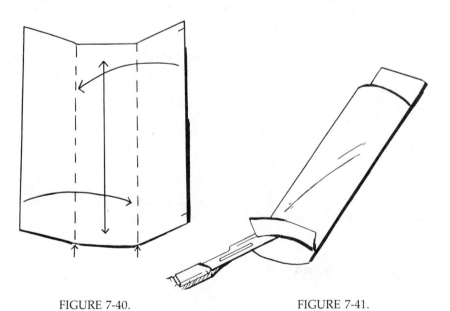

FIGURE 7-40.   FIGURE 7-41.

such a position that the excess length of the tube is evenly divided between the head and tail. Mark the tube at both ends at a point about 1/4 inch in from the headbands. Slit the tube in both folds, at both ends, from the ends to the marks (Fig. 7-41). Fold the single pieces of paper back on themselves and cut them off along the folds. The cut-off side of the tube is attached solidly to the spine of the book, and the covering leather is attached to the double-thickness side and turned into the center of the tube. If these portions of the tube were not cut away, they would show after the book was covered.

Run water through the tube and strip away the excess moisture by pulling the tube between the fingers. Insert a strip of wax paper in both ends of the tube (the width of the tube and about 2 inches, or 5 cm, long). Leave it protruding beyond the end of the tube so that it can be easily removed later. The wax paper is added to prevent the ends of the tube from sticking together in the process of attaching it. Glue the short or single side of the tube and lay it in position on the spine, lining it up carefully on the edges and centering between the headbands. Rub firmly with a bonefolder. While the tube is still slightly damp, to help it take the shape of the spine and maintain a firm bond with it, tie up the tube. Tighten the press so that the book cannot shift, and with an ace bandage or wide tape, wrap up both the book and the press, pulling the "bandage" firmly over the spine of the book (Fig. 7-42). Set aside to dry, preferably overnight.

When the tube is thoroughly dry, remove the wrapping and the strips of wax paper from the ends. Burnish the tube with the metal burnisher (Fig. 7-43) heated to the point where it sizzles when a drop of water is put on it. This is done to smooth out any irregularities or possible air bubbles and to make the tube adhere firmly to the spine. Start the burnishing near the middle (from head to tail) and center (from side to side) of the spine and work out toward the edges and the ends with firm pressure. Normally this should require only a few minutes. Reheat the burnisher when it ceases to sizzle.

The 6 strips are now added to the tube. Their purpose is to provide

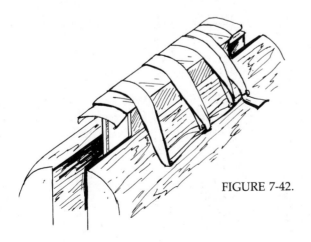

FIGURE 7-42.

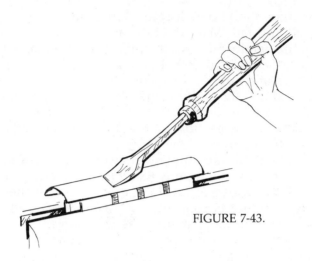

FIGURE 7-43.

sufficient thickness to allow for sanding it smooth and to serve as a firm foundation for titling and tooling. Glue 1 of the strips, lay it on the tube with the excess width evenly divided on each side. Rub with a bone-folder and then burnish as just described. Cut the second strip short enough to fit between the sewing of the headbands; glue, lay in position, rub, and burnish. The area of the spine at the headbands is usually a little higher than the rest of the spine, and the shortened strips help to counteract this. Make the third strip full length, the fourth short, and the fifth and sixth full length, added in this order and burnished in the same manner.

Leave the excess width free; in other words, do not let it adhere to the boards. It should look somewhat like the overhang of the eaves on a roof. When all of the strips have been added and burnished, again tie it up and set aside until thoroughly dry—several hours or more.

When dry, remove the wrapping and cut the tube at both ends flush with the boards as described in the earlier section for the bristol board bonnet on a Bradel binding. Take the sandpaper file and, with a circular motion, sand the surface of the tube until it is smooth. In sanding the sides of the spine, tilt the file so that the sanding motion conforms to the shape of the overhanging edges. The excess width of the tube is not removed while sanding the spine. If in the attempt to get the spine smooth, the tube is sanded through or air bubbles burst, add an additional strip or strips of paper.

When the sanding of the spine is completed, lay the edge of a ruler in the center of the spine, running from head to tail, and check to see if the ruler comes in contact with the tube over its entire length. If the ruler touches the tube only on its ends and there is space between the tube and the edge of the ruler in other areas, additional short strips of paper should be added as previously described. When dry, sand again.

After the work on the spine is completed, remove the book from the press. Lay it on a pressboard with the spine just off the board so that the surplus material of the tube will not get bent. Lay a strip of bristol along the spine edge of the top board (Fig. 7-44); hold the file in a

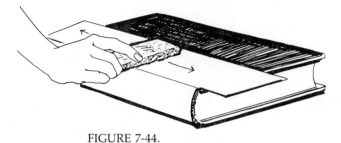

FIGURE 7-44.

horizontal position and sand away the overhang until the edge of the spine is level and even with the piece of bristol. Turn the book over and repeat on the other side.

For raised bands The same general procedures are followed as just described. More time will be required, however, in both the burnishing and the sanding in order to get the tube and the strips to conform to the shape of the cords. In sanding the sides of the bands, it is advisable that the portion of the file—or its edge—that comes in contact with the spine be free of sandpaper; otherwise, it will tend to cut too deep. All bands and both ends should be tied down when the burnishing is completed on the tube and again after the strips are added.

Tying up the bands is done with a heavy sewing thread as follows: Start at the tail; tie the thread securely to a tack on the press that is approximately 1 inch to the left of the first band; bring the thread up across the spine and as close as possible to the far side of the band—or the side toward the head of the book—down on the other side; attach it to the tack opposite the one started at, pulling the thread tight and close to the side of the band; secure the thread by winding it around the tack several times (Fig. 7-45). Carry the thread to the tack that is about 1 inch from the band toward the head, wrap it around the tack. Then carry it up and across the spine on the other side of the band and secure it on the tack on the opposite side of the press. Continue until all bands have been so tied down. The ends are tied down with a wide tape simply by securing the tape on one side of the press, bringing it up across the spine, and securing it on the opposite side of the press. Be sure that the tape covers the spine in the area of the headbands; or the book and the press can be wrapped with an ace bandage.

Covering the boards with bristol This has a twofold purpose: It provides a smoother surface for the covering leather, and it balances the pull that will be created when bristol is later added to the inside of the covers. Cut 2 pieces of bristol slightly larger in both dimensions than

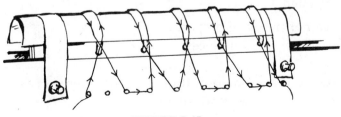

FIGURE 7-45.

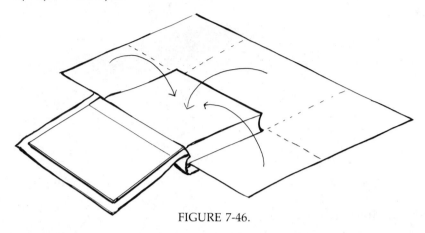

FIGURE 7-46.

the boards. It is easier and usually more accurate to work with these slightly oversize than it is to cut them to the exact size and get them attached properly.

Apply glue to the bristols and put 1 on each board. Exercise care in lining them up exactly along the spine edge of the boards—do not let them cover the little spacers on the edges, and be sure that the entire board is covered; rub down firmly. Put the book between pressboards and weight down for several hours. When dry, sand away the surplus bristol on the edges and back-corner it. If the edges of the book have not been protected earlier, fold a piece of paper around the book, inside the covers, to protect the edges during the sanding (Fig. 7-46). Then sand the surface of the bristol in the area of the cords or tapes if there are obvious irregularities.

At this stage the bristol will warp the boards, so keep the book under weight when not working on it.

The book is now ready for its cover. See the earlier section on Cutting Leather to Size and Paring for the preparation of the covering leather. If the spine is to be titled on a stamping press, this is done before the leather is attached to the book (see Patch Labels or Titles in Chapter 8). The following instructions are for covering when the titling on the spine is to be done by hand.

Covering the Book

This is done in 2 stages; first the leather is attached to the spine and, when this is dry, it is laid down on the boards.

Materials Needed

Covering leather properly prepared
Wastepaper clean, several pieces
Water
Wheat paste fresh and smooth, thin enough to spread easily
Cotton tape wide, or ace bandage
Sewing thread

Finishing press, nails on the side preferred
Pulpboard
Pressboards 2
Bricks
Right-angle triangle
Bristol board

Put the book in the finishing press with the spine and about 2 inches (5 cm) of the boards exposed, and tighten it well.

For a smooth spine Mark the center of the spine area at both ends of the leather and the center of the spine at both ends of the book. Moisten the entire outside surface of the leather with water. Paste the flesh side of the leather in the spine area, covering it all the way out to the edges at both ends. Let it stand 1 or 2 minutes and then apply a second coat of paste. If the paste does not seem evenly spread and tends to bead up when brushed, lay a piece of wastepaper over it; rub the paper lightly and remove it immediately.

Lay the pasted leather on the spine of the book, lining up the center marks on the leather with those on the spine at both head and tail and allowing an equal amount of leather to extend beyond the length of the book at both ends (Fig. 7-47). When in position, moisten the surface of the leather on the spine with water; lay a clean piece of paper over it and rub it gently with the hands for 10 to 15 minutes. As it begins to dry, put a fresh piece of paper over it and rub it lightly with a clean bonefolder. Exercise caution in keeping the edges of fingernails, rings, and the like free from the leather. In a dampened state, leather is very vulnerable to the slightest impression, and such marks are very difficult to remove. Too much pressure will obscure or flatten out the grain, and it frequently bruises the leather, darkening it in areas thus treated. This can be particularly disfiguring with light-colored leathers.

Remove the paper and roll the sides of the leather up and secure in a rolled position with paper clips. Tie the spine up as previously described and set aside to dry for several hours or more.

For raised bands Follow the instructions just given for covering a smooth spine up to the point of getting the leather in position on the spine. It is, however, necessary that the finishing press used here have

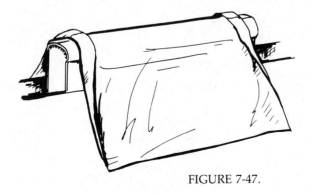

FIGURE 7-47.

tacks on the sides or some comparable provision for tying up the bands, for which linen sewing thread will also be needed.

When the leather is in proper position on the spine, keep it moist with water and shape it over the bands with the hands. Lay a strip of paper across the spine and against the bands, and gently but firmly push the leather snugly up against the bands. Continue until all bands have been so treated. Rub the leather between the bands down as described for a smooth spine. Put a fresh strip of paper against the bands; run a small bonefolder lightly along the edges of the bands to make sure that the leather is sticking at these points. Continue to rub for 10 or 15 minutes, or until the leather begins to dry.

Roll up the sides of the leather and secure in a rolled position with paper clips (Fig. 7-48). Tie the bands up in the manner described earlier under the German tube. Then cut 2 strips of bristol slightly wider than the spine and as long as the head and tail panels. Lay these on the spine in these areas and tie down with tapes secured to the tacks, or an ace bandage can be used as described earlier. Set aside to dry for several hours, after which the sides can be laid down.

Laying down the sides Remove the book from the press. Moisten the surface of 1 side of the leather, and with the book resting on its spine on a clean smooth surface, paste the inside of the leather. Let it stand for 1 or 2 minutes, then apply a second coat of paste. Be sure the paste is evenly spread and free of lumps. Lay the book flat. Hold the pasted leather up away from the board and gradually lay it down on the board, smoothing it out with a wad of moistened cotton until the board is covered. Pull the leather only enough to get it smooth; try not to stretch it. Put a clean piece of paper over the leather and rub it gently for a few minutes with the palm of a hand from the spine area toward the fore edge. Turn the book over and repeat on the other side. Place it between clean pulpboards and pressboards, and put sufficient weight on it to ensure that the boards will lie flat—a lithographic stone or 4 bricks will generally suffice. After 1 hour or so, replace the pulpboards with dry ones and put the book back under weight. Let it dry overnight before proceeding.

The next steps are to set the boards and remove the spacers. Moisten

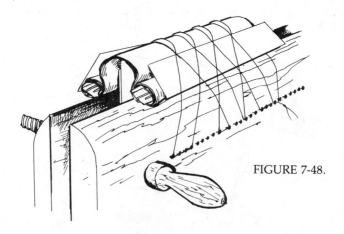

FIGURE 7-48.

the joint area on 1 side of the book with water and swing the board back and forth slowly, extending the arc a bit each time, until it lies all the way open easily. Lay the cover back on a pile of pressboards and a piece of clean pulpboard equal in height to the thickness of the book. Check to see if the board is in proper position in relation to the joint on the book. The edge of the board should lie parallel with the edge of the spine, and both joint and board should form a right angle with the book. If this is not the case, moisten the joint area on the outside again and carefully work the board into its proper position by holding it upright and putting pressure on it in the area that is out of line.

While the board is open and supported, remove the spacer from the edge of the board (Fig. 7-49). This is most easily done with the point of a thin blade such as a scalpel. Turn the book over and repeat these steps on the other side.

Turning the leather in at head and tail and setting the headcaps A headcap is the shaped, folded leather over a headband. For a tight back binding, insert a small bonefolder at both head and tail and move it across the width of the spine to be sure that the portion of the paper strip added earlier and left free or unglued is still free. It is this area into which the leather is turned. For a German tube, insert a small bonefolder in the ends of the tube at both head and tail and split the folds on both sides for about 1 inch, or the estimated width of the leather to be turned in. Again, this is the area into which the leather will be turned.

Start at the tail of the book. Moisten the leather to be turned in on the outside along the entire edge of both boards and in the spine area. Apply 2 coats of paste to the flesh side of the edges in the area of the spine and for about 2 inches (5 cm) along the boards. When the leather is soft and pliable, turn it into the center of the space previously provided and bring it over the edge of the boards for the distance that was pasted. Keep the entire edge moist during this process. When the leather is turned neatly along the spine, pull it toward the fore edge of each board before turning it firmly against the edges of the boards. Stand the book on its head and with the thumb and forefinger of both hands—1 on each board—ease the leather away from the spine. This should help smooth out the turned-in portion and pull any wrinkles or surplus leather out of the joints. Then turn the pasted edges of the leather onto the boards, pulling it firmly against the edges of the boards.

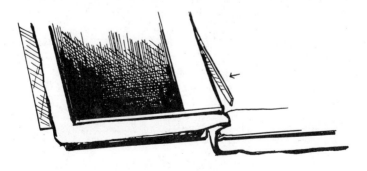

FIGURE 7-49.

With a small bonefolder, start in the center of the spine and gently pull the tucked-in leather in the area of the spine out in its folded state to the point where when folded over and flattened, it will be the approximate thickness of the boards. After the leather is pulled out, flatten it with the bonefolder so that the spine is even with the edges of the boards. If it is uneven or the fold is too heavy or too thin, work at it a bit; these things do not always come out just right with the first try. Again with a small bonefolder, press the leather into the area of the back cornering; hold this with a finger and with the bonefolder pull the flattened leather or the headcap toward the boards on both sides of the spine.

After doing the tail, keep it moist until the head is done in the same way. When both headcaps are formed, tie them up with a piece of sewing thread by placing the thread in the back-cornered area and wrapping it securely around the book along the joints (Fig. 7-50). Keep the thread in the notches of the back cornering at all 4 points, and tie securely with a square knot in the center of the spine area at 1 end or the other. If tied on the edge of 1 of the boards, the knot is likely to leave a mark. Moisten both headcaps and reshape them. Finish the job by hitting them lightly against a clean flat surface; this will ensure their being even with the edges of the boards.

Put the book between pulp and pressboards and weight down until dry. If the headcaps are to retain their shape, they should be thoroughly dry—preferably overnight—before proceeding with the work.

Cutting the corners and turning the edges The objective here is to cut away the surplus leather so that the corners can be covered and mitered neatly without reducing the strength of the leather appreciably at these points that are so subject to wear. Moisten 1 joint and swing the cover slowly until it opens easily; then support it in its opened state and weight down. Moisten the edges of the leather and pull it firmly over the edges of the board; at the corners pinch the surplus together and fold it first to 1 side then the other. Slip a piece of scrap board under the corner; lay the leather back on this, and with a sharp knife—a scalpel works well—cut the corner off the leather at a bevel just beyond the creases made by the folding (Fig. 7-51). Feather the edge of the cut and thin the portions of the leather that will overlap when in position on the inside of the board. At the very corner of the board, leave the leather unthinned (except for its initial paring) for the estimated thickness

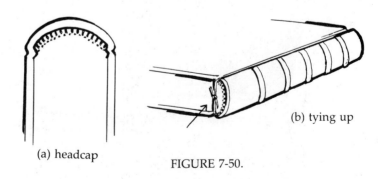

(a) headcap

(b) tying up

FIGURE 7-50.

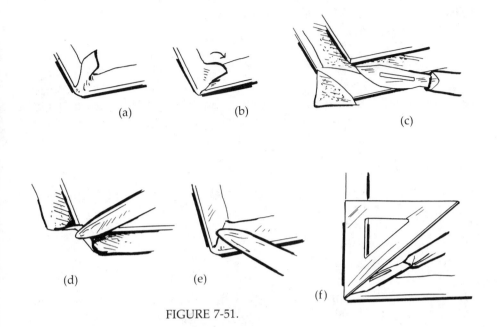

FIGURE 7-51.

of the board and thin it from this point out to the edge. The safest way to get the corners prepared properly is to make the initial cut, then do the feathering and thinning gradually, checking it at intervals in the process.

Moisten the leather to be turned in at either the head or tail of the book. Lift up any part of the 2 inches (5 cm), previously turned near the spine, that is not snug against the board. This often wrinkles when the book is closed.

Paste the inside of the leather and pull it firmly over the edge of the board. Shape the leather around the corner and ease the fullness back toward the spine. Keep the edge moist until the leather is well stuck to the board and free of wrinkles or other unevenness. Repeat at the other end and on the fore edge.

When all 3 edges are turned, the corners will probably require a bit more work. Start with 1 corner, keep the leather moist, and with a bonefolder spread any remaining fullness right at the corner out in tiny little pleats—not 1 big fold. If this cannot be done, open up the corner and thin the leather a little more at this point. Do this additional thinning with a stainless steel blade. Ordinary steel in contact with dampened leather tends to stain it—particularly in the case of light-colored leathers. When this is satisfactorily accomplished, lay a small right-angle triangle in position in the corner and miter the corner by cutting the top layer of leather away on the bevel so that the bevelled edge starts at the surface of the leather and works back. In other words, the bevelling should not expose the flesh side of the leather. Remove the fragment just cut away; repaste the leather, if necessary; reshape the corner, and rub the mitred edge down with a bonefolder. Insert a piece of bristol between the book and the cover and close it.

Turn the book over and follow the same procedures on the edges of the other board.

Lining Inside of the Boards

This serves a twofold purpose: It balances the pull of the bristol previously glued to the outside of the board, and it brings the inside surface of the board up even and flush with the edges of the turned leather.

Materials Needed

Bristol 2 pieces cut with right-angle corners 1 1/4 inches (3.1 cm) shorter in length and width than size of boards
Glue
Wastepaper several pieces
Weight

These instructions are for a book with leather hinges. If the hinges are paper, cut the bristol in width only 5/8 inch (1.7 cm) narrower than the boards.

Open the book and support the cover as described earlier. Lay 1 piece of the bristol in position on the inside of the cover; mark both the bristol and the board in some way so that when ready to attach the bristol to the board, the 2 can be brought together in the same relative position.

Center the bristol from head to tail and from fore edge to spine edge. A margin of 5/8 inch (1.7 cm) of leather should be showing at head, tail, and fore edge and the bristol set back or offset from the spine edge the same distance. This area will be covered by the leather hinge in a later step.

When the bristol is properly positioned, weight it down. Lay the straightedge along the edges of the bristol—1 at a time—and cut away the uneven and surplus leather. When all 3 edges are cut, lay the bristol aside and pull away the surplus leather, pulling it toward the outer edge of the board. Lay the bristol on a sheet of wastepaper, glue it, and place it in the frame made by the cuts snug against the edges of the leather. This is best done by getting 1 corner of the bristol in properly before laying the rest of it down. Rub down firmly. Turn the book over and repeat this step. When both sides are done, put the book between pulp and pressboards and weight down to dry overnight. Be sure there is sufficient weight on it to hold the covers flat.

Putting Down Hinges

As noted previously, these instructions are for a book with leather hinges.

Materials Needed

Right-angle triangle
Tweezers

Paper several strips
Binder's board scrap
Water
Cotton
Mixture wheat paste and water-soluble PVA equal parts
Pressboards

Open 1 cover and support it with pressboards as already described. Check the position of the board to be sure that its edge is still parallel with the edge of the spine; and using the right-angle triangle, check to see that the board and the joint are at a right angle with the book. If adjustment is necessary, moisten the surface of the leather in the joint and work the board into position as previously described.

Tear away the protection sheet along the joint. Remove any fragments of this sheet that remain exposed in the joint; tweezers work well for this.

Put weights on both the board and the book that are heavy enough to keep them from shifting. Free the hinge from the bristol board and pull it firmly across the joint onto the board; mark it at both ends from the spine edge of the board to the point where it meets or crosses the edges of the bristol and the turned-in leather. Lay the hinge flat; slip the scrap board under the ends and cut off the corners—as indicated by the marks—at a bevel and feather the edge of the end of the hinge in its entirety.

Lay the hinge in position again, and with a small bonefolder draw a line on the turned-in leather along the edge of the board, marking off the area in which the hinge will eventually rest. Feather the edge of the leather in this space; moisten the area and burnish or flatten it with a bonefolder (Fig. 7-52). This is done in order to make the hinge as flush as possible with the rest of the turned edge. If the hinge is appreciably higher after this is done, sand the area a bit and rub it down again. In doing this, be careful not to mar the surface of the leather that will remain exposed.

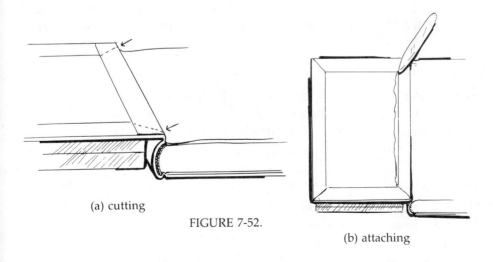

(a) cutting

FIGURE 7-52.

(b) attaching

Slip a strip of paper under the hinge; moisten the right side of the hinge and apply 2 coats of mixture to the inside, allowing 1 or 2 minutes between applications. Also apply mixture to the edge of the board and the joint area. Hold the hinge up and rub it firmly in the joint and against the edge of the board; then lay the rest of it down on the board. Put a piece of paper over the hinge and rub it firmly for a few minutes, paying particular attention to the joint and the ends.

The cover should remain open only long enough for the hinge to dry to the point where the adhesive has set and it can be closed without wrinkling the hinge—10 minutes is generally long enough, although it depends somewhat on how damp the hinge is and the humidity of the room. After 10 minutes, remove the weights and close the cover. Open it immediately and check the hinge. If it has wrinkled, lay the cover back in its original position; return the weights, moisten the hinge, and rub it some more; then try closing the cover again. If all is well, lay the cover open and cut away the surplus hinge—that portion that overlaps the bristol—along the edge of the bristol. Mark the edge of the bristol on the surface of the leather at both ends, lay the straightedge on the marks, hold it firmly, make the cut, and peel away the fragments.

Place a piece of pulpboard between the cover and the bristol board that is protecting the endleaf, offsetting it at the joint about 1/4 inch. Close the cover. Turn the book over and put the other hinge down in the same way.

When both hinges are down, moisten the joints on the outside and put the book under weight between pulp and pressboards until the hinges are thoroughly dry—1 hour or more.

The book is now ready to be titled, tooled, or decorated (Chapter 8).

It is customary to put the board papers in after all finishing has been done. If, however, the title was put on by using the stamping press, and no tooling or other decoration is planned for the covers, the board papers are added as soon as the hinges are dry.

Putting Down Board Papers

These papers presumably were rough cut and laid aside in a safe place at the time the endsheet sections were being prepared. If not, locate the same type of paper that was used for the endleaves.

Materials Needed

Board papers 2, cut 1/16 inch shorter in length than book pages, 1/4 inch narrower in width than inside measurement of board
Bristol 2 pieces slightly larger in both dimensions than boards
Wastepaper several sheets, clean
Pulpboard
Pressboards
Wheat paste smooth, thin enough to spread easily
Mixture wheat paste and water-soluble PVA equal parts

Open 1 cover of the book and support it properly. Lay the board paper facedown on a sheet of wastepaper; hold it firmly and apply paste to it. If the paper tends to curl, continue to brush it, without adding more paste, until it relaxes and lies flat. Pick it up; lay it in position 1/8 inch in from the fore edge, and center it from head to tail. Rub this edge gently. Pick the rest of the sheet up and lay it down gradually, smoothing it out as it goes down. Put a clean sheet of paper over it and rub firmly from the center out in all directions for a few minutes. Wipe away from the edges any paste that might have oozed out during the rubbing. Remove the pieces of bristol that were used in constructing the endsheet section, insert a fresh piece of bristol between the endleaf and the board paper, and close the cover. Turn the book over and add the other board paper in the same way.

When both papers are in place, put the book again between pulp and pressboards and weight down. In about half an hour, check to see that all is well. If so, replace the bristols with fresh ones; put the book back under weight and leave to dry overnight.

For tipping colored or decorated endleaves to the flyleaves, see earlier in this chapter under Case Binding.

Leather and silk doublures For leather, cut the leather 1/4 inch bigger in both dimensions than the space between the turned leather on the inside of the board. Pare the edges to the estimated thickness of the turned edges on the book. Paste it and lay in position, allowing 1/8 inch overlap on all 4 edges. When dry, make a bevelled cut on all edges through both pieces of leather. Moisten and remove the surplus. Lay the 2 edges down with the bevels overlapping; cover with a piece of clean paper and rub with a bonefolder. Cover with a pulpboard and pressboard, and weight down until dry.

For silk, make a bevelled cut on all leather edges on the inside of the board. Cut a piece of paper—the same as used for the silk flyleaves—the exact size of the exposed board. Check it to be sure that it fits; then cut off of 2 edges the estimated thickness of 2 layers of the silk used. Cover the paper with the silk as described under silk flyleaves (Chapter 6, General Techniques, Endsheet Variations); weight down until dry. Line the inside of the board with bond paper. Put a narrow line of mixture around all 4 edges of the bond paper; lay the prepared silk in position. Cover with a clean pulpboard and weight down until dry.

8 Finishing

Finishing is a "process of completing or perfecting; that which completes or perfects." The person doing the work is a finisher, and the tools used are called finishing tools. In hand bookbinding, the term specifically refers to the titling and decorating of the binding on a book. Titling can be done by several methods, and decoration can take the form of blind or gold tooling, inlays, onlays, bas-relief, intaglio, and the like.

This section deals primarily with the techniques used in producing various effects, with a few general guidelines. These principles can be applied to an infinite variety of decorative combinations. In a manual of this kind, it seems more meaningful to suggest that bindings be observed and studied— in libraries, at exhibitions, and in the number of available exhibition catalogs—for ideas in decoration rather than to attempt to illustrate here what could be only a very small number of possibilities.

First, the tools and materials most frequently used are described, followed by the basic techniques or principles employed in their use and suggested practice exercises. These exercises begin with the simplest and easiest form of decoration—blind tooling. It is strongly recommended that no work on a book be undertaken until all or at least a part of these practice suggestions have been tried successfully.

Tools for Finishing

Finishing tools are an essential part of every hand binder's equipment, and the cherished possessions of many. A large variety gives the binder a greater number of decorative possibilities, but much interesting and creative work can be done with relatively few tools, if carefully selected. The number and variety of tools needed by any binder are dependent, of course, on the amount and kind of work planned. So give some thought to this before stocking up.

The tools listed here are generally available from bookbinding supply houses either new or secondhand. Few suppliers today stock any quantity of them new, so there is likely to be a waiting period between ordering and delivery. The availability of secondhand tools depends on the dealer's prior purchase. Occasionally collections are offered by retiring binders or binderies that are overstocked either privately or at auction. Availability is, however, at best unpredictable.

If you contemplate purchasing secondhand tools, be careful in selecting them. If feasible, take a stamp pad and paper along and make an ink impression before purchasing. The smallest defect or damage to the surface or face will produce defective work—thus rendering the tool a disappointing, if not totally worthless, purchase. It is seldom economically practical to purchase a defective tool in expectation of having it recut or retooled.

Once purchased, treat your finishing tools with respect. Although they may seem sturdy and rugged, the edges or faces are quite delicate and vulnerable to damage. When in use, take care not to drop them or bang the edges against a table. Store them in some fixed position where the tooling surface is readily visible and where they are kept out of contact with other objects.

Handle letters (Fig. 8-1) These are letters cut on the end of a brass shaft. The other end of the shaft is inserted in a short wooden handle with a hole in it. Their use is probably the oldest method of titling a book with individual letters (other than written ones), and some binders today still consider them the only proper letters to use in the titling of a hand-bound book. Work produced with them has a more individual and less mechanical appearance, and they offer flexibility in opening or condensing a title to conform to the available space.

They are manufactured in different point sizes and typefaces, although both are somewhat limited. They do not always conform to the standard point system of measurement, and their faces are not always identified. Also, they are rather costly. A set customarily consists of 38 characters: the alphabet, figures 0–9, a period, and a comma; sometimes the diphthongs "ae" and "oe" are included or are available separately. Three sizes of the same typeface are desirable, if all titling is to be done with these letters.

Type pallets (Fig. 8-1) Sometimes referred to as type holders, these are vises with a handle. There are 2 basic styles: 1 with adjustable open jaws and the other, a channel or groove designed to take a specific size type, with an adjustable screw at 1 end. The open jaw model is the more useful and versatile, for it will accommodate almost any size type. These are made in varying widths; 1 with a jaw opening of 3 to 3 1/2 inches (7.6 to 8.8 cm) is as large as can be comfortably handled by most binders. This style also comes with a heating unit attached, although this addition hardly seems necessary for most hand binders. In the other style, it is necessary to have a series of them, 1 for each size of type. The type made for these does not follow the standard point-size system, so purchase only if accompanied by type that fits the channel.

Type Type is defined by Webster as "a rectangular block typically of metal or wood bearing a relief character from which an inked print is made." In bookbinding, however, it is used hot to make an indented impression and in the application of gold leaf or colored pigments.

The size of type is measured in points, and the area of the type measured to determine its size is from "belly-to-back." A point is about 1/72nd of an inch, so the body of a 72-point type measured in this way is 1 inch (2.5 cm) thick. The size of the letter or character on this body varies with the design of the typeface.

Three kinds of type are described here, all suitable for use in titling. The chief differences are their composition, the manner in which they are packaged, and their relative cost. Most hand binders use only capital letters in titling work. So capitals, along with figures and punctuation marks, are all that must be acquired in an initial purchase.

Brass type (Fig. 8-1) This is the best type for titling. It makes a nice, clean impression, wears well, and is not adversely affected by heat or pressure. Brass is an alloy. Its chief component is copper, which has a melting point of 1065°C (1949°F). It is available in a number of point sizes and a limited, but adequate, number of typefaces. It is packaged in fonts of 136 characters or pieces, or in half fonts (68 pieces), distributed as follows:

A B C D E F G H I J K L M N O P Q R S T U V W X Y Z ( ) . , - & : ; ' ' '
6 4 4 4 6 4 4 4 6 4 4 4 4 4 6 4 2 4 4 4 6 4 4 2 4 2 2 2 4 4 4 2 4 2 2 2

Figures are sold as figure fonts and consist of 42 pieces—6 of the number 1 and 4 each of 2–0.

Disadvantages are that it is not routinely a stock item, there is a waiting period for delivery, and the initial cost in purchasing an adequate variety of point sizes and typefaces. For handwork, 1 font of 2 or 3 sizes in one typeface should suffice. If used in a stamping press, 2 fonts of the same point size and face are highly desirable, if not essential.

White metal type This is a type made especially for hot stamping; it is a good thermal conductor and holds up well under pressure. Its basic component is a zinc-magnesium alloy, which is considered the hardest of the white metals. It has a melting point of about 453°C (850°F). Considerably cheaper than brass type, it is sold in fonts of 100 characters, distributed as follows:

A B C D E F G H I J K L M N O P Q R S T U V W X Y Z
4 3 3 3 5 2 2 2 4 2 2 3 2 4 4 2 1 4 4 4 2 2 2 1 2 1

1 2 3 4 5 6 7 8 9 0 & . , ' -
2 2 2 2 2 2 2 2 2 2 1 3 3 2 1

The quantity needed would be similar to that for brass type, mentioned above, although individual characters can be purchased, and it is readily available. Its chief disadvantage, possibly its only one, is that its typefaces, unfortunately, are not made up from well-designed alphabets.

Printer's or foundry type This type is made from a lead-based alloy, and lead is rather soft and malleable, with a low melting point of 330°C (626°F). It is made primarily for printing that requires no heat and little pressure. It does not hold up well under a combination of heat and pressure, but if reasonable care is taken, it can be used quite successfully for many impressions.

Its chief advantages are that it offers the greatest variety of sizes and typefaces at modest cost. For many years, it was readily available in many faces in point sizes from 4 to 72. With the relatively recent changes that have taken place in the printing industry, it is, however, not so plentiful. It is still available from a few sources, although not always immediately. Its disadvantages are its softness when heated and the fact that lead is not a good conductor of heat.

It is packaged by a fixed weight in fonts, which consist of "a complete assortment and just apportionment of all the characters of a particular face and size." Thus, fonts of the same point size, but a different face, may vary in the number of characters, and the larger the point size the fewer the characters to the font. For instance, an all-caps font of 12-point Caslon Old Style 471 has 296 characters, while the same font and point size in Goudy Old Style 178 has 345 characters, and a font of 24-point Caslon has 132 characters.

It is also packaged and sold in small or incomplete fonts—all lower-case, all capitals, and figures, consisting of numerals and punctuation marks. The weight of these is based on a percentage of the total weight of a font, so again, the number of characters vary.

One font of any given size, particularly the smaller sizes, usually has enough characters to serve most needs. It is desirable to have on hand several sizes of whatever typefaces are chosen. Twelve, 18, and 24 represent a reasonable range in sizes. Caslon Old Style 471, Goudy Old Style 178, Centaur, and Perpetua are pleasing classic faces, and Futura Book is a good modern sans serif.

Type manufactured in foreign countries, for use in the country of origin, includes accented letters that are characteristic of the language. Titles in the Arabic, Oriental, Slavic, Yiddish, and other languages can sometimes be obtained in the form of linotype slugs from newspaper offices printing in these languages. These, however, are probably available only in large urban areas, or where there is a concentration of particular ethnic groups.

Titling can also be done by building letters with gouges and pallets, described later in this chapter under Titling.

Quadrats and spaces Both of these will be needed in using any of the 3 types discussed above. A quadrat, or quad as it is commonly known, is a block of type metal lower than the letters, used in spacing both letters and words. These are packaged in assorted thicknesses. Brass spaces are 1 point in thickness and copper 1/2 point. They are packaged in small quantities by point size, and all 3 are available in all point sizes. They should be stocked in the same point sizes as the type purchased.

Tools for decoration (Fig. 8-1) These include rolls, fillets, line pallets, gouges, short pallets, and ornamental stamps. They are usually made of brass, although some are made of other copper alloys such as bell metal or bronze. They are all mounted in wood or asbestos handles for ease in handling. Established manufacturers mark their tools with their name and some identifying mark, either a letter, numeral, or catalog number. These marks are not, however, always easy to interpret. The best source of information regarding them is probably makers or dealers catalogs. Line tools are generally more useful and versatile if they are of the same line thickness.

Rolls and fillets (Fig. 8-1) These are also known as wheels or roulettes. A roll is a continuous or solid disc, and a fillet is a roll that has had a small section cut out of the edge and the ends mitred to permit neat corners in the tooling of a panel or rectangle.

The center of the wheel is attached to a metal shank in a way that permits it to turn freely, and the shank is mounted in a wooden handle.

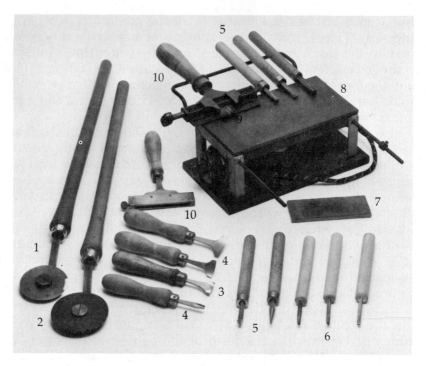

FIGURE 8-1. Finishing Tools. (1) Fillet, (2) Roll, (3) Ogee gouge, (4) Gouges,
(5) Decorative tools, (6) Handle letters, (7) Board for cleaning tools,
(8) Tooling stove, (9) Brass type, (10) Type pallets.

There are at least 2 styles of shanks. One is a single piece of metal, and
the wheel is attached to 1 side of it with a screw that turns counterclock-
wise. The other is 2-pronged—referred to as a French fork—and the
wheel is mounted between the prongs and riveted. There is generally
less play in a wheel on a single shank, and with no visual obstruction
on 1 side, it is easier to see the edge of the wheel.

These tools are generally numbered in Arabic numerals. Starting with
no. 1 for the thinnest line, this will produce a gold tooled line .010 inch
in width; no. 2, .015 inch; no. 3, .020 inch; and so on. They are made in
a great number of single-line thicknesses, double and triple lines, and
combinations of thin and thick lines and decorative faces. They are
available in various diameters—3 to 3 1/2 inches (7.6–8.8 cm) is a good
average size. In line thickness, a no. 3 and a no. 5 or 6 are good to start
with, and fillets are generally more useful than rolls. Handles are available in various diameters and lengths. Choose those that are comfortable to hold and long enough to rest on the shoulder, to help steady the
wheel when in use.

Pallets (Fig. 8-1) There are 2 different styles of tools that go by this
name. They are both mounted in short handles. One style is about 3
inches (7.6 cm) in length and made as individual pieces in the same line
thicknesses and ornamental faces as rolls and fillets. They are used
primarily in the tooling of horizontal lines on the spine of a book. This
can, however, also be done with a fillet, so these are not essential tools.

The other style consists of tools of the same line thickness, starting perhaps with one 1/16 or 1/8 inch long and increasing in length by a fixed measure up to 1 1/2 or 2 inches (3.8–5 cm). These are straight-line tools and are usually sold along with gouges as part of a set of design tools, and they constitute a necessary part of the set. Twelve or 15 pieces generally make up a set.

Gouges (Fig. 8-1) These are curved tools, and each tool represents an arc or segment of a circle. A group represents segments of a series of concentric circles. These are made up in 180°, 90°, 60°, 45°, and 30° arcs and possibly others in varying lengths and line thicknesses. The more usual are 90°, 60°, and 45°. What constitutes a set is seemingly the number of tools made by a manufacturer in the same arc and the same line thickness. This varies from 32 to 10 or 12. A set that would certainly serve most needs would be 16 pieces in 3 arcs each, accompanied by a graduated series (in length) of short pallets—12 to 15—all of the same line thickness.

Many binders accumulate miscellaneous gouges. These obviously will be of greater use if their line thickness and the degree of the arc can be determined. The following suggestions should help in this. The line thickness can be determined by making a tooled impression of it, preferably in gold. To ascertain the degree of the arc made by an impression of the tool, it is necessary first to determine the radius of the circle it will make. This can be done geometrically by making an impression of the tool, drawing 2 lines tangent to the curve and 2 intersecting lines at right angles to the 2 tangent lines. The radius of the circle will be the distance between where the lines intersect and the right angles.

Another way, and perhaps simpler for those not at ease with geometry, is to draw 2 straight lines perpendicular to each other, forming 4 right, or 90°, angles (Fig. 8-2). With a protractor, mark off 45°, 60°, and 30° angles. Fit the tool into 1 of the angles, the ends resting on the lines forming the angle, at points equidistant from the center. Using this measurement as the radius, draw a circle with a compass. If 4 impressions of the tool fit the circle and complete it, it is a 90° arc; 8, it is 45°; 6 it is 60°; and 12, it is 30°.

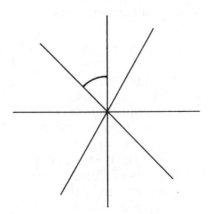

FIGURE 8-2.

Ogee gouges (Fig. 8-1) These are tools consisting of a double or reverse curve, formed by the union of a convex and a concave line. They are made in sets of graduated lengths and mounted in short handles. Although useful, they are not necessary to a collection of finishing tools, for their effect can also be produced by a regular gouge.

Ornamental tools (sometimes called stamps) These are dies cut on the end of a brass shaft and mounted in short handles. They have been made over the years in a variety of designs, both traditional and modern, and in a number of sizes. Dots, circles, stars, and the like are made in graduated sizes and sold either in sets or as individual pieces.

Many of these are copies of tools attributed to early binders, or copies of printer's devices, and many are just ornaments with no historic or other significance. Although available today, they are nowhere near as plentiful as they were at the turn of this century. The present trend toward freer and more modern decorations, and the high cost of production, are, no doubt, contributing factors.

No bindery is complete without at least a small collection of these tools. If buying them new, however, select with some particular job in mind; do not just stock them in anticipation of future use.

Other than stock items, a possible source for these dies is to have them custom-cut by an engraver from a black-and-white drawing. This is rather expensive, however, and hardly a practical expenditure for one job—unless, of course, it is a very special one.

Other finishing tools Some type of unit is necessary for the heating of tools—electric, gas, or denatured alcohol. The ideal one is a heat-controlled electric hot plate with an adjustable arm for supporting the tool handles. Any temperature-controlled hot plate, preferably with a solid top and no exposed coils, will serve the purpose. If exposed electric coils, gas, or alcohol is to be the source of heat, it is advisable to have some kind of metal plate that conducts heat between the source of heat and the tool.

Units designed for this purpose are available in most bookbinding supply houses. Before purchasing an electric unit from abroad, check the voltage to be sure that it conforms to American standards. Hot plates can be bought in most electrical appliance stores or departments, and these, along with gas and alcohol units, are available from suppliers of scientific equipment.

Gold cushions (Fig. 8-3) Two types are desirable: 1 for the cutting of sheets of gold leaf and the other for use with spools of ribbon gold. The 1 for gold leaf consists of a flat board, padded and covered with leather, the flesh side exposed. These are available in a variety of sizes, simply or elaborately constructed. An average and useful size is 6 × 9 inches (15.2 × 22.8 cm). These can also be made rather easily from 3/4 inch (1.9 cm) plywood, absorbent cotton, or other padding material free of lumps; a piece of leather; and round-headed or upholsterer's tacks. A gold knife should accompany the cushion. They are made in a variety of sizes and shapes and are generally available where cushions are found.

The cushion for use with ribbon gold is a long narrow strip of wood, covered with leather, flesh side exposed, and no padding. This seem-

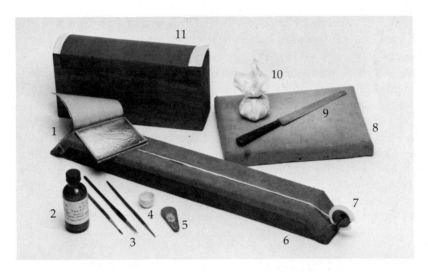

FIGURE 8-3. Tooling Equipment. (1) Gold leaf, (2) Glair, (3) Glair brushes, (4) Glair dish, (5) Shell gold, (6) Gold run, (7) Ribbon gold, (8) Gold cushion, (9) Gold knife, (10) Grease bag, (11) Tooling block.

ingly is not a stock item in bookbinding supply houses. One can be constructed with a 2 foot (.6 m) piece of 2 × 3 inch (5 × 7.6 cm) dressed lumber, sawed at a 45° angle at both ends; a piece of leather; brass fittings; a piece of 1/2 inch (1.2 cm) elastic; and round-headed tacks. The brass fittings, which hold the gold in position while permitting the spool to turn, consist of a 2 inch (5 cm) right angle corner bracket with 2 holes drilled in the half that is attached to the block and 1 hole in the upright portion; 2 large washers; a machine screw with a wing nut; and a small spring. The bracket is attached with wood screws to the block first; the leather is then added and tacked down on both edges; and the elastic is tacked across the end opposite the bracket.

Tooling block (Fig. 8-3) This is very useful in practice work. It is a block of wood with 1 rounded edge comparable to the round of a book spine. When a piece of bristol is laid across the rounded surface and attached solidly to the sides of the block, and a piece of leather is attached to the bristol, its curved surface and resilience simulate in shape and feel the spine of a book.

Dish for glair (Fig. 8-3) Any glass container small in diameter and holding about 1/4 ounce is suitable. A little glair goes a long way, and after its use any surplus should not be poured back in the main supply.

Brushes (Fig. 8-3) Two types of brushes are needed: 1 for applying glair and the other for testing a heated tool. For glair, a no. 00 sable, or camel's hair brush, is good. These are available in art supply stores. The other can be almost any type of small brush with a short handle; a 1/4-inch paintbrush with the handle sawed off works well.

Cleaning board (Fig. 8-1) This is needed for cleaning the surface of tools; a clean, bright finish on the gold cannot be obtained with dirty tools. This can easily be made by pasting leather, flesh side exposed, on both sides of a piece of binder's board, approximately 3 × 6 inches (7.6 × 15.2 cm), although size is not really important.

Grease bag (Fig. 8-3) This is used to grease the surface of a tool before picking up the gold, or in greasing the surface of the leather before laying gold down. Take a 6 inch (38.7 sq. cm) square of cotton flannel and a wad of absorbent cotton about 1 1/2 inches (3.8 cm) in diameter; add to the cotton a small amount, about 1/2 teaspoon, of vaseline, sweet almond oil, or coconut oil and work the cotton around a bit to get the grease evenly spread through it. Put the cotton in the middle of the flannel and fold the 4 corners up together and slip a tight rubber band over them, or tie together with a piece of string. These 3 greases are variously rated by different binders. More important than the type of grease, however, is the fact that it should be used sparingly.

Tooling Materials

Gold leaf (Fig. 8-3) This is the traditional metal used in titling and tooling. Pure gold is designated as 24-karat, but is considered too soft for most uses, so 23-karat is the purest that is beaten into leaves, and this is known as deep XX. Green gold, red gold, and white gold are less pure, having been alloyed with other metals to produce their colors. Green and white contain silver, and red is alloyed with copper. Both of these metals tarnish or oxidize rather quickly, so they are not recommended.

A sheet of standard gold leaf is 1/275,000th of an inch thick. The sheets are usually 3 3/8 inches square (about 20 sq. cm). They are packaged in specially treated tissue paper books, 25 leaves to the book and 20 books to the package. It is also available in leaves of double thickness. This is slightly easier to handle and requires fewer layers for a solid impression with greater depth of gold.

Palladium, or aluminum leaf, is the most satisfactory when a silver effect is desired. Palladium leaf has become increasingly difficult to obtain, but if you can get it, it produces a nicer effect than aluminum. Aluminum is made in 2 finishes— matte and glossy. The matte is considered preferable by most binders. These are packaged and sold in a similar fashion to gold leaf.

Ribbon gold (Fig. 8-3) This is deep XX gold leaf with a paper backing or support, made up in rolls of 67 feet (20 m) and cut into varying widths from 1/16 inch upward. The number of rolls to the box or package depends on the width. There are 22 rolls of 1/8 inch in a package. It is easier to handle and more economical to use in the tooling of lines than are the sheets. The 1/8 inch is a good general-purpose width.

Presized gold This is manufactured primarily for use with a stamping press. It is not gold leaf, but a 22-karat electrolytic gold supported on a mylar carrier and sized with a sizing or adhesive that is softened by heat, causing the gold to stick when heat and pressure are applied. This is sold in 100 foot (30 m) rolls in varying widths from 1 inch (2.5 cm).

Also available for machine use are presized aluminum and a variety of colored or pigmented foils. These are sold in 200 foot (60 m) rolls in widths varying from 1 inch.

The sizing on these presized products is not always the same composition, but varies for different materials. In purchasing, specify the type of leather or other material on which it will be used. None of these presized foils keeps indefinitely in usable condition, so it is advisable to buy them as needed rather than to stock up in anticipation of use. These foils are not recommended for any extensive use with hand tools on fine work. There is little chance of getting more than 1 layer of gold or color on an impression. It is, in fact, a 1-shot operation, and if the impression is imperfect on this 1 try, it is not easy—although not impossible—to remedy the trouble.

Glair (Fig. 8-3) This is a sizing or adhesive used in the application of gold or other metallic leaves in hand tooling. For many years binders made their own glair—and many still do—from egg white (see recipe in the Appendix). Today, however, a great number of binders find commercially prepared glairs both easier and more efficient to work with. These are sold under a variety of trade names, but most are packaged in nothing smaller than a pint or a quart. Roger Powell's B. S. glair is satisfactory, and it has the advantage of being available in quantities as small as an ounce. None of these products keeps indefinitely, so again, don't overstock.

Shell gold (Fig. 8-3) This is powdered gold or gold leaf mixed and ground up with gum water (gum arabic). It used to be marketed in a mussel shell, but nowadays the container is plastic, shaped like a mussel shell. It is made primarily for artists or illuminators. It is, however, often useful in touching up damaged tooling, particularly in conservation work.

All of the materials listed above are available in bookbinding supply houses in both large and small quantities, and most of them direct from the manufacturer as packaged, with the possible exception of shell gold. That is more likely to be found in an art supply store.

Tooling

Tooling can be defined simply as making a blind or gilt impression on leather or other material. It is, however, the most exacting and precise of the steps in the process of binding a book. It requires a steady hand, good eye sight, patience, and practice. The principles involved are relatively simple; it is their proper execution—which can be mastered only through the willingness to practice—that is the key to successful tooling.

Basic Principles

The cardinal principle in tooling perhaps is that the damper the leather, the milder the heat should be. In making the first blind impression in tooling, the leather is damp, so the tool should be only slightly heated and well below the sizzling point when a drop of water is applied to it. In fact, one should be able to hold it for a second or so without discomfort.

FIGURE 8-4.

The smaller the face or design of the tool is, the lighter the pressure should be. A small dot, circle, or serifs on type can easily cut the leather if too much pressure is applied. An ornament 1/2 inch (1.2 cm) in diameter will, on the other hand, require quite a bit of pressure; few binders have the strength to properly set down a tool 1 inch square (6.4 sq. cm). The same principle applies to fillets, pallets, gouges, and the like; the narrower the line, the milder the pressure.

A deep impression is neither necessary nor desirable, but uniform impressions are both for a nice-looking job.

Short-handled tools should be held firmly in the hand with the thumb on the top of the handle (Fig. 8-4); this helps to steady the tool and control the pressure. They are set down in a perpendicular position, rocked toward the top, back toward the bottom, straightened up, and then rocked from side to side so that a complete impression is made evenly. This should be done quickly and decisively, taking care to keep the tool firmly in position; delay, or the slightest shift of the tool, will create a blurred impression.

Most decorated tools and handle letters have a line or nick of some kind across 1 side of the shank to indicate the top of the tool. Letters, and tools having an up-and-down design, obviously should be set down right side up. Even when the design on the tool is symmetrical, each time it is set down in the same impression the nick should be oriented in the same direction. This is particularly important when working with hand-cut tools; there are likely to be minor variations that do not show when looking at it, but which would reduce the sharpness of the impression if set down a second time from a different orientation.

Fillets and rolls should be held in a vertical position, tipping neither to the right nor the left, and rolled slowly. The full face of the tool should receive even pressure; otherwise 1 edge of the line is more deeply impressed than the other.

All tools should be held so that one side or edge can be seen at all times.

Heating and testing the tools Many bookbinding manuals recommend as a time-saver that all tools to be used on a given job be kept on the stove while the work is in progress and cooled down to the proper temperature just before each use. This no doubt works for an experienced finisher who is doing an intricate design that uses a variety of tools in rapid succession. For the beginner, however, it is a much safer practice to heat each tool as needed. If the stove is kept hot, it takes very little time to heat a tool. If the tools are kept on the stove continuously, there is a very good chance that an inexperienced person will pick them up, forget to cool them, and burn the leather. Also, wooden handles can quickly become charred on the inside from overheating the portion of the tools that is inserted in them; when this happens, the tools drop out of the handles.

Test the temperature by applying 1 or 2 drops of water to the shank of the tool, or in the case of a fillet, to the wheel. If the water sizzles slowly, the temperature, generally speaking, is right for work with gold, but too hot for blinding-in. If the water gives 1 sharp hiss and flies off the tool in a "ball," the tool is definitely too hot for any work on leather. Cool it by laying the shank on a moist sponge or by brushing it several times with cold water. After cooling, test again before using it.

Moistening the leather For blind tooling or blinding-in, the leather is moistened. It is recommended that tap water be used for this purpose. For many years most binders used a solution of water and vinegar, or in some cases just vinegar. Vinegar had 2 advantages: It set the dye in the leather and it closed the pores. It is questionable whether any deteriorating damage ever resulted from its use (vinegar contains 3–9 percent acetic acid, which is rather mild, and diluted, it would be even weaker), but in the light of present-day concerns and knowledge regarding the adverse effects of acidity on leather, it seems advisable—psychologically if not practically—not to use it. In recent years some binders have used a diluted solution of potassium lactate; this, however, should be used only on vegetable-tanned leather, and it is not always easy to ascertain leather tannage. On light-colored leathers, test a sample to see if water stains it. If it does, try the other solutions, and use the 1 that gives the best results.

Practice work These instructions are for work on a natural-grained, unpigmented, leather. It is recommended that all practice work be carried out on the same type of leather as that used or to be used on books in progress. Both the amount of heat and pressure required vary with different types of leather.

Practice boards Make up several. Cut pieces of binder's board about 5 × 8 inches (12.7 ×20.3 cm), although the size is not of great importance. Cover 1 side with leather and counteract its pull on the other side with a piece of bristol or bond paper. It is important that the boards remain flat.

Blind Tooling

This is, perhaps, the easiest type of tooling practice. It consists of making an indention or impression with a heated tool on moistened leather. The easiest finishing tool to use is a single-line fillet—a no. 3 or 4. So single blind lines are a good place for a beginner to start. Work on a sturdy surface—not a wobbly table—of comfortable height, with lights that can be adjusted as needed; and if in a group of workers, seek out a quiet corner off the beaten path to the press, board shears, and such.

Materials Needed

Fillet single-line, no. 3 or 4

Practice board

Pressboard

Small weight

Straightedge stainless steel or plastic

Dividers

Bonefolder thin point

Stove

Water containers 2

Brush

Cotton wads

Carbon paper

Stamp pad

Lay the practice board on the pressboard, moisten the entire surface of the leather, and weight down. Using the straightedge, dividers, and the bonefolder, draw along 1 edge of the board on the moistened leather a series of straight lines about 1/4 inch apart.

Heat the fillet slightly (well below the sizzling point); grasp the handle at a point where it seems comfortable in the hand, rest the end of the handle on the shoulder, with the flat side of the wheel to the left so that the edge can be clearly seen. With a wad of dry cotton, catch the wheel at the mitred corner and place its edge at the beginning and in 1 of the drawn-off lines. Check the wheel to be sure that it is being held vertically, then roll it slowly along the line, putting only mild pressure on it. Repeat this on the other lines; then go back into each line several times, keeping the leather moist and reheating the fillet from time to time. The second time around, increase the pressure slightly. Learning to stay in an impression, or return to it, is a very important factor in learning to tool.

Indicate on the back of all practice boards the number of the tools used, so that these same boards can be used later on in practicing with gold.

The same moisture, heat, and pressure as described for single lines also apply to these other suggested exercises.

Next, draw off a series of panels or rectangles, starting near the edge of the practice board and working in toward the center, spacing them about 1/4 inch apart. This will give additional practice with the fillet and add the experience of making mitred, right-angle corners. Start at the lower left corner (Fig. 8-5), go up the left side of the board, and on around it in clockwise fashion; this will keep the angle of the mitre in

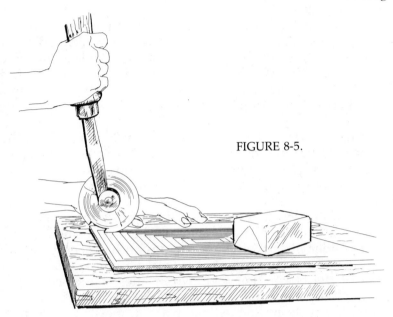

FIGURE 8-5.

proper position. Roll the fillet almost to the second or top corner, lift it up and turn the wheel so that when it is set back in the line, the other mitred edge will fit into the top right-angle corner. Ease up on the pressure as the mitred edge reaches the corner. Retool the panels several times.

Then try setting a small ornament down in each right-angle corner. A dot or a tool with a symmetrical design, neither of which can be set down crooked, is the easiest; then progress to something a bit more complicated.

Do this same type of practicing with pallets and gouges. With these try extending the length of the line made by doubling back a bit on the portion of the first impression; put very little pressure on the ends of these tools. It is very easy to come down too hard at these points and make a deeper impression than is made with the rest of the tool.

After practicing with the individual tools, make up a more intricate design that will require the use of a paper pattern. Build the design up with a number of different tools—gouges, pallets, ornaments—or make an overall design employing the repeated use of 1 or 2 tools in some planned geometric or orderly arrangement. This, incidentally, is known as a diaper pattern.

Cut several pieces of lightweight bond paper (8 or 10 pound), larger by about 4 inches (10.1 cm) in both dimensions than the practice board. Draw off in the center of these the exact size of the board.

Survey the available tools, then sketch a design lightly in pencil on 1 of the pieces of paper that can be built up with the tools on hand; adjust it by fitting the tools on it, and make an inked impression of them with a stamp pad. When the design is as wanted, and the tools selected, use carbon paper to transfer it to a fresh piece of paper. Position it on the paper exactly where it is wanted on the board, attach the 2 papers together so they will not shift, and impress the tools on the pattern.

Then go over the carbon copy with an inked impression of the tools, and mark on this pattern alongside the position of each tool its number.

In making a diaper pattern, select the tool or tools and experiment a bit with the spacing. When a pleasing arrangement has been decided on, draw any guidelines that will be helpful in properly placing the tool or tools. Then make inked impressions of the tool at all of the points indicated.

When the pattern is complete, cut it at all 4 corners, from the edges into the lines indicating the size of the board. Moisten the entire surface of the leather, lay the pattern in position, and secure it by folding the surplus edges of the paper around the board and attaching it with tabs of masking tape.

Straight lines of any length in the design need not be tooled through the pattern. It is more accurate to draw them off using a straightedge and a bonefolder after the rest of the design has been blinded in. For lines on the spine edge of the board, make all measurements from the fore edge of the board. These drawn-in lines should be blind-tooled.

Heat the tools for blind tooling and set each 1 down in its exact position on the pattern. Remove the pattern, moisten the leather again, and retool to sharpen the impressions.

Now try some practicing with handle letters or type. An 18-point type is a good size to start with. If printer's type is used, heat the pallet and put the type in it after it is removed from the source of heat; otherwise, the letters will be running around on the top of the stove in molten form. For the initial practice concentrate on setting the letters down several times in the first impression made, on 1 of the practice boards. Then try it on a rounded surface (see earlier under Tooling Materials for a tooling block and how to prepare it for use).

Handle letters are set down as described earlier for short-handled tools. For type in a pallet, start with the first letter in the word and set the rest of the letters down with a sort of rolling or rocking motion (Fig. 8-6). When all of the letters are down, rock the pallet from top to bottom so that an impression of equal depth is obtained.

The work should be at a right angle to the finisher, so that you can sight along the top of the type, below the flat surface of the pallet.

For additional practice with letters, see the following section on Titling.

Remedying troubles in blind tooling If the fillet goes off the line completely or doubles up a bit in places, moisten the affected area well; redraw the line, using the straightedge and bonefolder. While still moist, go over the line again with the fillet cold. This will generally "pull" the mistake out.

If handle letters or ornaments are not set down vertically and tend to lean a bit, moisten well. With the tool cold, set it back in the impression and give it a slight twist—just enough to straighten it up. This same technique also applies to type in a pallet.

If things are badly doubled up or very crooked, moisten well; slide the point of a needle horizontally under the surface of the impression and lift it up gently in several places. Moisten again so the moisture can

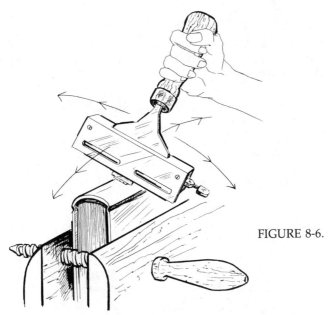

FIGURE 8-6.

run into the channels made by the needle and swell the leather, thereby obliterating the impression. Set aside to dry thoroughly. When dry, lay a piece of lightweight bond paper over the area and rub lightly with a bonefolder. If this does not remove the trouble, but improves it, repeat the process.

When the leather is burned by a tool, it is not only unsightly but it is very difficult to get gold to adhere to the spot. The best way to remedy this is to replace the damaged area with either an inlay or an onlay. If the damage is slight and the impression can be lifted up as described earlier, an onlay should suffice. If, however, the damage is extensive and the impression too deep to remove satisfactorily, then an inlay is advisable. In either case, try to locate a scrap of the same leather, matching as near as possible the texture and grain of the damaged area.

For an onlay, lift up the impression and let it dry thoroughly. Then sand the surface lightly. The new leather need not be faced with tissue as is done for a decorative onlay. Pare it paper thin; cut it about 1/8 inch larger all around than the sanded area; feather all edges until they look ragged or frayed. Paste the leather; lay it in position and moisten the surface with water; cover with a piece of paper and rub gently with a bonefolder. An inlay should be handled as described later under Other Decorative Techniques.

Practice Work with Gold Leaf

After practicing blind tooling until a degree of confidence is gained, use the same practice boards for work with gold. Gold tooling is a progression from blind tooling in the sense that in order to apply gold, a blind impression should first be made. Start again with the first practice board and follow the same sequence of exercises using gold.

The following instructions employ the use of a commercial glair (egg white glair is discussed later under Titling). This has several things in its favor: The leather does not have to be paste-washed; the tooling can be done some days, possibly weeks, after the application of the glair; it does not stain the leather; and any surplus can be sponged off or removed with a pencil eraser.

Materials Needed (in addition to materials for blind tooling)
Glair
Ribbon gold
Leaf gold
Cushions and knife for ribbon and leaf gold
Grease bag
Pencil eraser
Wooden toothpick rounded

The first step in gold tooling is to glair the blind impression, and the leather should be dry at the time of glairing.

Glairing It is the glair that causes the gold to adhere to the leather when a heated tool is applied to it. Some people have the erroneous impression that the heated tool melts the gold. Gold, however, has a melting point of 1064° C (1947° F); any such temperature would send the leather up in flames. In gold work, the tools are heated only to about 105°–110° C (225°–240° F).

With the small brush, carefully flood the glair into the impression; penciling it in lightly usually proves insufficient. An attempt, however, should be made to keep it within the impression; this makes for sharper tooling and reduces the time and work in "cleaning up" when the job is done. When all impressions on 1 board have been glaired, repeat with a second application. Set aside to dry for at least 1 hour—possibly longer if the humidity is high; it should feel dry and not tacky when touched.

Applying the gold There are 2 methods of applying gold to a blinded-in impression. One is to pick the gold up on the tool and go back in the impression; the other is to lay the gold over the impression and then set the tool down again in the impression. In the first method, the edge of the tool is slightly obscured by the gold, and in the second, the sharpness of the impression is slightly reduced. In practice these disadvantages are of about equal weight. If properly done by either method, the end result will be equally pleasing. Both methods will be explained, and it is recommended that they both be tried and that the practice work be continued using the technique that seems easiest.

Ribbon gold This is recommended for use with fillets and small tools—depending, of course, on the size of the tool and the width of the gold available. Its paper backing eliminates any problems in handling; and if properly used, little gold is wasted.

Handling gold leaf Due to its extreme thinness, gold leaf is very fragile and must be handled with great care, in an area free from drafts. If touched with a finger, it disintegrates, and the slightest current of air—even that created by the motion of the knife—can blow it away. It also tends to stick to the slightest trace of grease. The blade of the gold knife should never be handled, and both the cushion and the knife should be rubbed frequently with finely powdered talc. When not in use, the book of leaves should be placed between 2 pieces of board and secured with a rubber band or masking tape.

To protect the gold from drafts, make a shield to fit around 1 side and the 2 ends of the gold cushion (Fig. 8-7). This can be easily constructed from a strip of pulpboard or any wasteboard that is heavy enough to stand up when folded. Take a strip about 6 inches (15.2 cm) wide and as long as 1 side and the 2 ends of the cushion. Mark the length of the side of the cushion in the center of the strip, score it at these 2 points, and fold it. When needed, stand it up around the cushion.

Putting a sheet of gold on the cushion To get a sheet or leaf of gold onto the cushion, open the book part way at the last sheet of gold. Fold

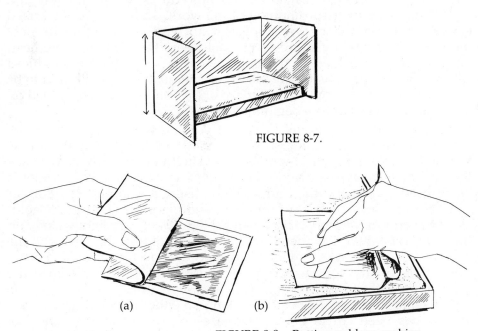

FIGURE 8-7.

FIGURE 8-8. Putting gold on cushion.

(a)   (b)

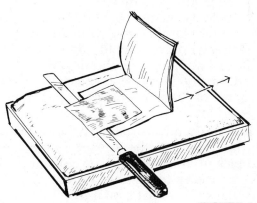

FIGURE 8-9.

the fore edge of the pages back toward the folded edge of the book (Fig. 8-8); keep a firm grip on the book so the other leaves of gold will not move. Flip the book over onto the cushion, laying the exposed or partly exposed leaf down. Tap gently on the back of the book; release the pressure to free the leaf and gradually lift the book off the cushion. Or the book can be laid on a portion of the cushion opened at a sheet of gold. Slide the edge of the knife under the gold, lifting it slightly (Fig. 8-9), and work 1 edge off onto the cushion. Hold this freed edge with the knife and carefully pull the book away—in the opposite direction—from the gold. If it wrinkles slightly, hold 1 corner with the knife and blow very gently on the center of the sheet.

Very little pressure is needed in cutting the leaf. Use a light-handed sawing or slicing motion. Estimate the size of the pieces needed and cut the gold only slightly larger.

Applying the gold The same general procedures for the holding and setting down of tools, positioning of the work, and so on, as described earlier for blind tooling are applicable to work with gold. The only difference is the temperature of the tools; here they require more heat. They should be heated to the point where a slow sizzle is produced when 1 or 2 drops of water are placed on them; and they will need to be reheated more frequently. The surface of the tools should be cleaned on the cleaning board before beginning the work.

Picking up gold on the tool First heat the tool to the proper temperature; then grease the tooling surface by patting it lightly with the grease bag. For ribbon gold, pull the ribbon the length of the cushion and stick the end of the paper between the cushion and the elastic. If a fillet is being used, catch it at the mitred edge—using a wad of dry cotton for protection against the heat of the tool—and place the edge on the gold. Hold the end of the ribbon firmly and roll the fillet very lightly along on the gold; repeat so that there are 2 layers of gold on the tool. Pull the end of the ribbon when more gold is needed on the cushion. With a wad of clean, dry cotton, gently pat the surplus gold flat against the sides of the fillet so that its edge can be easily seen.

The same steps are followed in picking up either ribbon or leaf gold—after it has been cut to the desired size—on other tools. Set the tool down on the gold ever so lightly; all that is needed is for the tool to come in contact with the gold. Pressure will cause the gold to crack and disappear. When the gold is on the tool, set it down in the glaired impression. Wipe away the surplus gold with dry cotton. For a more solid impression with greater depth of gold, repeat this. The impression need not be reglaired for 1 additional application of gold. If more than 4 layers of gold are desired, the impression should be reglaired after the second application. Some of the finest finishing has from 6 to 10 layers of gold.

Laying on the gold Rub the blind and glaired impression lightly with the grease bag, and rub the bag across the back of 1 hand—this will supply the grease needed to pick up the gold. Cut the gold into manageable size pieces; small pieces are easier to handle. Flatten a wad of cotton by pressing it down on a flat surface, pat it on the back of the greased hand,

and lay it lightly on the gold. If the cotton is greased too heavily, the gold will not "let go" when laid on the leather. Pick it up and lay the gold on the impression. Pat it gently with a dry piece of cotton. Breathe on it lightly and add a second layer. Pat this until the shape of the impression can be seen on the gold. If difficulty is experienced in laying the gold down and it becomes wrinkled and crackled, wipe it off and start again. A solid impression cannot be obtained if the gold is broken.

When the gold is successfully laid down, proceed with the tooling. Repeat for additional layers of gold, reglairing after the second application.

Cleaning up gold tooling If the gold was picked up on the tool, rub the tooling with a piece of dry cotton then lightly with a pink pearl or pencil eraser and again with the cotton.

If surplus glair is evident, rub with a piece of cotton moistened with water. If the glair was used too generously and spilled over the impression, and gold stuck where it was not wanted (this often happens in the open areas of letters), moisten the end of a round wooden toothpick by touching it on the end of the tongue and carefully scrape away the surplus.

Remedying troubles If the gold does not stick at all, the glairing was insufficient or the tool too cool. Reheat the tool and try again. If not successful, wipe the area clean and reglair; let the glair dry, and try again. If the gold sticks only in spots, reglair the areas where it did not stick and retool.

If there are minute breaks in the gold, they are probably due to slight defects in the tool. Touch up the spots with alcohol, lay a piece of gold on them immediately, and set the tool down again unheated.

If a fillet skids instead of rolling or turning, the glair is not dry enough or the fillet may need oiling at the point where it is attached to the shank. Oil it and give it a few turns to be sure that it is moving freely; be sure to wipe away the surplus oil. If the fillet continues to skid, delay the tooling until the glair is drier. It might save time, however, to reglair the area, for the skidding might have removed the glair.

If the gold appears fuzzy, the glair was not dry enough, the tool too hot, or it was held too long in the impression. Try cleaning it up as described above, and retool without additional glair.

If the impression was missed or doubled up in setting down the gold, it will be necessary to remove it. Lay a piece of moistened cotton over the area and leave it for a few minutes; cotton used in this way is sometimes referred to as "white mice." Take the end of a round wooden toothpick and gently scrape the gold away. The treatment would then be the same as described under blind tooling troubles.

Blind Tooling as Decoration

In cases where the design calls for blind tooling entirely or in part, it requires a bit more refining than is needed when gold is to be added. Greater care should be taken in keeping both the moisture and the heat uniform on all areas of the work. The combination of these 2 things darkens the tooled portions of the leather, and for a pleasing effect this change in color should be even. This is particularly important with light-colored leathers, where the color change is greater, and therefore more noticeable, than with darker leathers.

Sponge the whole surface with water; lay a piece of glass or cellophane wrap over it for some minutes, giving the moisture time to spread evenly. Then keep the area in which the work is being done dampened as the tooling progresses. The softer spongier areas of the skin will absorb more moisture more quickly than will the area close to the spine.

The tools should be heated as for other blind tooling, but they should be heated more often to keep the heat uniform. It is frequently necessary to increase the heat a bit (still below the sizzling point) when tooling the firmer areas of the skin in order to maintain an even color.

When the tooling is completed and the leather dry, "polish" the impressions. Heat the tools to a slow sizzle when tested with a drop of water. For ornaments and type, go back into the impression, quickly rock the tool as previously described, and pick it up immediately. On lines across the spine that have been made with a line pallet, slide the heated tool along the impression; and for lines made with a fillet, wedge the wheel so that it will not turn and slide it along the line. This is referred to as "jiggering" or "jiggling" the tool.

Tooling on a Book

Some suggestions for decorating a binding are found in Chapter 2 under Designing a Binding, and the techniques involved in tooling have been described in detail earlier in this chapter under Practice Work. Here the instructions deal with their application to a book.

The order in which a book is usually finished is, first, any lines or decoration on the inside of the covers; next, the outside of the covers; and, last, the tooling and titling on the spine.

Simple decorations such as lines or panels can be marked off directly on the covers by using a straightedge and bonefolder and measuring carefully. If only a few ornaments are used, they can be blinded in free hand. On the spine, lines can be marked off by laying a narrow strip of bristol across the spine and running a bonefolder along the edge. Care should taken to keep the lines parallel with the head and tail of the book and with each other.

For more intricate overall decoration, it is advisable to make a paper pattern. If the same design is to be put on both covers, make 2 patterns. The moisture from the leather and the pressure from the tools wrinkle and to some extent distort a pattern, so it is not advisable to use the same pattern twice.

In making a pattern, allow on the spine side a sufficient margin of paper to wrap around the spine and attach to the other cover and at head, tail, and fore edge about 2 inches (5 cm) to turn on to the inside of the cover.

When working on the covers—inside or outside—always keep the book, weighted down, on a pulpboard and a pressboard, and when it is desirable to shift the position of the book, do so by turning the pressboard. In tooling the inside of the covers, support them in their opened position with pressboards equivalent in height to the thickness of the book. Cover 1 edge—the 1 that will come in contact with the spine—and the surface of the top board with a piece of cotton flannel. Weight down both the cover and the book.

Before attaching a paper pattern to a cover, wrap a strip of plain paper around the other cover and secure it on the inside of the board with masking tape. This will supply a surface to which the pattern can be attached without damage to the cover.

A sheet of zinc, slightly larger than the book, with a sheet of paper folded around it, inserted between the book and the cover, will give support to the squares on the board and provide a firmer surface for tooling the cover.

For work on the spine, place the book between pulpboards and put it in a finishing press. Take care to screw the press tight enough to prevent the book from shifting under the pressure exerted in the tooling.

Remember to use a straightedge made of plastic or some metal that will not stain moistened leather when marking off lines.

It is a good idea to keep a scrap of leather, cut from the same skin as that used on the book, nearby the work, so if there is any uncertainty as to temperature or pressure, the tool can first be tested on the scrap.

Titling

The selection of an appropriate typeface and orienting the title are discussed in Chapter 2 under Designing a Binding. The techniques in both blind and gold titling are described earlier in this chapter under Practice Work. In this section are a few general rules dealing with the spacing and positioning of titles, along with the methods used in making a pattern and attaching it. The methods that are applicable to all 3 styles of letters—handle letters, type, and letters built up with gouges—are described first, followed by the techniques peculiar to each.

Making a pattern It is advisable to make a paper pattern for all titling or lettering, whether on the covers or the spine. A pattern for the covers is described earlier under Blind Tooling.

For the spine, select a lightweight bond paper (8- or 10-pound weight). Cut it the length of the book and the width of the spine plus 3 inches (7.6 cm). The extra width is used in attaching the pattern to the book. For a binding with raised bands, a separate pattern is made for each panel to be titled. These should fit comfortably and lie smoothly between the bands.

Mark the width of the spine off in the center of the pattern in its entire length—leaving 1 1/2 inches (3.8 cm) on each side. Draw a line, also its entire length, to indicate the center of the spine. Lay this aside until the letters or words have been letter-spaced and an inked impression made of them.

Letter spacing The proper spacing of letters in relation to each other is an important factor in obtaining an aesthetically pleasing effect. Although it slows up the completion of the job a bit, it is usually worth the time and effort expended. This is the spacing of letters within a given word so that there appears to be an equal amount of space between each 2 letters. It is not a matter of space by measurement, but rather a visual or optical thing. Probably no 2 people ever letter space exactly the same way.

There are no precise rules as to how much space should go between any 2 letters because the possible combinations are too numerous and the space would vary with each typeface. Generally speaking, letters that are open at the top or bottom and those that are rounded, when used in combination, appear to have more space between them than do the letters made up of vertical lines. The idea is to experiment until a pleasing result is obtained. Where built-up letters and handle letters are used, space by shifting or adjusting the position of the individual letters. Where type is used, it is a matter of inserting copper or brass thin spaces between the letters that appear too close together (more on this later under the three styles of letters).

Word spacing The spacing between words depends somewhat on the extent to which the letters have been opened up. In a condensed title or 1 with little letter-spacing, the general rule is to allow the width of the body of an "O" or an "M" between words. If the title has been opened up and space added between every 2 letters, increase the space between the words to the same extent.

Horizontal titling This is titling across the spine, parallel to the head and tail of the book. In determining what size type to use, draw the width of the spine on a scrap of paper or pulpboard and sketch the arrangement of the title and author's name. Then pick out the letters that make up the longest word or line and check its length against the width of the spine. It is advisable to leave at least 1/8 inch clearance on each side after it is letter-spaced. If the type first selected is too wide, try the next smaller size. Generally speaking, a smaller size type is preferable to hyphenating words in a title.

Such words as *the, of, by,* and so on, often look better if set in a smaller size than the main words in the title. If, for example, an 18-point letter is used for the main words, use 14 or 12 point for the prepositions. The author's name also looks better sometimes in smaller letters than the title; this is particularly true if it is to occupy more than 1 line.

The space between the lines of the title is usually about the height of the type; and if the author's name is to follow directly under the title, the space between the bottom of the title and the top of the author's name should be about twice this. It is customary to put some small ornament or a short line in this space between the title and the author's name.

In titling between raised bands, however, this rule of thumb has to be a bit more flexible. The space between the lines in the title should be even; the space between the title and author's name slightly more; and the space below the title in the panel should be slightly more than the space above the title. It is more important to have the title pleasingly arranged within the space than it is to follow a rule arbitrarily.

The position of the title and author's name on a smooth spine with no panels is a matter of personal choice. Consideration should be given to the number of lines, the length of the spine, and the effect desired. After an inked impression of the title and author's name has been made, with the proper spacing between the lines, lay this on the spine about 1 inch from the head of the book. Move it up and down until a pleasing position is found. Or check the book shelves for a title that seems appropriately placed and follow that.

The date of publication, if used, is traditionally placed about 1/2 inch (1.2 cm) up from the tail of the spine, in type several points smaller than the title.

Covers Titles on the covers, usually only the front, in order to appear centered generally need to be a little further away from the fore edge of the board than from the spine edge. A rounded spine gives the illusion of added width.

Vertical titling There are 2 schools of thought regarding the orientation of vertical titles. One thinks it should always run up the spine—from tail to head; the other, always down. If a book is going to stand on a shelf, it seemingly makes little difference. If the title runs down the spine, you must cock your head to the right to read it; and if it runs up the spine, you cock your head to the left. A definitive work has not yet been written—though it probably will be—on "the preferential cocking of one's head in reading vertical titles on books." Until such a work is published, the decision might well be that of the designer or binder.

If, however, it is a large book—or any book for that matter—that will lie, rather than stand, on a shelf, with the front cover up, then the title, to be read properly, should run from head to tail.

Conventionally, the title is centered on the spine, with both title and author's name in the same line and some small ornament or line separating the 2. When the title is to cover most of the spine, or if it is desirable that it appear to be centered from head to tail, place it a little bit closer to the head—about 1/4 inch. The amount of this space, however, will depend somewhat on the length of both the title and the spine. If exactly centered by measurement, it will appear to be closer to the tail.

Stringing letters down the spine 1 below the other is not discussed here; it is not a recommended use of the Roman alphabet.

One important thing to remember in all titling, regardless of the style of the letters, is always to check the first inked impression of the assembled words with the title page of the book. When concentrating on techniques, it is easy to inadvertently misspell a word or transpose letters.

Built-up letters The use of built-up letters is generally reserved for titles that would be equivalent in height to a 72-point type or larger. Such letters would normally be expected to be oriented vertically on the spine and horizontally on the covers. Pallets and gouges are the customary tools for this purpose. If, however, very large letters are desired—covering, for instance, the entire length of the book—a fillet for straight lines and a very small roll (3/4 or 1 inch—1.9 or 2.5 cm—in diameter) for curves can be used.

First, take a look at the available tools. With these in mind, sketch freehand, on a piece of paper the size of the spine, the letters in the title and the author's name in the approximate size and shape desired. Then select the gouges and pallets that come nearest to fitting the curves and straight lines of the letters. It is easier and simpler to alter the shape and size of the letters a bit—if it does not ruin their proportion—than it is to adjust the tools to fit the sketch (Fig. 8-10).

Letters can also be traced from a type specimen book or other source. If a suitable typeface is found, but the letters are not the right size, they can be enlarged or reduced, properly proportioned, with a pantograph. (Instructions for using a pantograph come with the instrument. It consists of 4 light rigid bars joined in parallelogram form for copying on any predetermined scale.) The gouges and pallets would be fitted to these in the manner just described above.

Make an inked impression of the selected tools on the drawn letters, and mark the number alongside the position of each tool. Then mark off on a fresh piece of paper the exact size of the space that the title will occupy, and stamp the letters out again, spacing them evenly within the area. It is helpful to have guidelines at both top and bottom of the letters and a third line through the center. When the letters are again stamped out, properly spaced, they are then transferred to the pattern, which was prepared earlier, by using carbon paper. Cut the ends off the paper with the impressions so that it is shorter than the pattern paper; cut a piece of carbon paper this same length. This will permit the center line on the pattern to be exposed when the carbon and the stamped impression are laid on it.

Lay the carbon in place and position the title or stamped impression exactly where it is wanted in relation to the head and tail of the spine, and line up the center line on the top paper with that on the pattern. Attach the top paper to the pattern with tabs of masking tape so there can be no shifting. Set the tools down again on the inked impressions. Separate the papers and make an inked impression of the tools on the carbon copy—again noting the numbers of the tools.

The pattern is now ready for use. Instructions for attaching it to the book follow under Attaching the Pattern and Blinding-In.

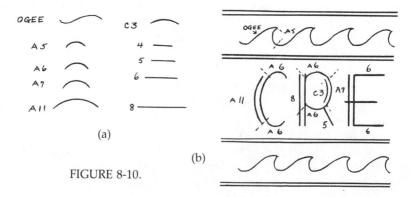

FIGURE 8-10.

Handle letters Select the size of letter from those available that best fits into the planned design of the binding. In making this selection, give consideration to the length of the title, the width of the spine for a horizontal title, and its length for a vertical title. Pick out the letters that are needed to make up both the title and the author's name and make an inked impression of them on a scrap of paper.

For a horizontal title, follow the general rules mentioned earlier as to the space between lines, and so on. When the arrangement and spacing are decided, letter space the words. Make several impressions of each word, moving or adjusting the letters until they appear evenly spaced.

Draw off the width of the spine on a piece of paper, and draw across this the same number of lines as there are lines in the title, including the author's name. Space these lines so that when the top of the letters are set down on them, the predetermined space will be between the lines. Then make an inked impression of the letters in each line of the title, leaving the proper space between words. Center each line, from left to right, within the lines indicating the width of the spine, and set the top of the letters down on the lines just drawn.

Next, decide exactly where on the spine the title is to be placed and draw the same series of lines on the pattern already prepared. Start the first line, toward the head of the book, at the point where the top of the first line of the title will be. Carry these lines all across the pattern.

To get the title in the proper position on the pattern, an inked impression can be made directly on the pattern, following the layout made above. Or the layout can be transferred with carbon paper as described earlier under Built-up Letters.

For vertical titling, the same general procedures are followed as given for Built-up Letters.

Instructions for attaching the finished pattern to the book follow under Attaching the Pattern and Blinding-in.

Type and pallet This method of titling, as stated earlier, offers the greatest choice of typefaces. Presumably a selection was made at the time of designing the binding, and the selected type is available. General rules regarding spacing of lines, positioning of the title, and making of patterns for both horizontal and vertical titles are given earlier in this section.

The primary differences between this and the other styles of lettering are in the letter spacing and in the fact that words or letters in each line of the title are handled as a unit, not as individual pieces or characters. Type is placed in the pallet a line at a time, with the first letter of the first word beginning at the right-hand side. Check the notches in the type and put them all facing in the same direction, oriented properly.

Pick out the letters that make up the title and the name of the author. Decide on their arrangement and the number of lines (suggestions for this have been discussed earlier). Mark the lines off on the pattern as described under handle letters. Put the proper space between the words. Put the first line in the pallet, tighten it, and make an inked impression on a scrap of paper or pulpboard. Look at the word or words critically to determine what letter spacing, if any, is desirable. If spacing is needed, open the pallet slightly and start the spacing by inserting a copper thin space between the letters that appear too close together. Tighten it and make another impression. Repeat until the space between all letters appears equal and the effect pleasing. When the spacing is completed, make an inked impression of this line of type directly on the prepared pattern.

Remove the first line from the pallet and lay it carefully on a scrap of binder's board where it will not be disturbed. Continue until all lines have been letter-spaced and stamped on the pattern.

If it is desirable to open up the whole title, first do the spacing between the letters, then add the same number of thin spaces between every 2 letters and the words. If a title or a line of type is too long to set down comfortably as a whole, set it down in sections, keying the letters in so that the proper spacing is maintained. For example, take the title ART OF THE PRINTED BOOK used vertically. First set down ART OF THE, remove ART OF, leave THE in the pallet and add PRINTED; then remove THE PRIN, leave TED, and add BOOK. SHAKESPEARE, used horizontally could be broken down as follows: first set down SHAKE, remove SHA and add SPE, then remove KES and add ARE. Three stampings will be necessary, SHAKE—KESPE—PEARE.

Attaching the pattern and blinding-in After the pattern is made, it is attached to the book and blinded-in through the pattern. For attaching to the covers see earlier under Blind Tooling. For the spine, place the book in a finishing press—protected on both front and back with pulpboards—with the book extending about 1 inch above the jaws of the press and the spine exposed. Screw the press firmly so that the pressure exerted in tooling will not cause the book to shift.

Raised bands Mark the center of the spine lightly with the point of a bonefolder on the sides of the bands in the panel to be titled. These marks aid in the centering of the pattern; they should not, however, be conspicuous enough to mar the surface of the leather. Position the pattern properly by lining up the center line on the pattern with the marks on the bands; from head to tail the inked impression of the title was presumably properly positioned at the time the pattern was made. Attach 1 edge of the pattern to the pulpboard on 1 side of the book with masking tape; turn the pattern back and moisten the area between the bands. Lay the pattern back in position and secure the other edge to the pulpboard on the opposite side.

Smooth spine The same general procedure is followed except that the center of the spine is marked at the head and tail and the center line on the pattern is lined up with these marks. The entire surface of the spine is moistened. If only the area to be titled is moistened, there is danger that the moisture will darken the leather a bit or leave a water mark around its edges.

Blinding-in Heat the letters or tools as for blind tooling and make a blind impression through the pattern, setting them down exactly on the pattern. Remove the pattern, remoisten the leather, and set the tools down again.

If the title is to remain as blind tooling, "polish" it as described earlier under Blind Tooling as Decoration. If it is to be gold, set aside to dry; then proceed with the glairing and tooling as previously described.

Personalizing a binding In cases where you want the name of the owner on the front cover, it is customary to put it in the lower right-hand corner. Allow the same amount of space between the end of the name and the fore edge of the board as that between the bottom of the type and the tail of the cover. One-half inch (1.2 cm) is average, although the length of the name and the size of the cover should be considered.

It is advisable to make and attach a pattern for this. The pattern need not, of course, cover the entire board. It should, however, be large enough so that it can be securely attached. The procedures for making the pattern, attaching it, blinding-in, and so on, are the same as those already described.

Egg white glair Glair made from the white of an egg has been used successfully for many years as the adhesive in gold tooling. It is still used by many binders and thought to produce superior results to those obtained with more modern commercial glairs. A recipe for egg white glair is given in the Appendix, and it should be made a day in advance of anticipated use.

The primary differences in use between this and one of the shellac-based commercial glairs are that both the glairing and the tooling are done with the leather slightly damp, and the tooling should be done just after the glair ceases to be tacky. It is the combination of moisture and heat that causes the gold to adhere permanently, and if too much time elapses between its application and the tooling, it loses this quality.

It is advisable to paste-wash the leather after blinding-in, with a mixture made by adding a level teaspoon of dry paste to four ounces of water. This serves to fill up the pores in the leather so that the glair is not completely absorbed. It is not necessary with some leathers, but determining the porosity of a piece of leather is not so easy, so this is recommended as a precautionary measure.

Two applications of glair should be used and extra care should be taken in applying them, for this tends to stain light leathers. An extensive overall design should be glaired in stages. Glair a small area and when this ceases to be tacky, glair an additional area; then go back and tool the first area glaired. This way the work can move ahead with a minimum amount of waiting time.

The tools should be heated to the slow sizzle stage, just as they are when used with other glairs. The drying time of this glair is dependent on the amount used and on the temperature and humidity of the work space; 20 minutes, however, is about average.

Methods for cleaning up the gold are the same as those previously described, as are suggestions for remedying troubles.

Patch Labels or Titles

These are labels that are tooled or stamped before they are attached to the binding. They are frequently used on cloth bindings to distinguish them from trade editions, where the title is generally stamped directly on the binding, and on leather bindings for decorative effect. They can be made of paper or leather (book cloth is not recommended because there is no satisfactory way to conceal the raw edges, and the job is likely to look "patchy" in the worst sense of the word) and are customarily made in a contrasting or harmonizing color rather than matching the color of the binding.

Follow the directions in the preceding section under Titling for the selection of type, letter spacing, and pattern making.

Lines at top and bottom of a label give it a more finished appearance. If used, the space between the bottom line of the type and the line on the bottom of the label should be slightly greater (1/16 to 1/8 inch) than the space between the top of the title and the top line on the label.

Paper label Cut a piece of the selected paper, grain direction running vertically, about 1 inch larger in both dimensions than the desired size of the finished label. Attach to a piece of binder's board—larger by several inches than the paper—at both top and bottom with masking tape.

Paper cannot be glaired satisfactorily with a liquid glair. There was a finely powdered dry glair available for this purpose, but it seems to be off the market, so the alternative is a presized foil. Place on the paper a piece of foil, sized side facedown, slightly larger than the area occupied by the title on the pattern. Lay the pattern on top and attach it to the board. If lines are to be added, top and bottom, draw them off on the pattern before attaching it.

Heat the tools a little hotter than the slow sizzle stage, for the pattern will serve to some extent as an insulator. Set the tools down squarely on the pattern and rock them in both directions. Tool the lines top and bottom while the pattern is in position.

Leather label For a cloth binding, any type of leather that seems appropriate can be used for a label. For a leather binding, however, the leather should be the same type as that of the binding—unless a contrast in textures is a part of the overall design. But don't use goatskin labels on traditional calfskin bindings.

Cut the leather 1/2 inch (1.2 cm) larger in both dimensions than the desired size of the label, after it is pared thin and evenly. Apply a coat of thin wheat paste to the flesh side of the leather and mount it on a piece of lens tissue; place it between clean pulpboards and weight down until thoroughly dry.

When dry, attach the leather to a piece of binder's board by applying a very thin line of glue to all 4 edges. Moisten the leather, lay in position, and secure with masking tape. Follow earlier directions for blinding-in. If lines are to be added, draw them in with a straightedge and bonefolder after the pattern has been removed, and proceed with tooling in the usual way.

If the spine of the book has been indented for a label, take the size of the indention into consideration when laying out the pattern.

Attaching the label Put a "flag" in the book to indicate its head and place the book, protected on both sides with pulpboards, in a finishing press and tighten the press well. Cut the label to size, using a straight-edge and a mat knife, before removing it from the binder's board.

For the paper label, if an indention was made on the spine, cut it to fit the indention. If not, cut it at top and bottom 1/16 to 1/8 inch above and below the lines. In width cut it about 1/16 inch narrower than the width of the spine. If the position on the spine has not already been determined, lay the label on the spine about 1 inch from the head of the book and move it up and down until a pleasing position is reached. Mark the position with a pencil dot on both edges of the spine. Check the distance from the head of the book to the dots to make sure that they are parallel. Apply mixture to the label; lay it in position; place a piece of paper over it; and rub it firmly with a bonefolder for a few minutes. Do not open the book until the label is thoroughly dry.

For a leather label, the same general procedures apply as for paper. If, however, the spine is indented, measure the indention carefully and cut the label to fit it, leaving an equal amount of leather beyond the lines at top and bottom. Then feather the edge of the label on both sides. If there is no indention, feather all 4 edges.

Stamping Presses

Some binders feel that a stamping press has no place in a hand binding shop. Skilled craftspeople, however, through the centuries have used gigs and other mechanical aids when their use did not jeopardize the quality or beauty of their work. A stamping press has no deleterious effect on materials, and if properly used it can produce work comparable in quality to good hand titling. Its gauges and its controlled heat and pressure are mechanical aids that eliminate to some extent human error. They are not, however, foolproof; it takes both skill and experience to use a stamping press correctly.

The time required for the "make-ready" is about the same as that for hand titling. Time is saved in that a precise pattern is not needed, in the ability to stamp more than 1 line at a time, and in cases where 2 or more volumes with the same title are being bound.

The instructions in this section are confined to the mechanics involved in using a stamping press. The setting of type, letter spacing, layout, preparation of the leather, and so on have been previously described and will not be repeated here.

The Kensol press The stamping press described here is a hand-operated Kensol. Other makes and models will, of course, vary to some extent, but this description and the instructions should be helpful in the use of other presses. The Kensol has an electric head or heating unit and is equipped with a thermostat. The head moves up or down vertically by an arm or lever, and it can be turned at any angle up to 90°. It is designed to take a chase, a long pallet, or a flat bed chase, all of which can be locked in position. The metal table is 18 inches square (116 sq. cm) with lines etched in the center in both directions and at right angles to each other. These lines aid in centering the work. The table can be raised or lowered for adjustment to the proper pressure and locked.

There are 2 gauges; one moves from back to front along the edges of the table. When in the desired position, it can be tightened with a screw provided for the purpose. The other gauge moves from side to side and is attached to the back gauge with a type of spring clamp. When the back gauge is tightened, a right-angle corner is produced where the two gauges are joined.

A chase is a vise in which 1 or more small pallets can be "locked up" for insertion in the press. It has a channel in the center of its bed into which a protruding tab in the center of the pallets fits. A separate pallet is used for each line of type. If the type in each pallet is centered and the tab on each is placed in the channel on the chase, all lines will be automatically centered on the center line in the table. Small pallets are available in several lengths. While they are designed primarily for type, type-high ornaments and brass rule (for lines) can also be used in them. Have at least 6 on hand.

The long pallet has open jaws and will accommodate a single line of type up to 9 inches (22.8 cm) long in any point size up to 72.

A flat bed chase is a smooth rectangular block of metal on which dies of varying sizes can be mounted.

All of these items are made to slide into the heating unit and are equipped with wooden handles for ease in handling.

It is essential that a press of this type be securely bolted to the top of a sturdy table or stand of some description, which in turn should be attached to the floor. It is a heavy piece of equipment and decidedly top-heavy.

Use of the stamping press The chase and small pallets are used for horizontal titles of 1 or more lines and for vertical titles that are short enough to fit in one of the pallets available. Fourteen-point type fits the pallets exactly in thickness. If more space is desired between the lines, strips of brass or aluminum can be inserted between the pallets.

When a smaller size type is used, there will be space between the type in 1 pallet and the back of the next pallet. To keep the type from shifting, this space should be filled in with binder's board equal in thickness to the space—and, of course, it should be lower than the type. When a larger size type is used, there will be space between the jaws of the first pallet and the back of the next. This again should be filled in to prevent the pallets from tightening up unevenly.

For a filler, cut strips of either bristol or binder's board the length and height of the pallets. Cut out of these the width and depth of the type, so that they will fit over the type and fill up the space between the 2 pallets.

If the line of type in the pallet is too short to permit tightening, block it out with quads. Be sure, however, to put exactly the same number and size of quads on both ends of the type; otherwise it will be thrown off-center.

Material used for letter spacing (customarily brass or copper thin spaces) and spacing between words (quads) should never be a larger point size than the type used. If larger, the type will not be properly tightened in the chase. They can, however, be a smaller point size.

Large pallet This is used for long single-line titles. After the type is in and the jaws tightened, the type should be secured in position from back to front. Place a strip of something rigid—preferably brass or aluminum, lower than the type—the length of the line, against the type and tighten the screw in the center of the pallet. Here, again, no thin spaces or quads should be a larger point size than the type used. If in tightening the jaws the line of type tends to bow out, creating a situation where the type is not parallel with the back of the pallet, place a copper thin space, lying on its side, at each end of the type. This will put more pressure on the base of the type than is on the top and will generally eliminate this problem.

Mounting of dies The flat bed chase is used here. Fish glue is the recommended adhesive. It retains its sticking power when heated, whereas most other glues do not. To protect the surface of the chase, first mount on it a piece of bristol. Cut the bristol to the exact size of the chase and apply the glue to it; lay it in position and weight down until dry. Mark off on the bristol the exact position for the die. It should be parallel with the edges of the chase and centered from left to right. Glue the back of the die; place it in the marked-off area and weight down for half hour or so.

Set the thermostat on the heating unit at 125°F; put the chase in the press and lock it in position. Lay several pieces of pulpboard on the table directly under the die and lower the head of the press so that the face of the die is resting on the pulpboard. Leave it in this position with the heat on for about 1 hour. This should fix or set the die. To remove the die from the chase, immerse it in a pan of warm water. It is advisable, however, to delay this until the entire job is completed.

The heat range for most stamping foils is 215°F to 225°F. This varies a bit because of different sizings and different materials. Always test the heat with a scrap of the material and foil to be used before doing the stamping on the job. If the foil does not stick, the heat should be increased. If the impression is fuzzy, reduce the heat.

The light on the thermostat remains on when the head is heating and goes off when the temperature at which it is set is reached. Do not stamp until the light goes off. It will, however, come on intermittently to maintain a constant temperature.

Adjusting the pressure The pressure should be adjusted so that the lever can be pulled all the way down, and in doing so a clearly defined blind impression is made. The impression should not be very deep. It is desirable, however, that the pressure be sufficient to flatten the grain in the leather. The pressure will require adjusting with each change in the thickness of material.

The motion in stamping should be quick. Pull the lever down and raise it immediately after the type makes contact with the material.

For all work with a stamping press, the gauges should be used, the chase or pallet locked in position, and both the heat and pressure tested and adjusted.

If satisfactory work is to be produced, it is necessary to prepare a stamping board to which the material can be attached. When this and the preceding rules are observed, it is possible to remove the job from the press and return it with the assurance that the type will hit the initial impression the second time.

Two layers of gold are usually sufficient to obtain a solid impression. Estimate the amount of foil needed for 2 impressions and cut this off the roll. It is a good idea to save all used foil, for any unused area can be used at some later date.

If gold leaf is to be used, make a blind impression. Then follow the directions for glairing and laying-on the gold given earlier under Practice Work with Gold Leaf (Tooling section).

When stamping on paper or book cloth, no preliminary preparation of the material is needed. Make a blind impression, lay the foil over it, and stamp it, adding 2 layers.

Foundry type is likely to be damaged if used in stamping on book cloth.

As soon as the chase or pallet holding the type or title is placed in the press and tightened, make an impression of it on a piece of paper or pulpboard, using carbon paper. Check it for accuracy with the title page of the book. If corrections are necessary, remove it from the press and make the changes before the type gets too hot to handle easily.

Stamping boards Use a lightweight binder's board (.059). Square 1 corner and mark it; orient the board so that this corner will be placed on the table of the press in the right angle formed by the gauges. If 2 or more volumes are to have the same title, make up identical boards for each volume.

Leather patch label For a horizontal title, cut the board several inches larger in both dimensions than the label material. Place a T-square against the right-hand edge of the board about 3 inches (7.6 cm) down from the top edge of the right-angle corner; draw a line across the board and a second line at right angles to the first in the center of the board. Put a hairline of glue on all 4 edges of the previously prepared leather. Lay the top edge of this on the line drawn across the board and center it from left to right on the center line on the board (Fig. 8-11).

To set the right-hand gauge, line up the center line on the stamping board with the center line on the table and bring the gauge in to the edge of the board. Pull the stamping board forward and make an impression of the title on the top of the board above the leather. Check this to see that it is centered on the center line on the board.

Next, position the board from top to bottom so that the title will be placed where you want it on the leather. Pull the board far enough to the left so that an impression of the title can be made on the right-hand side of the board without hitting the leather. Lower the head of the press until it almost comes in contact with the board and adjust the board until it appears to be positioned properly. Then bring the back gauge in and tighten it.

The squared corner on the stamping board can then be placed in the right-angle corner made by the gauges and the title stamped in its desired position.

Test the heat, adjust the pressure, make a blind impression, lay 1

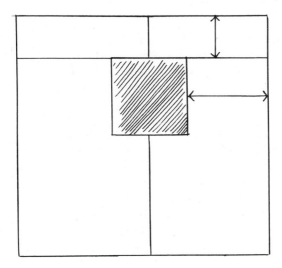

FIGURE 8-11.

layer of foil over it, bring the head down on it, and repeat. Remove the foil and stamp blind again.

Wipe away the surplus gold with a piece of dry cotton. If this does not clean it up sufficiently, rub it lightly with a pink pearl eraser. Erasers in the shape of a fat pencil are very useful for this.

Paper labels are stamped in the same way as just described for leather labels, although no earlier preparation of the paper is required.

Vertical titles In using the large pallet for vertical titles, follow the preceding directions for preparing a stamping board, attaching the material, stamping, and so on. The large pallet is not, however, self-centering, so the title has to be centered first by eye and any necessary adjustments made after it—or a portion of it—is stamped on the end of the stamping board.

Titling the spine of the covering leather Here, again, a stamping board should be prepared, but the leather is not attached to it until the proper position of the title is determined and the gauges on the table of the press are set. (Everything has to be more precise and accurate here than need be for a patch label.) Generally speaking, this is done by mounting a piece of bristol on the stamping board, positioning the title on the bristol, and then attaching the leather. The procedure varies a bit for the different styles of bindings, and a description of these differences follows. In each case, the stamping board should be large enough so that the leather when attached does not protrude beyond or overhang the edge of the board that will rest against the back-to-front gauge of the press and wide enough so that the leather can either be turned back on itself or lifted up over the right-hand gauge without disturbing the spine area on which the stamping is to be done. And in each case the leather is backed with paper to give it added body and to prevent stretching in the course of attaching it to the book.

For a case binding, cut 2 strips of acid-free paper (Permalife text is suitable) and 1 piece of bristol—all 3 exactly the same size—the exact width of the spine and the length of the boards cut for the case. One piece of the paper is mounted in the center of the leather (the other piece is laid aside until after the stamping is completed and is attached in the process of making the case). The bristol is used in preparing the stamping board.

For a Bradel binding, cut 2 strips of acid-free paper and 1 strip of bristol, all 3 the exact length and width of the spine. One piece of the paper is used to line the inside of the bonnet as previously described; the other is mounted in the center of the leather; and the bristol is used as mentioned above. For a tight back and German tube, cut 1 strip of paper—using the same paper stock that was used in lining up the spine or making the tube—and 1 piece of bristol, both the exact width and length of the spine. (For raised bands, see below.) The paper is mounted in the center of the leather, and the bristol is again used on the stamping board.

In all cases the paper is mounted on the leather by applying a thin coat of glue to the paper and laying it in position.

Attach the bristol to the stamping board by putting a spot of glue at each end of it. Lay it on the board parallel with the right-hand edge of the board. Draw a line down the center of the bristol and carry it over onto both ends of the stamping board. Decide on the desired position of the title and draw a line across the board and bristol at the point where you want the top of the first line of type.

Lay the stamping board on the machine table and line up the center line on the board and bristol with the center line on the table. Set the right-hand gauge. Position the board from front to back so that the top of the first line of the title falls on the horizontal line drawn across the board, and bring the back gauge in to the edge of the board.

With the right-angle corner on the stamping board placed in the right angle made by the gauges, stamp the title on the bristol using carbon paper and just enough pressure to make an impression. Be sure that both gauges and the chase or pallet are tightened.

Remove the board from the press and check the title to be sure that it is properly centered on the bristol and in the desired position from head to tail. If adjustments are necessary, make them and then make another impression.

If the stamping on the spine is to be done in 2 or more stages, draw lines across the stamping board indicating the position of each stage before attaching the leather to it. Once the leather is attached, these cannot be proofed on the bristol. Presumably the press is properly set for centering all lines, and the proper positioning from head to tail for additional stampings can be proofed on the side of the board as indicated by the additional lines.

Spot tip the paper (in 2 places) that was mounted on the leather earlier to the bristol on the stamping board and allow to dry. Put the spots of glue on some area of the bristol that will have no stamping on it. Line the paper up exactly with the bristol on all 4 edges. Exercise great care in doing this, for if it is not done accurately, the title will not be straight.

Return the stamping board to the press and proceed with the stamping as previously described.

Raised bands Follow the instructions for a tight back in cutting the paper and bristol and in preparing the stamping board. The paper, however, is not mounted in 1 piece on the leather. Mark off in the center of the leather the exact width and length of the spine and the position and width of each band. Cut from the strip of paper pieces to fit into the panels that are to be titled or stamped on and pieces for both the head and tail panel—even though they may not be stamped on. Make the pieces that are to fit between the bands 1/4 inch shorter than the space and those for head and tail 1/8 inch shorter. Mount these on the leather, leaving the areas of the leather that will be worked over the bands free of paper. Position the pieces at head and tail so that from top to bottom they will indicate the exact length of the spine; center the other pieces from head to tail in the panels. All pieces should be lined up evenly on both sides.

Stamping on book covers Any titling or stamping on the covers is done after the material is attached to the boards and before the edges are turned. This is to eliminate the possibility of a slightly bulky corner or a slightly thick spot on 1 edge from throwing the stamping out of line.

Cut a stamping board the exact size of the book's boards and 2 strips of the same binder's board as that used for the covers, about 1 inch (2.5 cm) wide and 10 inches (25.4 cm) or so long. Place 1 of these strips against the back gauge and 1 against the right-hand gauge. These are to accommodate the width of the unturned edges.

Mark on the stamping board the desired position of the title. Place the board in the right angle made by the 2 strips; adjust both gauges so that the stamping will be in the selected position. Make a carbon impression on the stamping board. If it is correct and properly placed, remove the stamping board from the press and replace it with the cover of the book. Take care to see that the unturned edges are resting on the 2 strips, that they are snug against the gauges, and that the edges of the book cover are snug against the strips. Be sure that the gauges and the chase or pallet are tightened or locked in position; proceed with the stamping as previously described.

Attaching titled leather to book Place the book in a finishing press. Mark the center of the spine of the book from left to right, at both head and tail, and mark the center of the strip or strips of paper previously mounted on the leather in the same fashion.

For a smooth spine, glue lightly with thin glue both the spine of the book and the strip of paper. Lay the paper on the spine, lining up the center marks on the two exactly. Cover with paper and rub gently for a few minutes. For raised bands, glue the paper on both the spine and on the leather as described above; paste the areas of the leather that will cover the bands. Lay the leather in position on the spine; work it over the bands, moistening if necessary; and rub down the glued areas. Tie up as described in Chapter 7 under German Tube Variations.

Other Decorative Techniques

Inlaying

This term, when properly used, refers to the actual removal of a portion or portions of the covering material and its replacement with another. If the design calls for a large area of a different material or different color of the same material, inlaying is the technique to use.

These instructions are for the inlaying of leather on a leather binding. The same general principles apply to the inlaying of other materials, and the possibilities are numerous. It is recommended, however, that if you are working with unfamiliar materials, make a sample before work on the book is begun.

The manner of handling the leather—moistening, pasting, and so on—is the same as previously described under covering with leather.

First, check the thickness of the leather to be inlaid with that used or to be used on the binding. It is essential that in the finished product they appear to be of equal thickness. If the piece to be inlaid is thicker than the covering leather, pare it overall to the same thickness. If thinner, the cut-out area in the covering leather can be built up with paper or bristol so that the 2 leathers will appear to be of equal thickness—in other words, flush with each other. When this is necessary, add the filler to the bottom of the package when cutting out the piece to be inlaid.

Where the inlay is to be a wide strip of leather that extends the entire length of the board and turns over the edges, the book need not be covered entirely. The area that is to have the inlay can be left uncovered, except that the covering leather should extend about 1/8 to 1/4 inch onto the portion of the board that eventually will be covered by the inlay. This is done so that a clean cut can be made through both leathers after they are attached.

If 1 leather is dark and the other light, when possible put the lighter on top. This eliminates the possibility of the darker leather discoloring the lighter where they overlap.

For a wide panel inlay, first cover the spine and bring the leather over onto the side or sides that are to have the inlay. Then cover the fore edge or edges; weight down and set aside to dry. Do not turn the edges at this time.

Cut the inlay leather large enough so that it will overlap both edges of the covering leather by 1/8 to 1/4 inch and from head to tail the same length as the covering leather. Moisten, paste, and lay in position; set aside to dry under weight.

When dry, cut away the surplus leather. First, support the leather that is overhanging the board at each end, so that the cut can be continuous in its entire length. Lay a straightedge along the top leather where the 2 overlap, and, holding the knife at an angle that will produce a bevelled cut, cut through both pieces of leather. Before removing the straightedge, run the knife down the cut again to be sure that the cut went completely through both pieces of leather.

Moisten the top leather and pull away the surplus or cut-off edge.

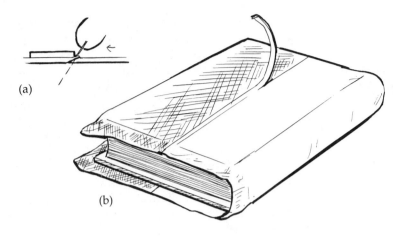

FIGURE 8-12.

Lift up the attached edge of this piece just enough to free the cut-off edge on the bottom leather; moisten and remove it (Fig. 8-12). Repaste lightly the edge of the top leather and lay it back in position against the edge of the bottom leather. Wipe away any surplus paste with a piece of moist cotton. Lay a piece of paper over the area where the 2 leathers meet and rub gently with a bonefolder in the direction that will bring the 2 leathers closer together. Place between clean pulpboards and pressboards and weight down until dry. Check this several times in the course of drying to be sure that the inlay leather is not shrinking and leaving a gap where the 2 leathers join. The smaller the area that is moistened in the process of removing the surplus leather, the less likely this will happen. If it does happen, moisten the edge of the inlay and gently push it until the gap is closed.

When introducing a different color leather that will cover only a portion of the board, this should be done with an onlay (following section) rather than an inlay. There are times, however, when circumstances make an inlay preferable. In such cases, follow these techniques. When the design has been decided upon, cut a pattern out of bristol or some board firm enough to use as a guide in cutting around it. Cut the inlay leather 1/4 inch larger in all dimensions than the pattern. Apply a coat of thin paste to the surface of the leather and cover it with lens tissue or some thin Japanese tissue. Weight down between pulpboards until dry. If a filler is necessary, lay this material in position on the covering leather, securing it with a spot of paste; add the inlay leather and the pattern, attaching them in the same fashion. Cut around the pattern through both leathers and the filler, holding the knife at an angle that will produce a bevelled cut. Remove the pattern, the inlay, and the filler from the covering leather, 1 at a time, by moistening the area where they were spot-tipped together. Then moisten the area of the covering leather that is to be removed and carefully lift it out.

Glue the filler and lay it in position in the cut-out area; let this dry under weight for 1 hour or so before continuing. Then paste the flesh side of the inlay and set it in. Moisten the tissue around the edge of the inlay and remove it so that the areas where the 2 leathers join can be seen and checked. Rub the edge as described above and set aside to dry. When the inlay is dry, moisten the remaining tissue with damp cotton just enough to remove the tissue and any surplus paste; return the book to its clean pulpboards and weight down until thoroughly dry.

In applying the lens tissue and tipping on the pattern it is esential that a water-soluble paste be used; straight wheat paste is recommended.

When the leathers are of equal thickness to start with and no filler is needed, simply eliminate filler instructions above.

After the leather is satisfactorily in place and dry, turn the edges, set the head caps, and so on in the manner previously described.

For inlays that cover only a portion of the board and do not extend over its edges, the binding can be carried to completion to the point of adding the board papers before the inlay is added.

Onlaying

This technique consists of attaching decorative pieces to the surface of a binding; they are usually different in color from the covering material, in varying shapes or sizes. Here, again, the instructions are for leather onlays on a leather binding. These might be classified into 3 groups— free form, punch-cut, definite shape—since there are slight variations in the handling of different sizes and shapes of onlays.

The binding can be carried to completion to the point of adding the board papers unless the onlay is to extend over the edges of the board. In this case the onlay should be in position and dry before the edges are turned. If the onlay covers a large portion of the board, it might be necessary to add a sheet of bond paper to the inside of the board to counteract the pull of the onlay. This can best be determined by leaving the volume completed, to the point of adding the board papers, over-night with no weight on it. If the boards remain flat, or nearly so, the board paper is all that is necessary.

Free form or abstract design Pare the leather extremely thin, to what might be described as "lacy" thin. Then pull or tear the design out of it. Apply a coat of paste to a piece of glass or a lithographic stone. Lay the design on the pasted area and press on it slightly so that it will pick up the paste. Then pick up the onlay and lay it in position on the cover in the desired shape (Fig. 8-13). Tweezers might be helpful in picking it up. After the onlay is in position, cover it with silicone-release paper or a clean smooth sheet of zinc, place it between pressboards, and give the cover—not the book—a quick nip in the press (Fig. 8-14). Remove from the press and set aside to dry under weight.

Punch-cut or cutting dies Onlays that are cut with punches or cutting dies are available as companion pieces to decorative finishing tools. Pare the leather very thin and paste-wash it on the flesh side with a thin paste solution. When nearly dry, put between pulpboards and weight down until dry.

Make a blind impression on the book cover with the finishing tool that matches the punch.

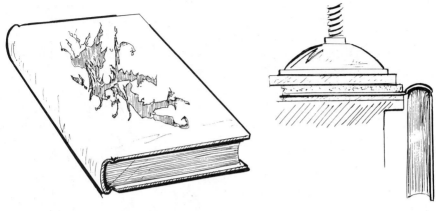

FIGURE 8-13.   FIGURE 8-14.

Lay the onlay leather faceup on a piece of binder's board and place on a firm surface. Set the punch on the leather and give it a blow with a hammer—and the onlay is cut out. Paste the flesh side of the onlay and position it in the blind impression; lay a piece of paper over it and rub it gently with a bonefolder. Then weight it down until dry. When dry, it can be blind or gold-tooled with the same tool that was used to make the blind impression.

If the onlay is very small, lay it on a pasted area rather than attempt to apply paste to it. It can then be picked up with the point of a needle.

Definite shape or form These onlays represent, perhaps, an original design, or at least 1 for which no cutting die is available.

The leather is again pared very thin. If the design is no larger than 1 square inch, the leather can be paste-washed on the flesh side; this will give it all the body it needs to hold its shape. If it is larger, the beginner should cover the surface of the leather with lens tissue. (Skilled craftspeople often do not find this necessary.) Both of these techniques have been described above.

Cut a pattern of the design out of bristol. When the leather to be onlayed is dry, lay it faceup on a piece of scrap board. Place the pattern in position on it; weight it down or hold it firmly and cut around the edges of the pattern. Hold the knife at an angle that will produce a bevelled cut or edge. This serves a twofold purpose: It further thins the edge of the onlay and it removes the possibility of the flesh side of the leather showing when the onlay is in position.

Moisten the area of the cover where the onlay is to go; spot-tip the pattern in the desired position of the onlay. Place the cover—not the book—between zinc sheets and give it a quick squeeze in the press. This should produce an indented impression of the pattern. If tooling is desired around the edges of the onlay, blind tool around the pattern before removing it.

Remove the pattern and sand the indented area lightly. Paste the flesh side of the onlay; lay it in position in the impression; replace the zinc sheets—be sure they are clean. The cover can now be given a quick nip in the press or set aside to dry under weight. The press will flatten it better, but it also tends to remove the grain from the leather to a greater extent. When dry, retool the edges if an impression was made earlier and lightly sponge off the tissue.

For narrow straight-line borders, a fillet of the desired width can be used to make the indention. For wider borders an outline should be tooled indicating its exact width before the onlay is applied, and the onlay should be carefully mitered at all right-angle corners or any angular corner.

Bas-Relief and Intaglio

Other decorative effects can be made with the techniques of bas-relief and intaglio. In bas-relief the figures or designs are raised slightly, or in relief, above the background. Intaglio is just the reverse; the figures or designs are depressed, or sunk, below the surface. In applying these techniques to bookbinding, the end results are different, but the basic problems are the same.

In past years, in each case this was done by paring the covering leather very thin in the areas that were to be stretched over a raised or protruding object, or worked into a depressed or sunken area. The leather was then dampened and a bonefolder used to shape the leather over the object or work it into the depression. If the design was intricate, a sharp definition of it was not easy to attain.

A technique that apparently has been used by industrial designers for some years has now been applied to bookbinding by Norman Gardner, a well-known designer. It works beautifully with both bas-relief and intaglio, and is described here. (Gardner's use of this technique in bookbinding is, to the best of the author's knowledge, its first. No reference to it has been found in the literature in the field, although an exhaustive search has not been made, and Gardner, himself, makes no such claim.)

Bas-relief Cut the figures out of bristol board or some good quality board (acid-free matting board) that is the thickness of the desired height. In determining the desired height, bear in mind that the leather has to stretch over it. The surest way to get the desired effect is to make up a sample or samples.

Glue the design and lay it in position on the covering board; weight down until dry. Cut and pare the leather as described earlier. In addition, thin the leather slightly in the area or areas that will cover the design, either by paring or sanding. Moisten the surface and paste the flesh side; let it stand for a few minutes until the moisture has soaked in and then put it on the covering board. Shape the leather over the design gently with the hands and smooth it out on the rest of the board.

Place the covered board—not the book—on a pressboard, lay on top of it a piece of polyurethane foam 2 or 3 inches (5 or 7.6 cm) thick and slightly larger than the cover in both dimensions. Put a zinc sheet on top of the foam and add a pressboard. Place the "package" in the press and screw it down tight. After about 10 minutes, remove it from the press, turn the sheet of foam over, and return to the press until thoroughly dry.

The board to which the design and leather have just been added should not be allowed to warp—it might ruin the design. As soon as the book is removed from the press, add a piece of bond paper to the inside of the board. Cut this the exact size of the board and attach it by applying glue to the paper and laying it in position.

Intaglio The procedure is the same as that just described for bas-relief, except in the cutting out of the design. Select a board equal in thickness to the depth of the depression desired. Cut it to the exact size of the covering board. Draw or transfer the design to this board and cut around it, removing the board from the areas that are to be depressed. Attach it to the covering board with glue; balance the pull with bond paper, if necessary. Then proceed with the covering.

In employing these techniques, it is always wiser to make up a sample. In this way the extent to which the leather should be thinned can be determined and a check can be made on the effect, if any, that pressing with the foam has on the texture of the leather.

9 Other Binding Styles

Covered in this chapter are a few types of specialized bindings that differ in one way or another from the 4 styles discussed thus far—case, Bradel, tight back, and German tube. Detailed instructions are given for these specialized styles only when they differ from instructions already given for the other bindings. Frequent references are made to earlier instructions.

Limp Binding

This is a case binding with flexible covers. It has been produced commercially with no stiffening material between the covering material and the board papers and with a thin flexible board. It is usually executed in leather. For a number of years its use has been restricted almost entirely to small Bibles, prayer books, and "gift items" for the Christmas season.

The instructions here are for a leather binding with a hollow back, using lightweight bristol as covering boards. Follow the steps in Chapter 7 for case binding through the rounding of the book.

These bindings are not backed, because the thinness of the covering bristol eliminates the necessity of compensating for the thickness of binder's boards. Skip this step and proceed with filling in between the tapes with Hosho, the headbanding, and the lining up of the spine with lawn; do not add the paper. Headbands are customarily made of leather; color is a matter of personal preference.

Add a tube to the spine, as described in Chapter 7 for the German tube (under Tight Back and German Tube Bindings). Eliminate the additional strips and burnishing. Cut the tube 1/2 inch (1.2 cm) shorter than the length of the book. The covering leather is not turned into the tube in this style. Glue the tube and lay it in position on the spine, centering from head to tail between the headbands.

Making the case Use a lightweight bristol (220M) for the covering boards, and the same paper for the spine strip that was used in making the tube. Allow the usual 1/8 inch square at head and tail and 3/16 inch square on the fore edge. Offset them at the joint the customary 1/4 inch. The spine strip is cut as usual, the width of the tube or spine and the length of the boards.

Cut the leather to size and pare it; sand the joints lightly. Then paste-wash the flesh side of it (see Chapter 8 under Titling). When almost dry—when the paste is no longer tacky—put it between clean pulpboards and weight down until dry. The bristol boards are not attached solidly to the leather, and the paste-washing serves to balance the pull caused when the board papers are added.

Apply hot glue to the spine strip and lay it in the center of the leather. If the case is to be titled on a stamping press, do so at this stage (see Stamping Presses in Chapter 8).

Attaching the boards Lay the 1/4-inch joint spacers snugly against the edges of the spine strip. Apply a 1/8-inch line of glue along the spine edge of each bristol and lay them in position against the spacers. Weight down until dry. Then cut the corners and turn the edges of the leather onto the bristol. Moisten the surface of the leather on the edges and paste the inside. Weight the bristol down to prevent buckling during this process.

If the book has round corners, cut the bristols on the fore edge to conform to the same round or arc. Locate a small circular object that fits the rounded book corners—a dime often works well (Fig. 9-1)—lay it in the right-angle corner of the boards, draw around it, and cut on the line.

Turning a round corner Cut the corners with a bevelled edge, leaving 1/4 inch of leather at the curve; pare this thin and feather the edges of the entire cut. Moisten the surface and paste the edges. Place the circular object used as a pattern in cutting the corners of the bristols on the bristol corner and shape the leather around its edge. Remove it and lay the leather down, easing it into small pleats on the curve. If necessary, to make a neat corner, snip a few little wedge-shaped pieces out of the edge of the leather that covers the curved area (Fig. 9-2). Then turn the remaining edges. Slip a clean piece of board under the corner, lay a scrap of binder's board on top of it, and give the corner a couple of mild blows with a hammer. When the edges are all turned, place the case between pulpboards and weight down until dry.

The covers can be left undecorated or tooled as desired. Traditionally, limp bindings have a single blind-tooled line around the edges of both boards and across the ends of the spine.

Attaching the case to the book Put the book in a finishing press after flagging its head (a strip of paper protruding at the head) protected by pulpboards. Leave 1 inch or so of the book exposed on the sides. Mark the center of the tube and the center of the spine strip in the case at both head and tail. Apply thin glue to both the tube and the spine strip; lay the spine of the case in position on the tube, lining up the center marks just made. Take care to see that the square on the boards at head

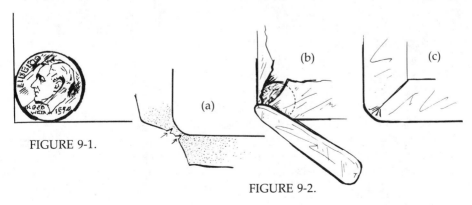

FIGURE 9-1.

FIGURE 9-2.

and tail is even. When properly positioned, lay a clean piece of paper over the spine, and rub it gently but firmly with the hands for about 15 minutes. Remove the book from the press; close the covers; place between protective boards and weight down for several hours.

The hinges and the board papers are then put down following instructions for a case binding (Chapter 7). Add 2 pieces of bristol between the board paper and the endleaf: 1 that goes all the way back to the spine, next to the board paper; the other from the edge of the hinge to the fore edge. Put the book between pressboards and weight down; do not put the book in the press.

If the cover is to be titled on the stamping press, do so after the bristols have been added and before the edges are turned. If titling is to be done by hand on either the spine or the cover, do so after the case is complete and before it is attached to the book.

Yapp Binding or Edges

This is a limp leather binding with overhanging (Yapp) edges or flaps on head, tail, and fore edges of both front and back covers, which when folded down against the book protect the edges of the pages. It was designed by William Yapp of London in the mid-nineteenth century as a suitable binding for pocket-size Bibles. The edges are also referred to as "circuit edges" and the binding as a "divinity circuit" binding.

Follow the instructions for a limp binding (preceding section) up to the point of cutting the bristol used for the covering boards and the paper for the spine strip. Here the boards do not have the usual overhang or square. Cut them in length 1/16 inch longer than the height of the book—allowing only 1/32 inch square on head and tail. In width, offset the bristols 1/4 inch at the spine edge, as usual, and make the square on the fore edge only 1/16 inch. The spine strip is the width of the tube and the length of the bristols.

The piece of leather required for this type of binding is considerably bigger than that needed for a binding on which the edges are turned snugly against the board. Here the overhanging edges are made by folding the leather back on itself. The Yapp or overhanging edges can be made any desired width. Traditionally, they met, or almost so, thus protecting all edges. For a book 1 1/2 inches (3.8 cm) thick, the edges might be 1/2 inch (1.2 cm) in their finished state. These directions are for a 1/2-inch overhang. If less or more is desired, adjust the measurements accordingly. In any case the amount of leather required is twice the width of the finished edge plus 1/2 inch.

Lay the bristols, the spine strip, and the joint strips out on the leather and cut so that there is a margin of leather 1 1/2 inches (3.8 cm) wide on top, bottom, and both fore edges. Pare this 1 1/2 inches thin enough so that when folded the 2 layers about equal the thickness of the rest of the leather and are soft and pliable. Feather all 4 edges.

Paste-washing the leather and making the case are as described earlier under Limp Binding; titling and tooling also. The turning of the edges are, however, handled a bit differently. Measuring from the edge of the boards, draw a line on the leather on all 4 edges at the point where it will

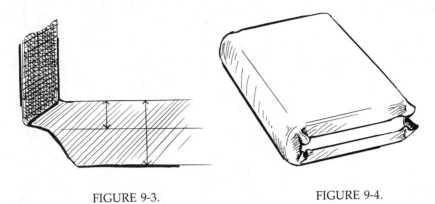

FIGURE 9-3.   FIGURE 9-4.

be folded. This is the finished width of the Yapp edge. Moisten the surface of the leather and paste the flesh side of the edges. Keep the surface moist, and when the leather is soft and pliable lay a straightedge on the lines just drawn and fold the leather up against it by running a bonefolder along its edge. Let this sit a few minutes to set the fold; then remove the straightedge, repaste the leather, and lay it down flat on itself. One-half inch (1.2 cm) of leather should fall on the bristol boards (Fig. 9-3). Pinch the leather at the corners together. Cut away the surplus, open them up, and feather the edges of the cut; repaste and lay the leather in position, easing it a bit at the corner. If the corners are to be round, follow the instructions earlier for Limp Binding.

When all edges are turned, weight the cover down between protective boards until thoroughly dry.

Before attaching the case to the book, fold the Yapp edges (Fig. 9-4). Moisten the outside edges of the case—the portion that makes up the Yapp edges. Lay a straightedge along the edge of the bristols on the inside; run a bonefolder along the outside of the leather, folding it against the edge of the straightedge. Fold all 4 edges in this manner.

Follow the remaining steps given earlier under Limp Binding.

Vellum Bindings

Vellum was a commonly used binding material from the sixteenth century into the nineteenth. It was not used extensively during the last half of the nineteenth century or the first half of the twentieth. There has, however, been a revival of use in relatively recent years.

Vellum has 2 characteristics that do not exist in leather: It has a grain direction that runs from head to tail of the skin, and it is also porous and unstable. Vellum constantly changes with changes in atmospheric conditions. In a humid atmosphere, it picks up moisture and expands; and in a dry atmosphere, it dries out and contracts. For these reasons books bound in vellum should be housed where the heat and humidity remain constant.

Most vellum made today for binding comes from the tannery with a coating of zinc white on the flesh side. This is done to make it opaque and possibly to reduce porosity.

FIGURE 9-5.

The techniques used in producing a vellum binding do not differ greatly from those described for other bindings. A vellum binding does, however, incorporate in its construction the techniques used in several types or styles of bindings.

Two types of vellum bindings are described here—hollow back with a French groove and a limp binding. Only variations in the use of techniques are detailed.

Hollow back It is customary to sew these bindings on vellum strips. Three strips about 3/16 inch in width, evenly spaced on the spine, are suitable for an octavo volume; and they should be cut 3 inches (7.6 cm) longer than the thickness of the book (Fig. 9-5). The preparation of the endleaves, sewing, rounding, and backing are similar to those described under Case Binding in Chapter 7. Sewn headbands are generally used on these bindings, and they should be worked in the usual fashion and at the same stage that headbands would be attached to the spine of a case binding. The spine is lined up and a tube put on the spine as described earlier in this chapter under Limp Binding.

The boards are then cut to size, again as for a case binding, and a strip for the spine is cut from the same paper used for the tube, the exact width of the tube and the length of the boards. The boards should be lined on both sides with bond paper. Apply paste to the paper, lay in position on the boards, smooth out, and give them a nip in the press.

Cut the vellum to size as for a case binding, and remember that it has a grain direction. Pare all 4 edges to a feathered edge. Vellum pares rather easily if it is moistened first. Sand the joints if the skin is unduly thick and stiff. If the zinc white is sanded away and the vellum in these areas becomes transparent, recoat them with zinc white. Allow this to dry, which will take about 24 hours.

At this point consider the question of titling. If it is to be titled by hand, complete the case. If on the stamping press, attach the spine strip and title the spine before adding the boards.

Make the case following the instruction in Chapter 7 under Case Binding, with the exception that the vellum is pasted. Moisten the vellum on the grain side with water, paste the flesh side with thin paste, let it soak in for a few minutes, and paste a second time. If the paste seems streaky or unevenly spread, lay a piece of clean wastepaper on it, rub gently, and quickly lift it off. Put 1 board in position, turn it over, and rub firmly. Do not stretch the vellum any more than is necessary to remove the wrinkles. Add the joint spacers, the spine, and the other board; put the whole case between clean pulpboards and pressboards and put in the press with firm pressure. Check it in a few minutes; if all right, change the top pulpboard for a dry one and return to the press until dry. If the vellum is wrinkling, moisten it thoroughly and return to the press.

Next, cut the corners as usual. Moisten the outside of the edges with water; paste the inside; wait a few minutes until they become soft and pliable; turn them in. Again put it to press as described above. Check in 10 minutes or so, and if all is well return to the press and leave until dry.

Put the book in a finishing press, spine exposed. Apply thin glue to both the spine strip in the case and the tube on the spine of the book. Lay the case in position, checking to be sure that it is centered from left to right and from head to tail. Lay a clean piece of paper over the spine and rub it firmly for some minutes.

Remove the book from the press, open the front cover, and mark in the joint area the exact position and width of the 3 vellum strips on which the book was sewn. These are now laced into the covers. Slit the vellum in the joint at these points along the edge of the spine. Pull the strips through the slits, lay them across the joint and slit the vellum again about 1/16 inch from the edge of the board, and slip the strips through these slits. The strips will then be on the inside of the board. Repeat on back.

Using brass-bound boards—be sure that the brass edges are clean—case the book in, thus producing a French groove. This will also set the position of the vellum strips in the joint.

Open the covers, cut the strips about 3/4 inches (1.9 cm) long and angle the ends. Paste the side of the strips that will go against the board. Slip a strip of wax paper between the board and the endsheets, close the book, and return to the press. Leave in the press until the strips are thoroughly dry—at least 1 hour.

The hinges and the board papers are then put down in the usual way. If the boards show signs of warping appreciably, line them out on the inside with bond paper before putting down the hinges and the board papers. Leave in the press until thoroughly dry. It is now complete except for any finishing that might be desired.

Limp vellum binding These bindings were originally executed centuries ago as an economical type of binding. Due to the durability of vellum, a number of such bindings are around today. For the most part they are, however, rather unattractive in their present condition. The vellum is wrinkled and cockled and the high spots are rubbed and dirty; frequently, the covers have shrunk or contracted to such an extent that they no longer cover the book pages, and the board papers are invariably torn along the vellum turn-ins. For some reason, for which no one seems to have an explanation, limp vellum has regained its early popularity in the last quarter of the twentieth century. One enthusiast says they eliminate the problem of warping boards! So they do—but they create the problem of cockled covers.

Directions are given here for a limp vellum binding. It is recommended that, if produced, it be put promptly in a Solander case (see Chapter 10) and housed in a room where the heat and humidity are maintained at a constant level. Otherwise, it will be a disappointing undertaking in a relatively short period of time.

These directions are for a binding that wraps around the book. The book is held in the covers only by the lacing of the vellum strips on which it and the headbands are sewn into the covers and by the Yapp fore edge and ties. There is no practical way to attach the book to the cover in the joints; board papers could only be attached to the turned edges of the vellum where they would be far from durable.

Detailed instructions are given only for variations from standard practices. Flyleaves can consist of 2 folded sheets—one inside the other. Since there are no endleaves and no hinges, a double fold will be stronger to sew through than a single one.

The sewing is done and the headbands worked as described earlier under Hollow Back vellum binding, except that the vellum on which the headbands are worked should extend 1 1/2 inches (3.8 cm) beyond the width of the spine, on both sides. After the book is sewn, reduce the swell; glue the spine; round it; work the headbands; and line the spine up with Hosho, lawn, and an acid-free paper. Set aside to dry and proceed with making the cover.

Cut the vellum—grain direction running with the vertical measurement of the book—allowing 1 1/2 inches (3.8 cm) turns at head and tail and 2 1/2 inches (6.3 cm) at fore edges. In measuring the height or length, allow 1/8 inch square at head and tail. Mark off these turns, moisten the outside with water, lay a straightedge on the flesh side, and with a bonefolder score and fold the edges.

Mark the width of the spine in the center of the vellum; moisten, score, and fold. Slip the book into the cover, pushing the spine firmly into the spine area of the cover. Mark the position of the fore edge of the book on the inside of the vellum both front and back. Make another mark 1/4 to 1/2 inch beyond the fore edge. This is the portion of the cover that will fold down over the fore edge of the book—the Yapp edge. If the thickness of the book permits, make this 1/2 inch (1.2 cm). Moisten, score, and fold both front and back at these points.

Lay the vellum flat and cut the corners so that the turns at head and tail lock into the fore edge turns. At the point where the scored lines at head and tail intersect with the scored lines on the fore edges, mark 1/2 inch (1.2 cm) on the scored line at the head and tail turn-ins—all 4 corners; at a right angle to the scored line, draw a line 1/2 inch on the head and tail turns (Fig.9-6). From this point draw a diagonal line intersecting the point where the 2 scored lines meet; carry this line onto the fore edge turns for about 2 inches (5 cm). Cut along the scored lines at both head and tail and fore edges from the edges to the point of intersection; remove this piece. Then cut the triangle drawn out of the head and tail pieces and snip off the point that is left. Mark 1/2 inch (1.2 cm)

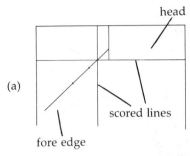

(a)

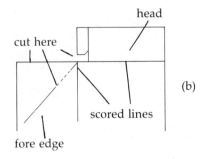

(b)

FIGURE 9-6.

from the point of intersection along the diagonal line on the fore edges. From the mark, slit the vellum along the diagonal line for 1 inch (2.5 cm). Fold the edges and slip the ends of the head and tail turns into the slits in the fore edge turns.

Put the book in the cover, centered from head to tail, and mark the position of the vellum strips along both sides of the spine; slit the cover along the spine edge the width of the vellum strips on which the book was sewn—slits running parallel to the spine; and for the strips on which the headbands were sewn make the slit at a 45° angle to the spine. Pull the strips through the slits; make another row of slits about 1/4 inch toward the fore edge from the first ones, and take the slips back into the inside of the covers. Pull the book snugly into the cover. Mark the position of the fore edge, front, and back; moisten the vellum and score and fold the Yapp edges. Remove the cover from the book for this.

Cut 2 pieces of lightweight bristol—preferably white 1 1/2 inches (3.8 cm) wide and the length of the inside of the cover from head to tail; slip these inside the folded fore edge up to the Yapp edge. Make 2 slits in the fore edges, evenly spaced from head to tail and about 1/2 inch (1.2 cm) back from the fore edge of the book. Make slits in the bristols at these same points. Insert silk ribbons or linen tapes through the vellum and the bristol—the width of the slits should be governed by the width of the material selected. Pull these through for about 1 inch and paste them to the bristol with mixture.

Sharpen up the folds by moistening all turned edges and putting under pressure until dry. Return the book to the cover, relace the vellum strips in the spine area; and tie the ribbons or tapes on the fore edge in a bow.

Bindings of this type were often not titled; if they were, the title was written on informally by hand.

One-Signature Book

The early steps in the binding of a one-signature book are described in Chapter 6, under Sewing, through the sewing and treatment of the edges. Rounding, backing, headbanding, lining up the spine, and so on are not necessary here; in fact, most of these steps would be impossible or difficult to execute on 1 signature. So, after the sewing and the trimming of the edges, if desired, are completed, the book is ready for its case.

The instructions here are for a hardcover, cloth case binding. Since this type of binding for a multisignature book is described in detail (Case Binding in Chapter 7), only the variations are discussed here. The use of other materials or combinations as given in Chapter 7 is applicable here.

Since there is no backed joint, the selection of binder's board is based solely on the size of the book. Generally speaking, an .059 is suitable for octavos and smaller books, and an .082 for quartos and larger ones.

Cut the spine strip out of lightweight binder's board (.059) instead of bristol. Its width is not the usual width of the spine of the book; it should be the thickness of the book plus the thickness of 1 of the covering boards. Place the boards on the book and squeeze the 3 together at the spine. Measure the width of 1 board and the book and cut the spine strip this width.

Increase the width of the joints from the usual 1/4 inch to 1/4 inch plus the thickness of the binder's board used as the spine. If .059 board was used, the increase would be 1/16 inch and the joint spacers cut 5/16 inch.

Construct the case in the usual fashion and check its fit on the book. When ready to case it in, remove the tabs of masking tape that are holding the protection sheets in place, but leave the sheets in position. Cut the ends of the cloth hinges at the usual angle.

Lay the case on a brass-bound board with the spine edge of 1 of the covering boards against the brass edge. Glue the hinge on 1 side of the book and lay the book in position on the case, taking care that the square on the board is even head, tail, and fore edges. Glue the other hinge, and while holding the book firmly in position, bring the case around the spine and lay the other cover down, or close the book. Weight it down and check to be sure that all 3 edges of both covers are even, and that the spine of the book is snug against the spine of the case. If not, make the necessary adjustments by freeing the hinges and starting over. If so, add the second case board and put the whole in the press for about 15 minutes.

Remove the book from the press, and add the board papers in the usual way. For titling, follow the instructions under Titling (Chapter 8). If a job backer and case boards with brass on only 1 edge are available, it is easier to case-in a thin book by putting it in the backer rather than the press. There is more room to adjust it, and both the edges and the spine can be seen more readily than they can in the press.

In this type, because of the lack of backing, the case does not fit the book firmly in the spine area. There is a slight hollow space on both sides of the spine of the book (Fig. 9-7). For this reason it is advisable always to use a cloth hinge and not to rely on paper being strong enough to withstand the strain.

Oriental Bindings

These bindings are quite different in appearance from Western bindings. They consist of 2 separate covers, which are sewn or laced onto the book through punched or drilled holes. The spine of the book

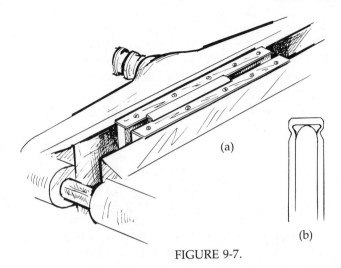

(a)

(b)

FIGURE 9-7.

remains exposed except for a small area at head and tail, which is usually covered with a piece of some solid color, thin silk (this varies).

Materials Needed

Binder's board 2 pieces, lightweight (.059), slightly larger in both dimensions than book, square up 1 corner on each piece before cutting to exact size

Paper 4 pieces for endleaves and board papers, same size as binder's board

Material 2 pieces selected for covers, large enough to allow 3/4 inch (1.9 cm) turn on all 4 edges

Hinges 2, same material as above, 1 inch (2.5 cm) wide, length of vertical book measurement (if material is woven fabric other than book cloth, see Case Binding in Chapter 7 for preparation)

Material 2 pieces, solid color, thin, 1 inch (2.5 cm) in length, 1 inch wider than book thickness

Silk or linen thread several yards

Newsprint unprinted

Wastepaper strips

Awl or hand drill

Hammer

C-clamps

Mixture wheat paste and water-soluble PVA equal parts

Glue

Wheat paste

Pulpboard

Pressboards

Brick

There seems to be no set pattern in the selection of the material used in Oriental bindings, although it may be based on tradition.

Preparation Do any cleaning and make any page repairs that are necessary. No guarding of the folds or hinging in of plates is required, for the "sewing" is done in the gutter margin (the margin on the spine edge of the pages) and not through the folds. Gluing up the spine, rounding, backing, and so on are omitted here, with the possible exception of trimming the edges. This depends on the nature of the book and the condition of the edges.

Cut the endleaves to the exact size of the book pages and tip one onto the spine edge of the first page and the other onto the last page. If the book has no flyleaves and you want them, they should be attached in the same way before the endleaves are put in place. If the edges of the book are to be cut, this is done after these pages are in position.

Square the book up, lining all 4 edges up even; weight it down. Place scraps of binder's board on both front and back of the book in the spine area at both head and tail, leaving the 1/2 inch (1.2 cm) at both ends free. Secure them in position with C-clamps.

Mark the spine lightly 1/2 inch (1.2 cm) in from the head; apply mixture to the area and lay 1 piece of the selected silk or cloth on it; attach the other 1/2 inch of the cloth to the tail of the book in the same fashion. Fold the sides down onto the flyleaves both front and back and attach with mixture. This will leave a triangular piece of cloth of double thickness; fold this down both front and back and attach with mixture on top of the piece previously attached to the flyleaves. Repeat this with the piece at the tail. The book is now ready for its covers; lay it aside, with the C-clamps still on it (Fig. 9-8).

Before constructing the covers, consider the manner in which the book will be titled. If with a paper label, no preliminary preparation is needed. If you wish an indented label, prepare the front cover as described for Case Binding in Chapter 7.

The adhesive used in constructing the covers depends on the type of material selected; if a sized cloth, use glue; if a tissue-backed fabric, use mixture.

Covers These consist of 2 separate pieces of binder's board. Cut the boards to the exact size of the book in both dimensions, grain direction with the vertical measurement. These bindings customarily have no overhang or square on the boards. Then cut off of each board, from head to tail, one strip 5/8 inch wide and one strip 1/8 inch wide. The

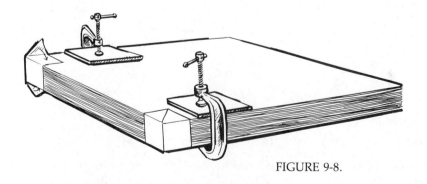

FIGURE 9-8.

wider strip represents the spine of the book in that this is where the covers are attached to the book, and the 1/8 inch strips are gauges or spacers for the joints.

Lay 1 board and 1 each of the 2 strips just cut out on the covering material, and cut it allowing a 3/4 inch (1.9 cm) margin on all 4 sides. Cut a second piece the same size. Cover both boards following directions previously given. Before turning the edges, add the hinge on the inside of the joint. Cut these 1 inch shorter in length than the height of the book. Draw a line on the board 1/2 inch (1.2 cm) from the joint; apply adhesive to the hinge; lay 1 edge of it on the line just drawn; rub it down; work it into the joint along the edge of both the covering board and the spine strip; and lay the rest of it down on this strip. Cut the corners and turn the edges in the customary way. On the spine side, cut the edge of the cloth short enough so that when it is laid down it does not extend into the joint.

Cut the board papers 1/4 inch smaller in both dimensions than the boards. From spine to fore edge, take the measurement from the joint to the fore edge. Paste the papers and lay in position, centering them on the boards or allowing 1/8 inch margin on all 4 edges. Weight down until dry.

Attach the covers to the book by putting several dots of mixture on the inside of the narrow strip on the spine edge. Lay in position, lining them up evenly with the edges of the book and with each other. Weight down until dry.

Sewing or lacing Make 2 identical templates to use as a guide in punching or drilling the holes, 1 for the front and 1 for the back. Cut 2 strips of pulpboard the exact height of the covers and about 2 inches (5 cm) wide. Draw a line 3/8 inch from 1 edge on both strips. Mark the position for the holes on both strips. Mark first the head and tail 1/2 inch (1.2 cm) in from the ends; and make the other marks about 1 inch (2.5 cm) apart, or evenly spaced between the end marks. Place 1 template on the front of the book, the other on the back, with the 3/8-inch area toward the spine of the book. Line them both up evenly with the spine and secure in position with C-clamps as described above.

If the book is thin, the holes can probably be punched with a thin, sharp-pointed awl or by driving a small nail or brad through them with a hammer. If, however, it is too thick for 1 of these methods, use a hand drill with a very small bit. In either case, the holes should go straight through, starting at the marks on the top template and coming through on the corresponding marks on the bottom one. (This is the reason for the 2 templates.) When the holes are made, remove the C-clamps, 1 at a time, and push the templates forward away from the spine and free of the holes. Replace the clamps so that they are still in contact with the templates.

Start the lacing on the back cover at the hole nearest the center. Use a piece of thread about 5 times as long as the height of the book; the amount needed, however, somewhat depends on the thickness of the book. Take the thread through the cover, the book, and the front cover; leave a 3 inch (7.6 cm) tail of thread at the starting point; go down

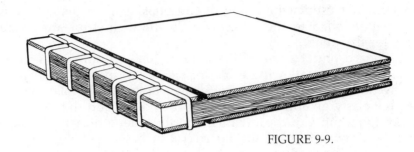

FIGURE 9-9.

through the next hole toward the head, up through the next, and so on until the last hole at the head is reached; carry the thread around the head of the book and back through the last hole from the other side; carry it around or over the spine and back into the same hole; then on to the next hole, around the spine again, and so forth until the center hole is reached. Then carry the thread in a running seam down to the last hole at the tail of the book; go around the tail of the book and return to the center hole in the manner just described. Bring the thread out on the back cover at the hole nearest to the center. Tie it and the "free tail" together with a square knot. Cut the surplus thread away about 1/4 inch from the knot (Fig. 9-9). Remove the C-clamps.

10   Protective Cases

Many authors in the field do not touch on the subject of protective cases. Some type of case, however, unquestionably protects a binding and adds additional protection to the book itself.

There are 3 well-known types of protective cases—a slipcase, a Solander case or folding box, and a fireproof case. Each has been constructed in a number of ways and with minor variations.

Although it is desirable that a protective case be aesthetically pleasing and the material selected for its construction in keeping with the binding, its primary function is protection. So it should be made of durable and serviceable materials. An elaborate case made of delicate materials, or that is highly decorated, in itself would need protection. Some restraint should be used in the desire to protect a "beautiful" binding in a "beautiful" case. Particular attention should be paid to the selection of the material used for the lining of any protective case. It should be acid-free, or nearly so, and free of any decorative motif that might transfer to the book; otherwise, it would tend to disfigure or hasten the deterioration of the item it was meant to protect.

In bookbinding terminology, a slipcase is a box that has front and back covers, is closed at head, tail, and fore edge, and is open at the spine. It is possibly suitable and appropriate protection for a cloth-covered book and for the storing of pamphlets and unbound magazines or periodicals, although with its open spine it offers only partial protection. It is not recommended for full-leather bindings, unless the book is first enclosed in a wrapper or chemise. For a number of years it was thought to be an excellent way to store fine bindings because the beauty of the spine was exposed on the shelf. Time, however, has shown that only the covers were protected, while the spine became faded, and in many cases disintegrated.

Hand binders generally make slipcases of binder's board by cutting the various pieces to size and setting them together with glue—as against most commercially made ones that usually use a thinner board, scored and folded.

A Solander case or folding box is basically a double box, or 2 boxes, which when closed or folded together simulate the appearance of a closed book. A true Solander case was originally constructed with a wooden frame and reputedly was designed by Dr. Daniel Charles Solander in the latter half of the eighteenth century while serving on the staff of the British Museum. This type of case offers, perhaps, the best overall protection. The book is completely encased, and it can be removed or returned to the case easily and safely.

Today, these cases are customarily constructed of binder's board, and like a slipcase, they are built or "set together." The prevailing belief is

215

that the most durable of the many variations is 1 with a flat spine that opens or "falls down" and lies flat on the table when the case is opened.

A fireproof case is made up of many layers of paper, sometimes including a sheet of asbestos, which are molded around the book or a block built to the exact size and shape of the book. The lining is usually chamois or cotton flannel, and the covering material generally leather. Aside from its fire-resistant characteristic, it has little to offer in the way of a protective case. A book has to be slipped into it tail first (or head first) and shaken out of it. Any book would have to be in very good condition to withstand the rigors of such protection. In addition, if properly constructed these cases are virtually airtight, and it is highly questionable as to whether this is a proper atmosphere in which to store any book, particularly a rare item. For these reasons, instructions for this type of "protective case" are not given here. (Edith Diehl in her book—see Bibliography—refers to this type of case as a Solander. The British, however, say that this is a misnomer. This is another example of the desirability of some standardization in bookbinding terminology.)

Instructions included here are for making a slipcase, a chemise and wrapper, and a Solander-type folding box, with variations. If a book is to be housed in a chemise and a slipcase, the chemise should be made first and the slipcase made to fit the book and chemise as a unit.

Slipcase

This case is made up of 5 separate pieces of binder's board set together with the aid of a bristol board flange and an adhesive. The boards are lined on what will be the inside of the case before the individual pieces are cut to size. For books or other material of octavo size or smaller, use an .059 binder's board; for quarto and larger, use an .082 or heavier board.

These instructions are for a simple, rectangular box, lined on the inside with paper and covered on the outside with linen-finish book cloth. Some variations follow. It is suggested that this entire section, plus the following section on chemises and wrappers, be read before any work is started.

Materials Needed

Binder's board 2 pieces, 1 large enough to cut 1 cover or side and fore edge strip, the other large enough to take care of second cover and head and tail strips

Paper 2 pieces selected for lining, same size as boards

Bristol 3 pieces 1/2 inch (1.2 cm) or so larger in both dimensions than cut sizes of head, tail, and fore edge strips; grain direction same as strips

Book cloth 2 pieces, grain direction with vertical book measurement (do not cut from roll until box is set together or constructed)

Triangle

Glue

Wheat paste
Pressboards
Bricks
Sandpaper
Rubberbands large

Line the binder's board on 1 side with the paper. Paste the paper, lay in position, smooth it out, and weight down until dry. If the paper tends to wrinkle, give the boards a quick nip in the press. (Fig. 10-1)

Cut 1 right-angle corner on each board. The strips for the head, tail, and fore edges are then cut off the boards. The strips for the head and tail are cut off the longer of the lined boards and the 1 for the fore edge off the wider board. The widths of these strips are the thickness of the book plus about 1/16 inch. To determine their exact width, lay the book flat on a table. Place on top of it at its thickest point (usually the spine area) a piece of .059 binder's board and measure from the surface of the table the thickness of the book and board combined. If a board shears is available, set the gauge to this measurement and cut all 3 strips by this setting. Then cut a piece of bristol for each strip. These pieces should be 2 board (.059) thicknesses wider than the strips. It is this additional width that constitutes the flange used in setting the box together.

All 6 of these strips are cut to the proper length along with the cutting of the 2 sides. Lay them aside, under weight, for the moment.

Cutting the sides In length, these are cut the vertical measurement of the book plus 3 board (.059) thicknesses, and in width, the width of the book—from fore edge to the curve in the spine—plus 2 board (.059) thicknesses.

Lay the head and fore edge of the book in the right-angle corner on 1 of the boards, lining the edges of the book up evenly with the edges of

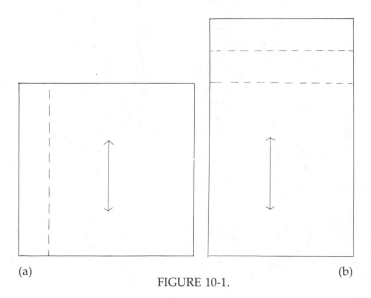

(a)　　　　　　　　　　　　　　　　　　　　(b)

FIGURE 10-1.

the board, and weight it down. Pinch 3 scraps of the lined board to-gether and lay them against the tail of the book (Fig. 10-2). Draw a pencil mark on the board along the outermost edge of the 3 scraps. Set the gauge on the board shears as indicated by the mark, and cut both boards and the strip of bristol for the fore edge to this length. With the gauge still set, place 2 scraps of the board used above in measuring against the gauge, place the strip of lined board for the fore edge up against the scraps, and cut it (Fig. 10-3). If properly done, this strip will be 2 board thicknesses shorter than the length of the sides.

Lay the book on 1 of the boards again, lining up the fore edge of the book with the edge of the board, and weight down. Place 2 of the scraps of board vertically against the spine of the book (Fig. 10-4) and mark the board as described earlier. Set the gauge on the cutter by the mark and cut both sides, head and tail strips, and the 2 pieces of bristol all to this width.

Now mount the head, tail, and fore edge strips on the pieces of bristol, lined side facing up. In each case glue the board and lay it in position on the bristol. On the head and tail strips, the ends will be flush with the ends of the bristol; in width the board should be centered on the bristol, leaving an equal amount of bristol—or a flange—exposed on both edges. The fore edge strip is centered on its bristol, leaving a flange of equal width on all 4 edges (Fig. 10-5). Weight these down and leave until dry.

Setting the box together Put a smooth piece of wastepaper on a large pressboard. Glue the edges of 1 of the side boards on head, tail, and fore edge; lay it on the pressboard and weight it down. It is necessary that the bristol board flange be no wider than the thickness of the binder's board. If it is, the box cannot be set together as described here, for the excess bristol will prevent the strips from fitting properly against the side board. If the flange is too wide, cut it to the proper width before proceeding.

With a small glue brush, carefully glue the bristol flange on all 4 edges of the fore edge strip and put it in position on the fore edge of the board, lining up the ends of the bristol with the head and tail of the board. Here the edge of the board of the fore edge strip will be resting on the face of the side board and the bristol board flange on the edge of this board. Rub the outside of the bristol for a few minutes with a bonefolder; check with a triangle to see that it is vertical and place a couple of small weights against it. Next, glue the bristol flanges on the head strip and the end that will go toward the fore edge of the box; put this in position at the head of the board as just described (Fig. 10-6). One end of this strip should be resting on the end of the fore edge strip (the binder's board) and flush with the end of the bristol; and on the spine edge it should be flush with the edge of the side board. Add the tail strip in the same way. Then glue the 3 edges of the second board and lay it in position (Fig. 10-7). If everything has been properly cut and fitted together, this board should fit nicely within the 3 bristol flanges. Rub the edges for a few minutes. If you have some large rubber bands, slip 2 or 3 around the box from head to tail; stick some pressboards

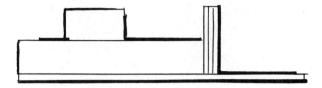

FIGURE 10-2.

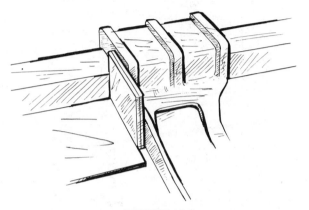

FIGURE 10-3.

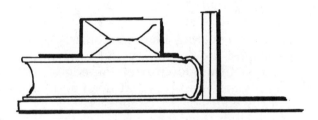

FIGURE 10-4.

FIGURE 10-5.

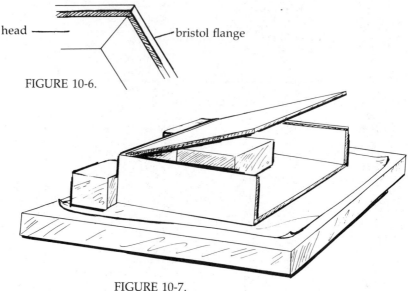

head ————   bristol flange

FIGURE 10-6.

FIGURE 10-7.

equivalent in height to the thickness of the box in the open side; lay it down on 1 side on a flat surface and weight down until dry.

Remove the bands, leave the pressboards in the box for support. Sand all glued edges or joints smooth on both sides and the ends of the box. It is now ready to be covered.

Covering the box The covering material consists of 3 pieces: 1 large piece that wraps around the entire box and turns into it at both edges on the spine side and turns down over the edges of the box at both head and tail; and 2 small strips used at head and tail to cover up the seam or joining of the edges of the larger piece.

Cut a piece of the cloth several inches larger than the overall dimensions of the box, grain direction running with the vertical measurement of the box. Cut 1 right-angle corner on the cloth; draw a line in from the top edge at a point that equals half the thickness of the box and a line 5/8 inch in from the other straight edge on the cloth. Lay the head and spine edge of 1 side of the box on these lines; at the tail allow the same amount of material as that allowed at the head. Mark the cutting point. Then turn the box over on the fore edge and lay it flat on the other side and mark the cutting point 5/8 inch out from the edge of the box. Make these 2 cuts. This should produce a piece of cloth with 4 right-angle corners, that is, the length of the box plus its thickness and in width is 1 1/4 inches (3.1 cm) wider than the overall measurement of the 2 sides and 1 thickness.

Glue the entire piece of cloth with thin glue. Lay the box in position in the right-angle corner made by the first 2 lines—oriented the same way. Turn it over and lay it on the table so that the free cloth can hang over the edge of the table (see Fig. 7-30, Chapter 7). Rub the cloth down well, smoothing out any wrinkles; then pull it snugly over the fore edge. Turn the box over again and rub the cloth down well over the edge of the box; lay it down on the other side, rubbing well.

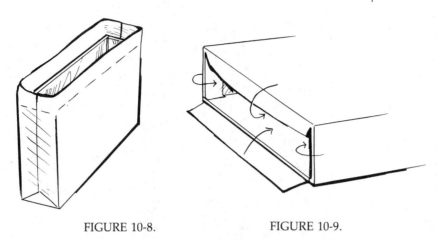

FIGURE 10-8.   FIGURE 10-9.

Pinch the corners of the cloth together at the head and cut away the surplus, producing a mitred effect. Reglue the cloth if necessary and lay the 2 pieces down on the head, pulling them firmly over the edges of the box (Fig. 10-8). These should meet in the center of the head strip. Repeat this at the tail.

Check the width of the cloth to be turned in on the spine or open side of the box. These pieces should be uniform in width—about 5/8 inch—and the edges straight. If it is necessary to cut them, the easiest way is to cut a strip of binder's board the length of the cloth and the width of the desired turn. Lay this strip against the edges of the box and cut away the surplus with a mat knife. Make a straight cut at both head and tail from the edge of the cloth overhanging the sides to the edge of the board on both sides. These cuts should be on the inside side of the head and tail strips. In other words, the cuts should be made so that when the edges of the cloth are turned into the box the cut edges or ends will lie smoothly along the inside edge of the joint.

First, turn the edges in at head and tail, working the cloth smoothly into the right angle joints; then turn the sides in (Fig. 10-9). Reglue them all lightly if necessary. If the cloth at head and tail do not meet exactly, either cut away the surplus if there is overlapping or fill in if there is a gap. Treat the mitred corners in the same fashion.

Cut the strips of cloth for head and tail with the grain direction in the cloth running from side to side, so when in position they will give the appearance of being a continuation of the pieces that cover the sides. In width cut them about 1/16 inch narrower than the thickness of the box, and in length—from fore edge to spine—1/16 inch in from the fore edge and extending 5/8 inch beyond the spine edge, or the same as that allowed for the turn of the sides. Glue these strips and lay in position. Before turning the ends into the inside of the box, cut the same amount off each side to make it the exact width of the inside measurement of the head and tail. Lay a piece of clean paper over the strips and rub firmly with a bonefolder, especially on the edges.

Cut a strip of binder's board the width of the thickness of the box, measured on the inside, and about 16 inches (40.6 cm) long. Fold this in half lengthwise, making it V-shaped. Slip this into the case with the bottom of the V supporting the open or spine side of the box. Put a pressboard on top of the box and weight it down with a brick until dry.

Slipcase with a door A door is a desirable feature, particularly when the case is to contain unbound material. In addition to protecting the contents more completely, it provides space for titling or identifying it, and it makes for a neater and more attractive item on a bookshelf.

The slipcase is constructed as described above, with 1 exception. The head, tail, and fore edge strips are cut the width of the thickness of the material plus 1/4 inch, or 4 thicknesses of an .059 binder's board. Regardless of the size of the slipcase or the weight of board used in its construction, an .059 board is appropriate for the door. If, however, a heavier board is used, adjust the above measurement accordingly.

The door described here is made as a separate unit and is not attached to the case in any way. It slips into the case, can be easily removed, and can be constructed to open from either the right or left side. It consists of 3 pieces of board, covered on the outside with book cloth and lined on the inside with paper.

Cut 1 piece of board the height of the slipcase—inside measurement—less 1/16 inch and in width the depth of the case, plus its thickness, plus 3 inches (7.6 cm). From this board cut 1 piece the depth of the case—inside measurement—less 3/32 inch; 1 piece the thickness of the case—inside measurement—less 3/16 inch; 2 joint strips 2 board thicknesses; and 1 piece 1 1/2 inches (3.8 cm) wide. Cut the corners on 1 edge of this strip (long dimension) at an angle. Mark 1 inch off on both edges of the right-angle corners; draw a diagonal line between the marks and cut.

If you want an indented label, follow the instructions in Chapter 8 under Patch Labels or Titles.

Lay the boards on the cloth, after getting 1 square corner; place a joint strip on both sides of the piece cut the thickness of the case less 3/16 inch. Mark the usual 3/4 inch (1.9 cm) turn on all 4 edges and then cut the cloth to size.

Glue the cloth and lay the boards in position with the joint strips. Cut the corners, remove the joint strips, and turn the edges as described under Making the Case. At the cut-off corners, or the diagonals, cut the cloth on the diagonal, leaving a 3/4-inch turn. Fold this over the edge of the board along with the other edges; pinch the cloth together and cut away the surplus; reglue the edges, if necessary. Lay the turn on the straight edges down first, then the diagonals.

A "pull" adds to the ease in opening the door. Make this of grosgrain ribbon or linen tape about 3/8 inch wide in a color that goes well with the covering material. Find the center from top to bottom on the inside edge of the 1 1/2-inch (3.8 cm) strip. This is the edge nearest the joint and the edge from which the corners were not cut. Slit the covering material at this point the width of the ribbon. Fold a 3 inch (7.6 cm) piece of ribbon in half lengthwise, slip the 2 ends through the slit, and pull 1/2 inch (1.2 cm) of them through to the inside. Lay them down on the 1 1/2-inch board and mark around them. Then cut out of the board

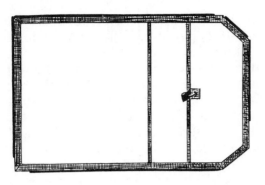

FIGURE 10-10.

an amount estimated to be the thickness of 2 pieces of ribbon; attach the ribbons to the indention in the board with mixture (Fig. 10-10).

Cut 2 strips of the covering cloth 1 1/2 inches (3.8 cm) wide and 1 inch (2.5 cm) shorter than the length of the door. Draw 2 lines on the center board 5/8 inch from the edges. Glue the cloth strips and lay them on the lines, centering them from top to bottom. Work the cloth into the joints, and lay the rest of it down on the adjoining board. If the center strip is less than 1 1/2 inches (3.8 cm) wide, cut 1 strip of cloth 1 1/2 inches wider than the center strip. Glue it and lay it in position, covering the center strip and the joints and centering it from head to tail.

Variations

If a full- or half-leather binding is to be stored in a slipcase, it is advisable to give it the added protection of a chemise or wrapper. A chemise protects the spine and eliminates any wear on the sides of the covers that might occur in slipping the book in and out of the case. It does not, however, protect the edges of the boards at head and tail. Some protection is afforded the edges when putting it into the case if the chemise is slightly longer than the book is tall and the book is carefully centered from head to tail in the chemise and slipped into the case in a horizontal position. Once the case is stood up vertically, however, there is nothing to prevent the book from sliding down and resting on the tail or bottom of the case; so the tail of the book gets no protection in the process of removing it from the case. For complete protection, a wrapper is preferable to a chemise. (See instructions for making a chemise and wrapper in next section.)

If the slipcase is to be covered with a material heavier than linen-finish book cloth, the added thickness of the material should be taken into consideration in cutting the boards to size.

If the slipcase is to be more than 1 1/2 inches (3.8 cm) thick, it is advisable to line the head, tail, and fore edge strips of binder's board with a piece of bond paper (grain direction same as the boards), before lining them with the lining paper. In such a situation these strips cannot be cut off the 2 boards previously described (or lined), but should be made up separately. This added bond paper along with the lining paper balances the pull set up by the bristol board and covering material on the outside—thus permitting these boards to remain flat.

If you wish to finish the edges of the open or spine side of the case with leather (generally done only if the spine of a leather binding is to be exposed—which is not recommended—or the chemise—see following section—is to have a leather spine), the 2 side boards are cut to cover the book just to the edge of the spine, and the spine edges of the boards are bevelled about 1/4 inch in from the edge. This bevelling is easier to do while the boards are flat and before the case is set together. The head and tail strips and the bristols on which they are mounted are cut about 1 inch (2.5 cm) longer than the side boards are wide. After the case is set together, the book is slipped into it; the shape of the rounding of the spine is drawn off at both head and tail, and the ends are cut to this shape and the edges sanded smooth (Fig. 10-11).

Leather for this edging should be pared very thin and all edges should be feathered. The pieces cut for the head and tail should be about 3/4 inch (1.9 cm) wider than the inside measurement of the case and long enough to extend into the case at the corners about 1/2 inch (1.2 cm) and to cover both sides of the portion of these strips that protrude beyond the body of the case (in other words, to cover both sides of the rounded ends) plus 1/2 inch. These pieces are attached to the inside of the case first, using paste, worked well into the corners, and allowed to dry before turning them over the rounded ends.

When ready to turn, repaste the leather and moisten well; pull snugly over the rounded edge and work down smoothly by easing the leather into little pleats (Fig. 10-12). This often looks impossible, but if the leather is thin and is kept moist it can be worked down very nicely, although it takes a bit of time and patience. The edge strips for the sides are cut about 1 inch wide and the exact length of the inside measurement of the case. Paste and moisten the leather; put 1/2 inch (1.2 cm) evenly in position on the inside of the case and fold the remaining leather down smoothly over the bevelled edge. The covering cloth is then cut to allow an even amount of leather exposed on each edge. The strips of cloth on head and tail can be cut off square or rounded to take the shape of the ends.

When a slipcase is very thin, it adds to the ease in removing a book from it if a ribbon or pull is attached. This is attached to 1 of the side boards after they are lined and cut to size and before the case is set together. Either grosgrain ribbon or linen tape about 3/8 inch wide works nicely for this (Fig. 10-13). In length the piece should be 1 1/2 times the width of the side, plus the thickness of the case, plus 2 inches (5 cm).

Find the center of 1 of the sides in both dimensions. Slit the board at this point, lengthwise, the width of the ribbon. Make the cut on the inside; poke the ribbon through the slit and pull about 1/2 inch (1.2 cm) of it through to the outside. Lay this down on the board, mark around it. Lift it up and cut the board out along the marks. Remove a layer or so of the board the estimated thickness of the ribbon; apply mixture to the ribbon and lay it in the cut-out area. If not enough was cut away, lift the ribbon and remove more board. If too much board was removed, add a layer or 2 of bond paper, and when dry, sand smooth.

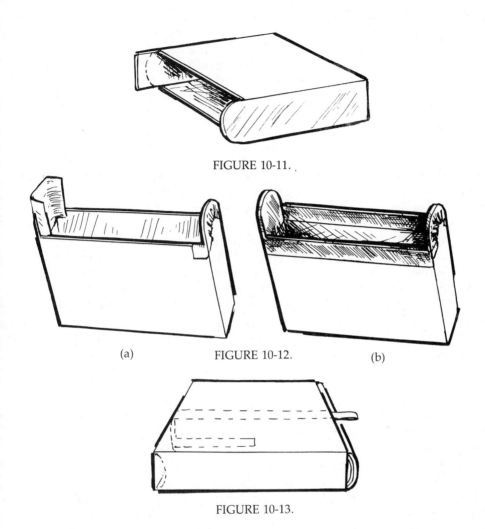

FIGURE 10-11.

(a)　　　FIGURE 10-12.　　　(b)

FIGURE 10-13.

Chemise and Wrapper

To give added protection for a book to be stored in a slipcase, a chemise is recommended. For more complete protection, use a wrapper (see preceding section, Slipcase—Variations).

Chemise This is constructed from 5 pieces of board—2 sides, a spine, and 2 fore edge flaps. The instructions here are for full cloth, lined with either paper or a lightweight, soft woven material. The same techniques used in making a cloth case binding (see Chapter 7) are applicable here, as are the variations in the use of other materials that follow in the same section.

Use a lightweight, acid-free bristol board. Cut all 5 pieces the length of the book plus 1/16 inch. In width, cut the 2 sides the width of the book less 1/8 inch measured from fore edge to the edge of the spine; the spine strip the exact width of the book spine; the inner fore edge flap, the thickness of the book less 1/8 inch; and the outer flap, the thickness of the book less 1/16 inch.

Make all joints 1/8 inch wide. Cut the covering material allowing the usual 3/4 inch (1.9 cm) turn on all 4 edges. Glue the cloth and lay the boards in position. Before turning the edges, line the spine strip on the inside with a piece of acid-free bond paper cut the exact size of the spine; attach with glue applied to the paper. This will produce a bit of warping that will aid in shaping the spine to fit the rounding of the book.

If a paper lining is used, first cover the joints with strips of the same cloth used in covering. These should be 3/4 inch (1.9 cm) wide and the length of the paper used for the lining. Then add the paper in 5 separate pieces, pasting the paper. If a woven material is used, it can be left in 1 piece, eliminating the necessity of the additional cloth joint strips. See Case Binding in Chapter 7, for handling unsized fabrics.

When the chemise is complete, fold it around a batch of boards that are equivalent in thickness to the book for which the chemise was made, and weight down until dry. This will give the spine a chance to dry in a slightly curved position. Do not, however, wrap it around the book until it is thoroughly dry.

For titling, follow the instructions for Titling in Chapter 8.

Wrapper This is made like a chemise with 2 exceptions: The sides, the spine, and the fore edge flaps are cut in length the exact height of the book and head and tail flaps are added.

Cut the head and tail flaps from the same bristol with the grain direction running as if they were a continuation of the side to which they are attached. Each flap is made from 2 pieces of board; 1 piece covers the head or tail and the other folds down against the cover of the book. In width, cut these the same as the sides; the 2 strips that will cover the head and tail the same thickness as the inner fore edge flap; and the 2 pieces that will fold down against the book about 3 inches (7.6 cm) high, or they can each be half the length of the book less 1/8 inch, so that they will meet, or nearly so, when in position on the book.

Before the edges of the covering cloth are turned, cut the cloth at the right angles formed by the addition of the flaps (Fig. 10-14). When the edges are turned at these points, there will be a small uncovered area. To avoid this, add a small piece of cloth at these 4 points before turning the edges.

When complete, put under weight as described for a chemise. However, leave the end flaps exposed and weight down separately.

Solander or Folding Box

This is sometimes referred to as a folding box, a telescoping box with a drop-down spine, or a clamshell box, although it in no way resembles a clam shell. It provides excellent protection for fine bindings, first editions, unbound catalogs, paperbacks, or collections of letters.

This style of box is built or set together from separate pieces of binder's board and covered. It consists of 2 boxes or trays, closed at

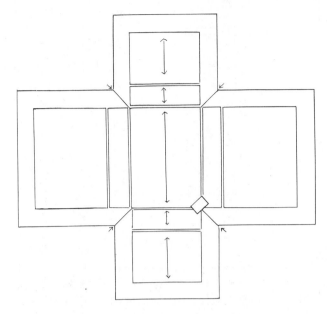

FIGURE 10-14.

head, tail, and fore edges and open at the spine. The inner, and smaller, box is made to fit the book or material that it is to house, and the outer, and larger, box is made to fit over the smaller box. Both boxes are attached to a case or cover, which in construction and general appearance is similar to the cover for a case binding (Chapter 7). The spine in this cover serves as the spine of the box and drops down, or lies flat on the table, when the box is open. The inner box is made first and covered before the pieces for the outer box are cut; and the outer box is completed before the case is cut.

An .059 binder's board is suitable for octavos and smaller material; an .082 for quartos and larger, unless the material is unusually large or heavy; then a heavier board is advised for the construction of the boxes.

The directions here are for a case constructed of .059 binder's board, covered in 1-color, linen-finish book cloth and lined with paper. Since this case is constructed in stages, a summary of materials is not given here. They are noted as the work progresses. Variations follow the instructions.

Inner Box Line up the head and fore edges of the book along 2 edges of a piece of binder's board on which 1 right-angle corner has been cut. The grain direction in the board should run with the vertical measurement of the book, as usual.

In length, the board should be the exact size of the book plus 1/16 inch, or 1 thickness of an .059 board. Mark the board and make the cut. In width, it should be the width of the book plus 1/8 inch or 2 thicknesses of an .059 board. Use a triangle against the spine in arriving at the width, and make allowance for raised bands, if any. Mark and cut.

The head and tail strips are cut the exact width of the board, with the grain direction running as if they were cut off 1 end of the board. The

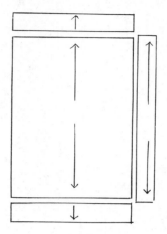

FIGURE 10-15.

fore edge strip is cut the length of the board plus 2 thicknesses of this same board, grain direction long (Fig. 10-15). In height all 3 strips are the thickness of the book, plus 1 thickness of the board being used, plus 1/16 inch; or the thickness of the book, plus 2 thicknesses of .059 board. To arrive at the proper height, lay the book on the board that is cut to size and place on top of it a piece of .059 board. Make the measurement from the surface of the table to the highest point, which is usually the spine area. Cut all 3 pieces to this measurement.

Setting the box together Put a smooth piece of paper on a large press-board. Glue the edges of the binder's board or bottom of the box at head, tail, and fore edge. Lay on the pressboard and weight down.

Attach the head and tail strips first, then the fore edge. Put a thin line of glue, estimated as wide as the bottom board is thick, on the face of the strips along the bottom edge; and on the head and tail strips glue the edge of the board that will rest against the fore edge strip. Set these in position against the glued edges of the bottom board, and line up the ends exactly with the sides of the board. Check with a triangle to be sure that the strips are vertical and at a right angle with the bottom; hold in position by placing small weights on both sides of the strips. Glue the fore edge strip along the bottom edge and along the face of the ends that will rest against the ends of the head and tail strips; set in position as described above; set the whole aside to dry (Fig. 10-16). When dry, turn the box upside down on a pile of pressboards for support and sand all glued edges smooth.

Covering the box The covering cloth is 1 long strip. Rough-cut a strip across the roll of cloth—from selvage to selvage—estimated twice the height of the sides of the box plus about 3 inches (7.6 cm). This should allow for squaring it up before cutting it to the exact size. Cut 1 edge and 1 end straight and at a right angle to each other. Draw a line, on the wrong side of the cloth, along its length 1/2 inch (1.2 cm) in from the edge just cut, and a line on the cut end also 1/2 inch in from the edge. This should produce a right angle. Wrap a long strip of paper or a cloth tape measure around the outside of the box; to this measurement add 1 inch (2.5 cm) and cut the cloth this length. In width it should be

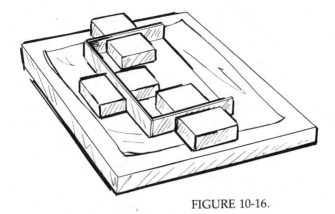

FIGURE 10-16.

twice the height of the sides plus 1 inch; mark and cut. After making the cuts and before gluing, check this strip with the box to be sure its size is correct.

Glue the entire strip, if it is no longer than about 24 inches (60.9 cm). If longer, it can be glued in stages. Working from 1 edge, set the spine edge of the tail and the bottom edge of the box in the right-angle corner made by the drawn lines; rub down well from the inside of the box. Turn the box along the line (Fig. 10-17), laying the fore edge on the glued cloth and rub down. Turn the box again so that the head is on the cloth and rub firmly. Pick the box up and check all 3 sides to be sure that the cloth is well stuck and free of wrinkles.

Turn the edges of the cloth at the bottom of the box first. Support the box in an inverted position with a pile of pressboards or something small enough to fit inside the box and high enough to permit the edges of the cloth to hang free (Fig. 10-18). Pinch the cloth together at the 2 corners where the fore edge strip joins the head and tail strips; cut away the surplus, producing a mitred effect. Reglue lightly all 3 edges of the cloth and lay them down onto the bottom of the box, pulling them firmly and evenly over the edges (Fig. 10-19).

Next, make the following cuts in the cloth. The finished box will be neater in appearance if the cutting points are first drawn off using a right-angle triangle against the edges of the boards. At both head and tail on the spine or open side of the box, cut the 1/2 inch of cloth that extends be-yond the edge at 2 places. At the bottom of the box make a straight cut from the edge of the cloth to the edge of the board that will permit the cloth on the edge to turn in flush against the inside of the bottom. On the top make a straight cut in line with the edge of the head and tail strips from the edge of the cloth to within 1/8 inch from the board. From this point continue the cut in a slightly curved fashion out to the edge of the cloth. The object of this cut is to remove overlapping material on the turn, leaving sufficient material to adequately cover the corner of the board.

On the fore edge make straight cuts at both head and tail, from the edge of the cloth to the edge of the board, which will permit the cloth on the fore edge strip to turn in flush against the inside of both head and tail strips (Fig. 10-20).

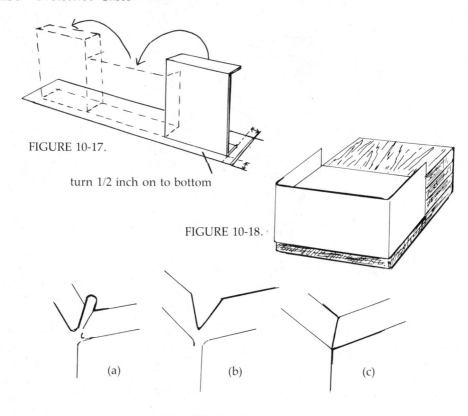

FIGURE 10-17.

turn 1/2 inch on to bottom

FIGURE 10-18.

(a)   (b)   (c)

FIGURE 10-19.

After these cuts are made, reglue lightly all edges as they are turned. The edges are turned in the following sequence at head and tail. First, turn the little tabs that are attached to the bottom of the box on the open side into the inside of the box and work the cloth smoothly into the right-angle joints. Next, turn the cloth at the spine edge of these 2 strips, working it down over the right-angle corners of the strips. Then turn the edges at head and tail and work the cloth smoothly into the right-angle joints formed with the fore edge strip; finally, turn the edge on the fore edge strip. The cloth on all turns should be pulled snugly

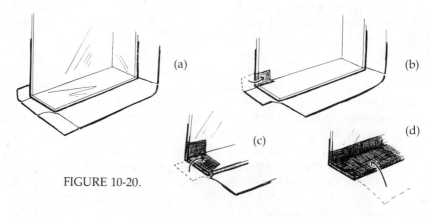

(a)   (b)   (c)   (d)

FIGURE 10-20.

and firmly against the edges of the boards and rubbed smooth with a bonefolder. Using a right-angle triangle and a scalpel, miter the cloth on the inside corners of the box.

When the job is complete, place the box on a flat surface and fill it up with pressboards the size of the interior of the box. If boards of the proper size are not available, place weights on both sides of the head, tail, and fore edge strips, so that they will dry in a vertical position.

Outer or top box The bottom of the top box is cut the size of the outside measurements of the inner box, plus 1/8 inch in length and 1/16 inch in width. The head, tail, and fore edge strips are cut in width the outside height of the inner box, plus 1 board thickness (representing the bottom of the top box) plus 1/16 inch. In length these strips are cut as described earlier for the inner box, and the whole is set together in the same manner. It is also covered in the same fashion as just described for the inner box.

Before making the case, give some thought to the manner in which the box will be titled. For an indented title label or for titling directly on the spine, see Chapter 8 under Titling, and Patch Labels or Titles.

The other steps are the same as those given for the inner box.

Making the case Cut the 2 boards for the case 1/4 inch longer and 1/8 inch wider than the outside dimensions of the larger box; this will give 1/8 inch square at head, tail, and fore edges. Cut the spine strip of the same board the length of the boards, and in width the outside height of the inner or smaller box, plus 1/2 the difference between the height of the 2 boxes. To arrive at this measurement, place the fore edges of the 2 boxes back to back on a flat surface and measure the space between the top edge of the smaller box and the top edge of the larger one (Fig. 10–21). Add half of this measurement to the outside height of the smaller box and cut the spine strip to this width. Cut 2 strips to be used as gauges for the joints 5/32 inch or 2 1/2 board thicknesses (.059).

Cut the cloth and make the case as described under Case Binding, Chapter 7.

Line the inside of the case—the 2 boards and the spine—and the outside bottom of both boxes with bond paper, grain direction running with that of the boards. Cut the paper to fit within the turned edges of the cloth; most of the exposed surface of the board should be covered, although an exact fit is not necessary. Glue the paper, lay in position, and weight down until dry.

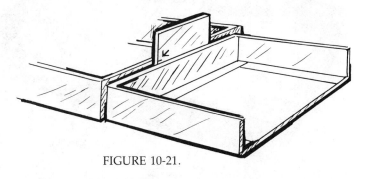

FIGURE 10-21.

Setting the boxes on the case Before starting this step, make a mark on the inside of the spine indicating the head or top of the case, and assemble a number of pressboards that are as near the size of the box as possible and will produce a stack slightly higher than the interior height of the box (Fig. 10-22).

The larger box is set on first and is attached to the front board of the case or to the left-hand side. Lay the case on a pressboard; glue the bottom of the box; put it in position on the case, centering it from head to tail, and lining the open or spine side up exactly with the inside edge of the board. Hold this in position for 1 or 2 minutes; then fill the box with the pressboards and put it in the press, while still resting on the pressboard. After tightening the press, check to be sure that the box is still in proper position. If so, leave it in the press for at least 30 minutes. If, however, it has slipped out of position, remove it from the press, reposition it, and return to the press.

The smaller or inner box is attached in the same way. Immediately after getting it in position, weight it down with weights that are shallower than the box and close the outer box over it. If all is well, fill it with pressboards and put in the press as described above.

Lining the spine and joints Cut a strip of the cloth used in covering the length of the inside of the smaller box, and in width, the width of the spine, plus the joints, plus 1 1/2 inches (3.8 cm). Draw a line on the smaller box 5/8 inch in from the spine edge. Glue the cloth; lay 1 edge of

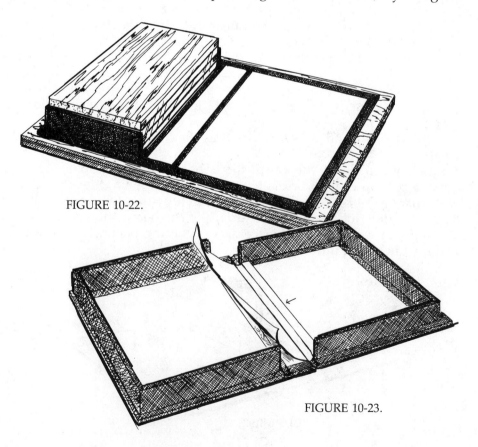

FIGURE 10-22.

FIGURE 10-23.

it on the line while holding the rest of it free from the case, and rub down well. Next, work it into the first joint with a bonefolder. Lay it on the spine; work it into the second joint; and finally lay the remaining cloth onto the floor of the larger box (Fig. 10-23). Rub it down well and weight down until dry.

Lining the boxes In selecting the paper for the lining or floors of the 2 boxes, bear in mind that the book will come in contact with the material selected and that 1 of the functions of the lining is to aid in the protection of the book.

Two pieces of paper will be needed, 1 for each box. They are not, however, cut the same size. The grain direction in the paper should run with the vertical measurement of the box. For each box cut a piece of paper 1/4 inch shorter and 1/4 inch narrower than the inside measurement of the box. Some papers stretch more than others and nearly all stretch more cross-grain than with the grain, so take this into account in cutting these pieces. Paste the paper and lay in position; center it from head to tail; offset it 1/8 inch in from the spine edge of the box and let it fall where it will along the inside of the fore edge. Cover the linings with pieces of clean wastepaper and rub well. Then cover them with clean pulpboards and weight down until dry.

Dust strip This is a covered strip attached to the spine. It gives added protection to the contents of the box in that it helps prevent dust from seeping into the head of the box in the spine area.

Cut a strip of .059 binder's board 1/16 shorter than the interior length of the smaller box, and in width 3 board thicknesses (.059) narrower than the spine strip. Cover 1 side of this with the same type of paper used to line the boxes; cut the paper 1 inch (2.5 cm) wider and 1 inch longer than the board. Paste the paper; lay the board in the center of it, leaving a 1/2 inch (1.2 cm) margin of paper on all 4 edges. Cut the corners on the paper and turn all edges down onto the board. Attach this to the spine of the box by putting a narrow line of mixture around all 4 inside edges. Lay in position, centering from left to right and from head to tail position it so that it will fit into the smaller box when the case is closed. Cover with a pulpboard and weight down until dry.

If the spine was not titled earlier, title now as planned.

Variations

When constructing a box from binder's board heavier than .059, the only measurement that need be adjusted or changed from the preceding instructions is the width of the joints in the case. The width of the joints have a direct relationship to the thickness of the board used. They should consistently be as wide as 2 thicknesses of the board used, plus 2 thicknesses of the material used to cover the inside of the joints.

If a case is 2 or more inches (5 cm) thick, many binders feel it desirable to line the inside of the smaller box with paper instead of bringing the covering cloth all the way to the floor on the inside of the box. In this case, the covering cloth turns into the box only about 1/2 inch (1.2 cm) and should be cut accordingly. The paper lining is cut in 4 pieces, grain direction running with that of the board to which it will be attached. In height, cut the strips for head, tail, and fore edges the interior depth of the box plus 1/2 inch (the extra width covers the joint and goes onto the floor). In length, cut the head and tail strips the width of the box plus 1/2 inch (here again the extra length covers the joints), and the fore edge strip the exact length of the interior measurement of the box.

The head and tail strips are added first. Paste the strip for the head; lay it in position, setting it back about 1/8 inch from the spine edge, and 1/8 inch down from the top edge of the box. Rub smooth; work the added length into the right-angle corner and onto the fore edge strip, and the added width into the joint and onto the floor or bottom of the box. Pinch the surplus in the corner together and cut it away. Add the strip at the tail in the same way; then add the fore edge strip, working the surplus width into the joint and onto the bottom of the box. Mitre the corners.

Cut the piece of paper for the bottom 1/4 inch shorter and 1/4 inch narrower than the inside measurements of the box. Paste it and lay in position; center from head to tail and offset it at the spine edge 1/8 inch and let it fall where it will on the fore edge. Cover with clean wastepaper and rub well, then cover with a clean pulpboard and weight down until dry.

If you wish a fabric lining such as silk, velvet, or suede cloth, this must be taken into account in determining the size of the smaller box and in the depth of the larger box. The fabric is not attached directly to the inside of the boxes, but mounted on lightweight bristol, which is then tipped in—not solidly attached.

Select the bristol and the fabric and make up 2 small samples that can be used in arriving at the proper size of the smaller box. Cut 2 pieces of bristol about 2 inches (5 cm) long and in width the estimated height of the box. Cut 2 pieces of cloth 1/2 inch (1.2 cm) larger in both dimensions than the bristol. Lay the bristol on the wrong side of the cloth in such a position that 1/2 inch of cloth can be turned onto the bristol at 2 edges. Apply mixture to the 2 edges of the bristol (Fig. 10-24), cut the corner on the cloth, and turn the edges onto the bristol.

Add the combined thickness of both of these samples to the measurements given earlier in arriving at the length of the bottom board for the smaller box; 1 thickness to both the width and depth, and 1 thickness to the depth of the larger box.

When the box is complete up to the point of attaching the fabric

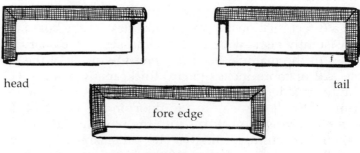

head   tail

fore edge

FIGURE 10-24.

lining, line all exposed board surfaces with bond paper to balance the pull from the covering material.

The sequence in attaching a fabric lining is the same as that for paper. Cut the head, tail, and fore edge strips of bristol in width the interior depth of the smaller box less 1/8 inch. In length cut the head and tail strips the interior width of the box less 1/8 inch; and the fore edge strip the interior length of the box less 3 thicknesses of 1 of the samples previously made up. Cut the cloth to cover these strips 1 inch (2.5 cm) wider and 1 inch longer than the bristols. Grain direction of both bristols and fabric should run with the grain direction of the component parts of the box.

On the head and tail strips, turn the fabric as described in making the samples, at the spine edge and the top edge. Leave the other 1/2 inch of fabric free at the fore edge and bottom. Let these dry under pressure before attaching to the box.

When putting these in position, apply mixture to the floor of the box along the joint and at the corner to the fore edge of the box. Then apply a thin line of mixture to the 2 turned edges of the fabric on the strips. Set these in position, 1/8 inch in from the spine edge and 1/8 inch down from the top edge of the box. Pull the fabric snugly over the bristol, work it into the joint and onto the pasted area of the floor, into the corner, and onto the pasted area of the fore edge. Put a strip of clean wasteboard on both inside and outside edges of the box and hold in position with 2 or 3 C-clamps. This will supply the necessary pressure to hold the lining in place until the adhesive is dry.

Turn the fabric at both ends and the top edge of the fore edge strip and attach as just described, applying mixture to the floor of the box and to the 3 turned edges of the strip. Mitre the corners and remove the surplus material.

Cut the bristols for the floor of both boxes the size of the interior measurements of the boxes less 1/4 inch in both dimensions. Cut the fabric 1 inch (2.5 cm) larger in both dimensions; turn all 4 edges and put under pressure until dry (described under Preparing Endsheet Sections —silk doublures— Chapter 6). When dry, apply mixture to all 4 edges, lay in position, and weight down. Prepare and attach the dust strip in the same fashion.

These cases can be covered with a variety of materials or combinations of materials. In general the techniques used in their construction are the same as just described. A few exceptions or suggestions follow.

If leather is used, it must be pared—and a lot of paring is required.

If the boxes are to be covered in paper, all joints should be reinforced with lawn or airplane linen before the paper is added.

For a two-tone effect on both the case and the boxes, first decide on the color for the spine and how much of this color should show on the boards. Once this width is determined, the head and tail strips of both boxes are covered with this same color, for the same width on the open or spine side of the boxes. The second color is abutted to the first.

If a rounded spine is desired, it can be made by gluing several layers of binder's board together (the number would depend on the extent of the rounding wanted). Start with a board the proper width of the spine;

cut each additional board a little narrower than the preceding one. Apply glue to both boards in putting them together. When dry use a carpenter's rasp to get the general shape; then finish it off with sandpaper. Attach it in a couple of spots with glue to the edges of pressboards held in a finishing press for ease in handling. If rounded molding can be obtained from a lumberyard, it is a bit easier and faster to use. If it is not the desired width, buy it larger, center the spine strip on it, and sand away the surplus edges. Cover it with a piece of acid-free paper before incorporating it into the case.

If a clasp or closure is wanted, fashion it in 2 pieces and attach these to the outside bottom of the boxes, centered from head to tail on the fore edge, before the boxes are attached to the case.

11 Conservation Work

To know what to do is Wisdom;
To know how to do it is Skill;
To do it as it should be done is Service.

This quotation sums up the 3 guiding principles that should govern all conservation work. Wisdom combines knowledge, insight, and judgment, and these qualities are developed only through years of experience and thoughtful study. Skill is the ability to execute effectively the fruits of wisdom. And service is the willingness to combine wisdom and skill in doing a job "as it should be done."

Conservation work is an extension of hand binding in that additional knowledge, beyond the mastery of techniques, is expected of a competent conservator. His or her horizons should be broad enough to see the book as a part of a cultural heritage, not just as an isolated item. This requires respect for the printed word and some knowledge of the history of the bindings and the techniques and materials used in their production. The conservator should know when certain techniques and materials were first used and be able to identify them; he or she should have some experience with their reactions to various treatments and some appreciation of their appropriateness for a specific job. It is not expected that every conservator carry on the tip of the tongue detailed information regarding these things. It is expected, however, that the conservator be aware of the significance of this information and familiarize himself or herself with the sources where it can be found.

The ideal objective in any conservation job is to return the item as nearly as possible to its original condition. Structurally, it should be sound and durable; any repair or replacement of missing portions should be skillfully and unobtrusively done; and the overall job should be historically accurate and aesthetically pleasing.

In putting these objectives into practice on books, other considerations, however, enter into the picture. A few of these are the quality of the paper on which the book is printed; the condition of the materials that make up the binding; its anticipated or potential use; its historic significance; and its value. It would, for example, be desirable to preserve all parts of a valuable binding of historic significance that in the future would be used primarily for exhibition purposes, even though the materials were deteriorating. If, on the other hand, the book were to be subject to frequent use, it would probably be wiser to replace with new materials, in the style and kind of the original, those areas most vulnerable to wear. Each volume requires individual consideration in the light of the knowledge at hand.

Obviously, the first decision that has to be made in handling any conservation job is "what to do." If the wisdom to "know what to do" is lacking, be smart enough to recognize this and do nothing to the volume until advice is obtained. Protect it, instead, in its present condition by either boxing it or simply wrapping it carefully in acid-free bristol or paper and storing it in some safe place. This same recommendation is applicable in cases where the money for a proper conservation job is unavailable, and in cases where it is questionable whether the value of the book justifies the expense. A delaying tactic is generally preferable to makeshift or shortcut repairs. Far too many interesting and valuable books have been defaced, and in some cases rendered valueless, by moves of false economy, or by well-intentioned—but not so well-informed—binders working under the supervision of or with instructions from unschooled and indifferent custodians or owners. Routinely, conservation work is not of an emergency nature. There is time for thought and consideration before action is taken. No volume that has survived 50 years or more is suddenly going to pieces tomorrow because it was not restored yesterday or today.

It is not feasible to attempt to anticipate every problem that might arise in the conservation of unknown volumes—the variables are many and the possibilities infinite. So rather than go into great detail on a few probable problems, the attempt here is to set down a few general guidelines applicable to all, or most, conservation work. Then some of the techniques peculiar to conservation work are described in the same order as those given earlier for the binding or rebinding of a book. The instructions that follow, when used in conjunction with those given earlier, should provide sufficient information for the proper handling of a great variety of problems.

General Guidelines

Broadly speaking, it is advisable to preserve all of an original binding, or all that has survived. It is especially desirable to preserve the original board papers and endleaves if they contain names, inscriptions, early bookplates, and the like. Information of this kind is often relevant to the provenance of the book.

In removing the binding, save every fragment, mark it in some way to indicate its proper position, wrap it up carefully, and store it in some safe place. Obviously, the format of the book should not be altered when the binding is to be restored, nor should the edges of a rare book be trimmed when it is necessary to rebind it.

In cases where it is necessary or desirable to introduce new materials, take the time and effort to locate or produce those that match the original in texture and color. Do not, for instance, reback or retitle a calfskin binding with goatskin, or vice versa. Do not use stark white machine-made wove paper as replacement for board papers and endleaves when the originals were handmade laid paper that has darkened or mellowed with age. Do not put exposed cloth or leather hinges in an early volume where the originals were paper. Do not replace sewn or worked headbands with commercially woven ones.

Some restorers have followed the practice of deliberately distressing new materials by mutilating them so that they take on the appearance of the original. New materials can, however, be made to blend or harmonize with the old through careful selection and dyeing, if necessary, without jeopardizing their strength. This would seem to be the sounder procedure. The accepted practice in introducing new materials in the rebacking (adding a new spine), corner repairs, re-edging of boards, and replacing or repairing broken inner joints is to lift up the original material and insert the new under it. In this way a minimum amount of the new material is exposed.

When the binding on a volume of value is missing completely, rebind it in the style of the period in which it was published. This information can be obtained by a visit to a rare book collection or by consulting the catalogs of historical exhibitions. In choosing new materials, always try to find suitable ones of known quality, strength, and durability.

Worksheets It is particularly important that detailed records be kept on all conservation work. This information should not only be retained by the conservator, but a copy of it, in neat and legible form, should remain with the volume. Had binders and conservators in the past kept such records, conservators today would know a great deal more about the causes of deterioration (see Chapter 6 under Checking and Taking the Book Apart).

Before any work is done, write a detailed description of the book when received. If possible, take a photograph or photographs of it. If not, make a rubbing of the spine. To make a rubbing, place a thin piece of bond paper over the spine, attach it so that it cannot shift, and rub it with graphite or a heelball (a combination of wax and lamp black made for this purpose).

Checking the book for completeness Follow instructions in Chapter 6 under Checking and Taking the Book Apart.

Taking the book apart and removing the binding Here the instructions differ from those when the binding is not to be saved. If the binding is already detached from the book, wrap it and put it away. If the joints are broken and the boards are still attached, carefully cut them free and lay aside in a safe place.

If a hollow back binding, removing the spine presents no particular problem, for it is more often than not free on 1 edge. If so, free it on the other with a knife or bonefolder, and put it away along with the boards. If it is still in position on the book, insert a small bonefolder in 1 end of the spine and work it over to 1 side freeing the edge; then free the entire edge by working the bonefolder or a thin knife along it. Repeat on the other side.

The spine on a tight back binding is considerably more difficult to remove and requires patient, careful work. After the boards are removed, place the book in a finishing press with protective boards on front and back. It is recommended that the spine be removed in its dry state. Some conservators advocate applying a coat of paste to soften the adhesive. This possibly works with some leathers, but is a hazardous practice since many old leathers shrivel up, take on a charred appearance, or disintegrate when exposed to moisture for even a short period of time. It is safer to remove it dry, even if it cannot be removed in 1 piece.

Have on hand a strip of board on which the spine can be laid after it is removed. If it comes off in pieces, lay the pieces on the board in their proper order or position. This facilitates reconstruction.

Start at 1 edge of the spine and work a thin knife blade carefully under the leather. Keep the sharpened edge of the knife against the spine of the book, and pry the leather loose for about 1/8 inch along the entire length of the spine. Return to the starting point, lift up another fraction, and so on until the center of the spine is reached. Repeat this on the other edge until the spine is free.

While the book is still in the finishing press, clean up the spine of the book as described in Chapter 6 under Checking and Taking the Book Apart.

If the book appears to be in good condition, do not "pull" it. A simple way to test the strength of the sewing is to open up the volume at the center of several signatures and pull gently on the thread in 2 or 3 places with a fingernail or a small bonefolder. If it withstands this test, leave it intact. If, however, the threads are rotten and break easily, it is advisable to resew it; in which case follow earlier instructions in Chapter 6.

Inner hinges If no signatures of the book itself require resewing, but new endleaves and flyleaves will be sewn on, attach the inner hinges to the spine edge of the first and last pages of the book. Fold the hinge in half lengthwise. Attach half of it with mixture to the page, lining up the folded edge of the hinge exactly along the edge of the spine. The other half of the hinge is left free, and the endleaf and flyleaf are later attached to it. One hinge is attached to the first page of the book and 1 to the last page in this manner.

End sheet sections When the endleaves and flyleaves can be saved, do not replace them. Remove them from the book, make any necessary repairs, add new hinges as described in Chapter 6 under Preparing Endsheet Sections, and resew them. If the inner joints between the endleaves and board papers were originally paper, reproduce them in the same way. Use a paper matching the original in color and texture and reinforce it with lawn or airplane linen.

When the endleaves and board papers are marbled or patterned, try to locate some strong paper for the hinges the color of the predominant color in the original. Moriki, a strong Japanese paper, is made in several colors and works well for this. As in the case of other paper hinges, these should be reinforced with cloth. If no paper suitable in color is available, use a good strong paper, and after the hinge is in position, carefully paint with watercolors the pattern of the original paper on the exposed portion of the hinge.

In cases where it is necessary to replace the endleaves and flyleaves, do so with paper matching as nearly as possible the original (see Dyeing of Materials later in this chapter). Make these up and cut them to size following earlier instructions (Chapter 6), with this exception: Leave the fore edge of the section uncut. Cut this after the section has been sewn on and the book backed. In reshaping the joint of the book, there is an indeterminate pullback on this section. When it is in its proper position, the fore edge can be cut to conform exactly with the fore edge of the pages it adjoins.

Treatment of edges The edges of a restored volume should be left unaltered. If, however, they are unusually dirty and it seems desirable to clean them up a bit, follow the instructions in Chapter 6 under Treatment of Edges for cleaning with a pink pearl eraser.

When new endleaves or flyleaves have been added, or missing portions of pages have been replaced and their edges are conspicuously clean next to the edges of the book, color them. Place the book in a finishing press and screw it up firmly. Color the edges of the pages with a watercolor pencil, either dry or moistened, whichever works best. These pencils come in a great variety of colors and shades, and with a little care the "new" edges can be made to blend with the original.

Sewing Although the entire book does not need to be resewn, often the first and last signatures are loose or in need of washing, flattening, edge repairs, and the like. If so, remove the signatures by cutting the threads in the center of them. Pull the threads out at the kettle stitches so that they can be properly secured when the signatures are resewn. Make the necessary repairs, guard the folds, add the inner hinges, and resew through the folds. This is preferable, for reasons that should be obvious, to securing them in position by overcasting or whip stitching, or tipping them on—methods used by some conservators. Overcasting means sewing over and over through the spine into the joint on the first and last pages of the book.

Frequently, if a volume has previously been restored, the first few and the last few pages will have been glued in position. When this is so, remove the affected pages as a unit and soak them in lukewarm water until they can be separated without damage. Dry and flatten them in the usual way.

When the cords or tapes on which a book was originally sewn are broken off at the joints, attach linen tapes, using mixture, to the spine between the cords, allowing them to extend 1 inch beyond the edge of the spine on both front and back. These provide something around which the removed signatures or new endsheet sections can be sewn, and they serve as a substitute for the cords in reattaching the boards. This, in general, is safer than attempting to extend the original cords by splicing on additional lengths and reputedly is just as strong.

In resewing only a few signatures or just the endsheet sections, sew first through the outermost signature that is in position, leaving a tail of thread at the starting point; this provides an anchor to which the resewn signatures can be attached. Then add the signatures that are to be resewn in the usual fashion. In doing this, tie the tails of the original thread to the new thread at the appropriate points. (See the preceding page.)

Attaching the endsheet section to the inner hinge See Chapter 6 under Attaching the Endsheets.

Reducing the swell If the book has been resewn, follow instructions in Chapter 6 under Reducing the Swell. If not, omit this step.

Gluing the spine, rounding, and backing If the book has been resewn follow instructions in Chapter 6 (Gluing the Spine, Rounding the Spine) and Chapter 7 (Backing). If it has not been resewn, glue the spine in its rounded state. Reshape it if the rounding is uneven. Often the head of the spine is less round than the tail; this is due to the fact that a book tends to fall forward in its binding when standing on a shelf, because its fore edge is unsupported. Generally the backing needs very little attention. It is a good idea, however, to put the book in the backer, along the lines of the original backing, and sharpen up the joints. This is particularly desirable if signatures have been removed and replaced or new endsheet sections sewn on. Be sure that any loose threads created by removing a signature be secured on the spine before it is lined up.

Headbands These are attached or worked in the usual manner (see Chapter 7). In each case they should conform in style and color, if possible, to the originals. If any portion of the headbands was present when the book was received, it is generally not difficult to determine the type and color or colors of thread used and the style. If they were entirely missing, fragments of the original can sometimes be located inside the book. If no clue can be found, replace them in the customary style of the period in which the book was published. If no headbands are evident, it is possible, of course, that the original had none. If there is a small line at head and tail of the spine that is cleaner than the rest of the edges, this indicates that headbands were present at some time, in which case they should be added.

The final step in the restoration of the book itself is the lining up of the spine. This is done in the usual way depending on the style of binding (see Chapter 7 for binding styles). When this is done, put the book away and restore or repair the binding.

Leather Bindings

Many of the steps for leather bindings are also applicable to other types of covering material.

When new leather is to be added, the first step is to locate a suitable leather. If, in order to get a good color match, it is necessary to dye the leather, estimate the amount needed for rebacking, corner, edge repair, and so on, and dye all at the same time (see Dyeing of Materials later in this chapter). It is easier to do any necessary work on the boards while they are detached from the book; do so after dyeing the leather.

Board papers If these are to be replaced—although they should be saved if possible—remove them dry. A small amount of moisture can be applied to bookplates or other added notations if it is needed to remove them without damage. Perhaps the most efficient way to remove them is by using a wetting agent. (These are sold under various trade names and advertised for this purpose. Directions for use generally accompany them.)

For removing the paper, use a scalpel or thin-bladed knife. Hold the blade almost horizontal with the board. Work the blade under the

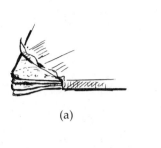

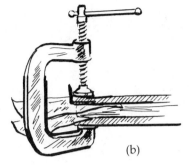

(a)

(b)

FIGURE 11-1.

paper, lift up an edge of it, and peel as much away as possible. Continue until the paper is completely removed. A small amount of moisture on the paper where it overlaps the covering material will clean up this area. Try to avoid digging into the board with the knife. When the paper is removed, sand the board and burnish it with a bonefolder.

Corner repairs and re-edging boards If the corners of the boards are soft and bent, lift up the leather on both the outside and inside of the board. If it is necessary to split the leather, make the cut on the inside edge of the board. Open up the affected area of the board in several places—split it, in other words—and insert an adhesive (mixture works well) between the layers of the board. Place a piece of wax paper between the board and the leather on both sides, add a scrap of binder's board for protection, and put one or more C-clamps on it (Fig. 11-1). This should straighten out the corner and stiffen the board. Set aside until dry. This same technique can be applied to damaged edges.

If a portion of the corner is missing entirely, open up the edge near the center; insert a piece of bristol board larger than the missing area and secure in position with an adhesive. While this is drying, pulp some binder's board by scraping with a knife. Mix this with paste to a puttylike consistency and rebuild the missing corner on the bristol board, first 1 side and then the other (Fig. 11-2). When this is nearly dry, compress it with a bonefolder, cut away the surplus, and put between C-clamps as described above. This mixture tends to shrink in drying, so make the application fairly generous. Set aside until thoroughly dry, then sand smooth.

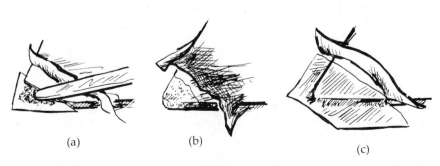

(a)

(b)

(c)

FIGURE 11-2.

There are available plastic wedges that work well for certain types of corner repair. The technique involved in their use is similar to that described above.

Recovering corners Cut the prepared leather for corner repair much the way it is cut for corners on a half-leather binding (see Chapter 7 under Cutting Leather to Size and Paring). It should be large enough to cover the missing area and extend about 1/8 inch under the original covering leather; the turn on the edges need not, however, be the usual 3/4 inch (1.9 cm), but just wide enough to handle easily and slip under the leather or board paper on the inside of the board.

Pare the edges that will be covered by the original material rather thin and feather them. Lift up only enough of the original to slip the new leather under it. Apply mixture to the board and lay the leather in position. When this is dry, turn the edges, slipping the edges of the new leather under the lifted-up area on the inside of the board.

After the corner or corners are covered, and before the original leather is laid down, sand the underside of it. Lay a piece of bristol on the new leather to protect it. Hold a small piece of binder's board on the surface of the leather to be sanded as a support, and using an emery board, bevel the underside of the leather and feather the edge. Blow or brush away all sanded fragments; lay the leather in position, and if it feels smooth, paste it down. The easiest way to get this down neatly is to apply mixture to a piece of bristol board; slip it under the unattached portion of the leather, press lightly on the surface of it, thus transferring the mixture to the leather. Remove the bristol, lay the leather in position, cover with a piece of paper, and rub lightly with a bonefolder. Immediately remove any adhesive that might have oozed with a moistened Q-tip; cover with wax paper and weight down until dry. Do not put under pressure in a press. Repeat this on the inside of the boards.

These same techniques again apply to replacing any leather missing in other areas on the edges of the boards.

If portions of the leather are missing on the surface of the boards, or areas have been badly skinned, lay a piece of bond paper over the area and with a pencil draw the outline of the area on the paper; cut a piece of matching leather this shape, allowing 1/16 to 1/8 inch extra all around. Pare this to the estimated thickness of the leather that it will adjoin; feather the 1/16 to 1/8 inch edge. Apply mixture to the whole piece and lay in position; rub down and set aside to dry under a weight.

To repair or fill small holes such as wormholes, scrape the surface of a piece of the selected leather with a knife. Mix the scrapings with a bit of paste to a puttylike consistency and fill in the holes. The first application will probably shrink a bit in drying. If so, add a second layer. This same mixture can be used to fill small gaps or cracks if the new and old leathers fail to meet neatly.

When the work on the boards is complete, they are attached or returned to the book. First, lift up the leather on the outside and the board papers on the inside along the entire spine edge of both boards for about 1 inch. Elevate the boards so that the knife can be held in a near horizontal position; keep the blade of the knife slightly tilted toward the board, and try to keep it between the leather or paper and the board. The ease with which this can be done or the difficulty is in direct relationship with the strength of the materials and the lasting qualities of the adhesive originally used. It is usually a slow and painstaking operation, but if care and patience are exercised, most materials can be successfully lifted. If fragments break off, preserve them; they can generally be returned to their proper position rather inconspicuously.

Next, put the boards in position on the book, following the instructions for attaching boards under Tight Back and German Tube Bindings (Chapter 7).

If the original leather is not flexible enough to permit lifting it to cut out the indention for the tapes, mark their position on the edges of the boards and sand the areas with a small emery board.

Rebacking This is the term used when new leather is added to the spine and is carried over onto both boards. Cut the selected leather the width of the spine plus 2 inches (5 cm) and 1 1/2 inches (3.8 cm) longer than the boards. If, however, portions of the original leather are missing in the spine area, cut the new leather large enough to cover these areas, plus 1/8 inch or so to slip under the original. Pare as described for a half-leather binding (Chapter 7, Cutting Leather to Size and Paring).

Covering Attach the leather to the spine as earlier described for leather bindings. If the spine is smooth, lay the leather down on the boards at the same time that the spine is covered. After it is in position, remove the book from the press, insert pieces of wax paper between the new and the old leather, and weight down until dry.

If the spine has raised bands, attach the leather to the spine only, leaving the sides unpasted and free, and tie up the bands as previously described in Chapter 7, German Tube Variations. When this is dry, lay the sides down.

The lifted edge of the original or covering leather is then laid down on the new leather as described above under Recovering Corners. After the underside of the leather is sanded and before it is attached, cut a clean straight edge along its entire length from head to tail. Cut away as little as possible. If the edge is very ragged with pieces missing, it makes for a nicer looking job to set in a few little patches rather than to cut the entire edge back to clear these areas. Often "little patches" can be salvaged from the surplus cut away.

Slip a narrow strip of binder's board under the edge of the leather. Lay a straightedge between the cutting points, previously determined; hold a sharp knife at an angle that will produce a bevelled cut and carefully cut a clean straight edge. Put very little pressure on the knife; rely on its sharpness to do the job. If the cut removed the edge just thinned, sand the edge of the new cut a bit more.

Clean all loose fragments between the 2 leathers. Lay the covering leather in position. If small bumps or irregularities are obvious, lift it again and sand these smooth or slice them off with a sharp scalpel. In doing so, however, be sure not to mar the new leather that will remain exposed. Apply mixture to the old leather, lay it down, rub it through a piece of paper, place the book between pressboards, and weight down until dry.

FIGURE 11-3.

Turning the leather in at head and tail and the setting of the head caps are done in the usual manner.

The hinges that cover the inside joints are attached next. These are put down as described earlier, except that they are inserted under the lifted-up board papers. If these consist of a paper hinge reinforced with a cloth hinge, the cloth goes down first, and when this is dry, the paper is laid down in the same way.

When the hinges on both front and back are in position, lay the lifted-up portion of the board papers down. Cut a clean straight edge on the paper as close to the edge of the board as possible, using the technique just described for the lifted-up leather on the outside. Remove from the underside of the paper any fragments of board that might have been lifted with it and any loose fragments. Apply mixture to the lifted portion of the paper, lay it down, and rub smooth. Insert a strip of wax paper between the board and the book before closing it.

Replacing the original spine Remove from the inside of the spine all lining paper, fragments of glue, and the like, and sand it smooth. Lay the spine on a clean, smooth surface when doing this work. If it has raised bands, cut several pieces of binder's board the width of the space between the bands and slip these, for support, under the section on which work is being done (Fig. 11-3).

If the spine has false raised bands and the strips of board on which they were formed are in position and in good condition, leave them, but cut them back about 1/4 inch from the edge on both sides. If, however, these strips are cracked and crumbling, remove and replace them with strips of leather, making them about 1/4 inch shorter on each edge than the width of the spine.

After the spine has been cleaned, cut the edges straight and sand or pare them to a feathered edge.

Put the book in a press. Apply mixture to the spine and lay it in position on the book. Place a piece of paper over it and rub it down firmly, starting in the center and working out toward the edges—giving the edges particular attention. Tie it up with wide tape; an ace bandage, pulled tight, also works well. Set aside to dry overnight.

If pieces of the spine are missing, make a pattern and cut pieces of new leather to fit the spaces. Pare these to the thickness of the original spine and abut the edges of the old and new.

In cases where it was not possible to remove the spine in 1 piece, lay the pieces out on a board in their proper position—after they have been cleaned, trimmed, and pared—and check to see which pieces should be attached to the new spine first. Often the leather will have split, and it is important to fit the 2 pieces back together properly.

Where tooling is missing due to parts of the binding having been worn away or lost, it gives the overall job a more finished appearance and reduces the conspicuousness of new leather if the tooling is carried to completion. This is possible, of course, only if suitable tools are at hand. There are, however, 2 schools of thought today regarding the replacing of missing gold, or blind tooling. One thinks that for aesthetic reasons it should be replaced; the other feels that it is a more honest restoration if tooling is not carried over onto new leather. Think about this or discuss it with conservators whom you respect.

If new gold is added, it blends better with the old if it is toned down a bit. This can be done by dissolving a very small amount of burnt umber or burnt sienna (artist colors ground in oil) in turpentine. Paint this carefully on the new gold with a small brush and wipe it off immediately with a piece of cotton.

The volume is now ready for its cosmetic treatment. Scuffed areas can be touched up with the dye that was reserved for this purpose, or if no dye has been used thus far, locate or mix a dye that matches the leather. Leather crayons also work well here. These are made in a great variety of colors and can be effectively applied by first dipping the end in a bit of British Museum leather dressing. This softens the crayon so that the color sinks into the leather. Watercolors and acrylics can also be used.

The final step is to oil and polish the volume. The best dressing for this—according to present thinking among conservators—is a combination of neat's-foot oil and lanolin. This can be purchased as a prepared dressing (the formula for it is in the Appendix). Apply with a soft cloth, and after it has dried for several hours or overnight, polish the book with a clean dry cloth. Cotton flannel works well for both of these steps. There are a number of leather dressings on the market sold under various trade names. Few, if any, list their ingredients. Unless you know their composition and that the ingredients are harmless, it is advisable to stay away from them.

Cloth Bindings

The techniques for restoring cloth bindings follow closely those given in the preceding section for leather bindings. The work on the book itself is the same, as is the desirability of matching the original materials in color and texture. Here, again, dyeing plays a significant role in producing an aesthetically pleasing end result (see Dyeing of Materials later in this chapter).

Much of the book cloth used in the nineteenth century and the early part of the twentieth was embossed. Since very little of the cloth manufactured today is embossed, matching textures presents something of a problem or a challenge. Fabrics other than book cloth can often be used successfully; various weights and weaves of linen are surprisingly adaptable.

There is 1 basic difference in the recovering of corners, re-edging of boards, and the laying down on the boards of new cloth in connection with rebacking. Since cloth can neither be pared nor sanded, to avoid a

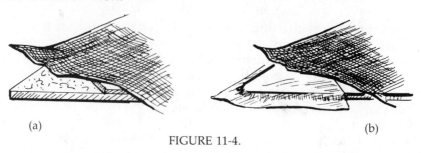

(a)

(b)

FIGURE 11-4.

noticeable stepdown at the point where the new cloth ends, the boards should be reduced in thickness the estimated thickness of the new cloth, in areas where the new cloth will be covered by the old.

In all of these situations, first lift up the original material, then decide where the new cloth will be placed on the boards. Make clean, straight cuts at these points and lift or peel away a layer of the board, using a scalpel (Fig. 11-4). Do this gradually, lifting very little off at the start. Lay a straight-cut edge of the cloth against the cut on the board and check to see if the board and the cloth are flush at the point of contact. If not, lift off another thin layer of board and so on until the desired result is attained.

After the corners and edges are restored, add the new spine. Lift the covering material and the board papers on the spine edge of the boards and thin the boards on the outside as just described, 3/4 inch in from the edge. The grain in all new cloth should run with the vertical measurement of the book; use mixture as the adhesive in cloth work.

Cut the cloth to be used in rebacking the width of the spine, plus 1/2 inch (1.2 cm) for the 2 joints, plus 1 1/2 inches (3.8 cm)—this allows for 3/4 inch (1.9 cm) to be attached to each board—and in length 1 1/2 inches longer than the boards. The bristol spine strip is cut the width of the spine and the length of the boards as usual and the gauges for the joints 1/4 inch.

Attach the new cloth to the front cover first; add the spacer for the joint; the new spine strip; the spacer for the other joint; and then the back cover. Turn the edges at head and tail. Try the case around the book, and if it fits satisfactorily, paste the original covering material down, using mixture, after cutting a clean straight edge on the cloth. Give the boards a quick nip in the press. If the case does not fit, take it to pieces and make the necessary adjustments.

If the original board papers were removed, case the book in the usual way (see Chapter 10). If these were retained, however, casing the book in is a bit tricky. Old board papers are frequently not strong enough to stand being folded back without breaking, and even if they were, the crease made by doing this is difficult to remove. Instead of the usual method, attach the hinge or hinges first on 1 side then the other. Lay the case on a brass-bound board; position the book on it (Fig. 11-5); apply mixture to the hinge, and with the cover in an upright position, slip the hinge under the board paper and close the cover. Rub it on the outside for 1 or 2 minutes. Open the cover, and if the hinge is smooth, put a strip of wax paper between the board paper and the hinge, and put the book in the press between case boards for 10 or 15 minutes. If

FIGURE 11-5.

the hinge is wrinkled, free it and try again. Repeat on the other side. Then cut a clean straight edge on the board papers and paste them down.

Clean up the original spine, trim the edges, apply mixture, and lay it in position on the new spine. Tie it up as described earlier.

Scuffed areas can be touched up with dye, and watercolors work well on cloth.

Paper-bound case bindings are handled in much the same way as cloth. The edges of paper can, however, be either pared or sanded, so use this technique where the old and new materials overlap, instead of thinning the board.

When the covering paper is marbled or patterned, use for the new material in re-edging a strong paper as near in color as possible to the background color in the original. After it is in position carry the pattern in the original paper onto the exposed areas of the new material using watercolors.

Vellum Bindings

The basic principles and techniques governing vellum conservation are similar in many respects to those described earlier for leather. The primary difference is that leather is usually in a deteriorated state, and vellum seldom is.

Vellum is invariably dirty, sometimes almost black. Limp bindings are usually wrinkled and cockled; board papers torn; and fore edge ties broken or missing. Sometimes it has contracted so that the covers no longer cover the pages of the book. The chief problem with hardcover bindings is the warping of the covers, the subsequent lifting up of the turns, and the tearing or breaking of the board papers. When the covers warp, the text pages usually expand. It is not uncommon to find the fore edge of a warped vellum book as much as a 1/2 inch thicker than the book is in the spine area.

The conservator does not generally see hardcover vellum bindings that are in good condition with flat boards. There are, however, many around, and more often than not they have been housed in identical or similar conditions to the bindings whose covers are badly warped. There must be some reason why 1 volume remains in good condition while its neighbor warps badly. A few questions posed, but unanswered, are were the boards or the vellum cut against the grain; was the vellum stretched unduly in the process of covering; was the pull of the vellum adequately balanced on the inside of the board at the time the book was originally bound?

There are many ways advocated for the treatment of vellum. You can clean it with milk, for it is the skin of a calf; you can make it supple with lanolin, for it is the skin of a lamb; it should or should not be washed with saddle soap; no moisture should be applied to it; and on and on.

The remedies or techniques suggested here are simple, and they work. They introduce no materials unfamiliar to vellum, which should make them safe, and perhaps they will be considered by some people as old-fashioned. The use of vellum in binding, however, dates back several centuries. The bindings for the most part have withstood the test of time very well, so the old-timers must have been doing something right!

The first thing to do to a vellum binding is clean it. This can be done satisfactorily and safely with a pink pearl eraser and an opaline bag. It is tedious and slow, but reasonably sure. Extreme care should be taken where either gold tooling or handwritten titles appear; these can sometimes be easily obliterated by an eraser.

Any page repair, resewing, or making of new flyleaves or endleaves is done as described in Chapter 6 or under Leather Bindings earlier in this chapter.

Limp covers If they are unadorned, limp covers can be flattened by pressing between damp blotters. Lay a pulpboard, a piece of wax paper, and a wet blotter on a pressboard in this order; add the vellum and cover in the same way. Put first under moderate weight. Check at intervals and, if necessary, redampen the blotters. When free of wrinkles and reasonably flat, put in the press under firm pressure for a short period. Remove, change the blotters, and put under weight again until thoroughly dry. The edges can then be refolded; the ties replaced in the manner in which they were originally attached; the cover returned to the book; and board papers, if any, pasted down, and set aside to dry under weight in the usual fashion.

If the covers are tooled in gold or titled with ink, they should be relaxed in a humidifier and carefully flattened on a vellum stretcher. If you do not have this equipment, it is recommended that you delay the job until it can be obtained.

Hard covers In the case of warped covers, remove the board papers. If they are blank, great care need not be taken. If they contain bookplates, signatures, inscriptions, or the like, every effort should be made to remove them intact. (See reference to this at beginning of this chapter.) Once removed, store them in a safe place.

Determine the grain direction of the board. If it is warping from spine to fore edge, the grain direction is running with the vertical measurement of the book. If the warping is from head to tail, the grain is running from spine to fore edge. Once it is determined, cut a piece of acid-free bond paper the size of the board—lifting up the turns of the vellum if necessary—in the same grain direction as the board. Paste it and lay it in position on the board. Lay the board flat on a smooth, firm surface or support it in its opened position. Cover it with a piece of wax paper, a pulpboard, and a pressboard, and put quite a bit of weight on it. As it begins to flatten, increase the weight. Repeat this process until the board is flat. After 1 board is flat, proceed with the other. At the same time, weight the book itself down; the fore edge will contract to its proper thickness under continued weight. When both covers are flat and the book has reverted to its normal size, continue with other repairs or conservation techniques as described earlier for leather in this chapter. Where an adhesive is called for, use wheat paste, and where moisture is needed in turning edges, setting headcaps, and the like, use water. When the job is completed, keep the book under weight for several days or until all work is thoroughly dry and seasoned.

It is recommended that all restored vellum books be promptly housed in a Solander case (Chapter 10), preferably with a clasp or closure of some kind.

Dyeing of Materials

Leather, cloth, and paper can all be successfully dyed with the same type of dye. There are at least 2 types of powdered aniline dyes available: those that are soluble in water and those that are soluble in alcohol. If purchasing these, be sure to get instructions from the distributor for their proper preparation.

For general use, however, Dr. Martin's prepared dyes are very satisfactory; they are ready to use and readily available in a wide color range. Various shades and colors can, however, be made from the primary colors, so they are the only ones that need be routinely stocked. An artist's color chart is useful to have on hand in mixing colors. These dyes are relatively expensive, but very concentrated, so a little dye goes a long way.

Before attempting to match the material on the original binding, do any cleaning that may be necessary. In the case of leather, sponge it with cotton moistened with water. Test a small area on the back cover before proceeding. Sometimes, particularly with old calf, water tends to cause the surface of the leather to crack, and a crazed appearance develops. In such cases it is better to confine the cleaning to an opaline bag.

In selecting new material to be dyed, try to locate pieces as near in color as possible to the original. Have on hand several swatches or samples of the material to be dyed. Select or mix a color that seems right; try it on a sample and let it dry thoroughly. Increase or reduce the strength of the solution as the result dictates. When a satisfactory color is arrived at, set aside a small amount of it for use later on in the touching up of scuffed areas on the original covers.

Leather can be immersed in the dye solution (although this is an extravagant use of dye) or sponge-dyed. If the leather is evenly moist beforehand, the dye will take better. If the right tone is reached, but it is not dark enough, repeated applications will darken it further. Allow for drying time between applications. Keep a record of the dye used, the amount of water, the quantity of dye, and the number of applications.

Book cloth should be sponge-dyed, and for successful dyeing, it should be a starch-filled cloth. A pyroxylin-coated or impregnated cloth will not take dye of this type.

The dyeing of paper can be done with either a dye or with watercolors. The amount of dye and the amount of water should be recorded and the period of immersion timed. A kitchen timer is useful for this. It is essential in the dyeing of paper that the samples used for testing be the same paper that is to be dyed. Two white papers of different make will not react to the same dye solution in the same way.

Start with a pan large enough to take the sheet of paper unfolded. (Any shallow pan such as a roasting pan, a baking dish, or a photographer's washing pan are satisfactory.) The paper should, of course, be cut to the approximate size needed. Add enough water to easily cover the paper. If only a slight darkening or toning is required, add 5 or 6 drops of dye. Mix this thoroughly with the water before adding the paper. Put the sample in the dye solution; press down on it to get it completely immersed, and leave it for 5 minutes. Remove it, rinse in clear water, and lay aside to dry. When dry, check it against the color desired. If it is right, proceed with dyeing the sheets. If it is too light, strengthen the dye solution, or leave the next sample in a bit longer; if too dark, dilute the solution, or leave the sample in for a shorter time, or both. If it is the wrong tone, introduce a bit of another color.

After the right color is obtained, put the paper in the pan for the specified amount of time. Remove it, rinse in clear water, put between pulpboards, and weight down until dry.

If watercolor is used, thin it so that it can easily be brushed on without streaking.

Appendix

Supply Sources

Supplies

Numbers indicate suppliers, listed below.

Adhesives, 9, 40
Board, all-rag mounting, 7, 40
Board, binder's, 14, 20
Board, bristol, 40
Board, chip, pulp, 20, 30
Board shears, 15
Book cloth, 10, 25, 27
Bookbinding suppliers, general, 2, 8, 11,
    23, 24, 41, 45
Brushes, 3, 9, 50
Chemicals, 5
De-acidifying products, 49
Dies, engraving, 4, 36, 37
Dyes and pigments, 9, 18
Edge gilding, 33
Encapsulating materials, 45, 47
Finishing tools, 26, 37
Foils, 41, 44
Glair, 45
Glue, 9, 51
Gold and pigmented foils, 41, 44
Grinding tools, knives, and scissors, 1,
    29, 50
Handles for finishing tools and others,
    43, 50
Headband silk, 21, 34, 51
Knives, scissors, 1, 50
Leather, 7

Lithographic stones, 7, 50
Marbling supplies, 16, 22
Mylar, 47
Newsprint, 20
Paper, 7, 30, 35, 38, 40
Paper cabinets, 19
Paper cutters, 13
Paper, decorated, marbled, 7, 10, 16, 22,
    38, 42, 46
Paper, handmade, 48
Paper, newsprint, 20
Paper, silicone release, 45
Parchment, 7, 45
Paring machines, 12
Polyurethane foam, 51
Presses, stamping, 28, 41
Scissors, knives, 1, 13, 50
Shears, 15
Silicone release paper, 45
Silk, 21, 34, 51
Skiving machines, 12
Stamping presses, 28, 41
Tape, double-faced (sticky), 45
Tissue, Japanese, 3, 7
Type, 6, 17, 31, 32, 37, 39
Vellum and parchment, 7, 45
Zinc plates, 51

Suppliers

Following the names of some suppliers are letters a–c: a = catalog, for which there may be a charge; b = samples, for which there may be a charge; c = minimum order required.

1. Ace Grinding Co.
   248 Mulberry St.
   New York, NY 10012

2. Aegis Binders Supply (a) (b)
   Box 103
   Floosmoor, IL 60422

3. Aiko's Art Materials Import (a) (b)
   714 N. Wabash Ave.
   Chicago, IL 60611

4. Alcon Engravers, Inc. (c)
   656 Broadway
   New York, NY 10012

5. Amend Drug & Chemical Co.
   88 Cordier
   Irvington, NJ 07111

6. American Printing Equip. & Supply (a)
   42-25 Ninth St.
   Long Island City, NY 11101

7. Andrews/Nelson/Whitehead (b) (c)
   31-10 48th Ave.
   Long Island City, NY 11101

8. Basic Crafts Co. (a)
   1201 Broadway
   New York, NY 10001

9. H. Behlen Bros. (a) (c)
   Rt. 30 North
   Amsterdam, NY 12010

10. Bookcraft (b) (c)
    65 Wright Lane
    Hamden, CT 06517

11. BookMakers (a) (b) (c)
    2025 Eye St. N.W., Suite 412
    Washington, DC 20006

12. Campbell, Bosworth Machine Co.
    152 W. 25 St.
    New York, NY 10001

13. Dahle U.S.A. (a)
    26 Berkshire Rd.
    Sandy Hook, CT 06482

14. The Davey Co.
    164 Laidlaw Ave.
    Jersey City, NJ 07306

15. Davis-Standard (a)
    U.S. Route 1
    Pawcatuck, CT 02891

16. Decorative Papers (a) (b) (c)
    Faith Harrison
    Box 281
    Eastford, CT 06242

17. Detroit Type Foundry
    1959 E. Jefferson St.
    Detroit, MI 48207

18. Fezandie & Sperrle, Inc. (c)
    111 Eighth Ave.
    New York, NY 10011

19. Fidelity Products Co. (a)
    705 Penn. Ave., South
    Minneapolis, MN 55426

20. Henry Fuchs & Son, Inc. (a) (c)
    94 Ninth St.
    Brooklyn, NY 11215

21. Greenberg & Hammer
    24 W. 57 St.
    New York, NY 10019

22. Don Guyot (a) (b)
    1902 N. 44 St.
    Seattle, WA 98103

23. Harcourt Bindery (a)
    9-11 Harcourt St.
    Boston, MA 02166

24. W. O. Hickok Mfg. Co. (a)
    Ninth & Cumberland Sts.
    Harrisburg, PA 17105

25. The Holliston Mills, Inc. (c)
    Warehouse Rd.
    Hyannis, MA 02601

26. Hoole Machine & Engraving Co. (a)
    334 12th St.
    Carlstadt, NJ 07072

27. Joanna-Western Mills Co. (c)
    2141 S. Jefferson St.
    Chicago, IL 60616

28. Kensol-Olsenmark, Inc. (a) (c)
    40 Melville Park Rd.
    Melville, NY 11746

29. A. Kochendorfer, Inc.
    413 W. Broadway
    New York, NY 10012

30. Lindenmeyr Paper Corp. (b) (c)
    53rd Ave. & 11th St.
    Long Island City, NY 11101

31. Los Angeles Type Founders (c)
    225 East Pico Blvd.
    Los Angeles, CA 90015

32. MacKenzie & Harris (a)
    460 Bryant St.
    San Francisco, CA 94107

33. R. Marchetti & Bro. (c)
    285 Lafayette St.
    New York, NY 10012

34. Margot Gallery, Inc.
    26 W. 54 St.
    New York, NY 10019

35. McManus & Morgan, Inc. (c)
    2506 W. Seventh St.
    Los Angeles, CA 90057

36. Merit Engraving Co.
    307 W. 38 St.
    New York, NY 10018

37. M. W. Engraving Co.
    Hanover Industrial Air Park
    Ashland, VA 23005

38. New York Central Supply (a)
    62 Third Ave.
    New York, NY 10003

39. Pittsburgh Graphic Products Corp.
    Foot of Jersey Ave.
    Jersey City, NJ 07302

40. Process Materials Corp. (b)
    301 Veterans Blvd.
    Rutherford, NJ 07070

41. Ernest Schaefer, Inc. (a) (c)
    731 Lehigh Ave.
    Union, NJ 07083

42. Peggy Skycraft (b) (c)
    8095 S.E. 282 St.
    Gresham, OR 97030

43. Swan Handle Co.
    1041 Garfield Ave.
    Jersey City, NJ 07304

44. M. Swift & Sons, Inc.
    Ten Love Lane
    Hartford, CT 06101

45. Talas (a)
    130 Fifth Ave.
    New York, NY 10011

46. Jean Teten (a) (b) (c)
    5 Broadway
    Kentfield, CA 94904

47. Transilwrap Co.
    135 English St.
    Hackensack, NJ 07601

48. Twinrocker Handmade Paper (a) (b)
    RR #2
    Brookston, IN 47923

49. Wei T'o Associates, Inc. (a)
    Drawer 40
    Matteson, IL 60443

50. Henry Westpfal & Co.
    4 E. 32 St.
    New York, NY 10018

51. Consult local Yellow Pages for hardware stores, notion stores or counters, plumbing supply houses, upholstery supply shops

pH and P.I.R.A. Tests

pH. The negative logarithm of the effective hydrogen ion concentration or hydrogen ion activity in gram equivalents per liter used in expressing both acidity and alkalinity on a scale whose values run from 0 to 14 with 7 representing neutrality, numbers less than 7 increasing acidity, and numbers greater than 7 increasing alkalinity (Webster's Dictionary).

The P. I. R. A. (Printing Industry Research Association) Test for Durable Leather. A piece of leather, 2 1/2 inches square (16.1 sq cm) and weighing from 2 to 5 grams, is placed on a glass plate and evenly treated on the flesh side with a normal solution of sulfuric acid in the proportion of 1 cc of acid per gram of air-dry leather. This proportion is just enough to dampen the leather (moisture content now about 65 percent) and to give it when air-dried a sulfuric acid content of 5 percent. The leather is allowed to dry at room temperature. Hydrogen peroxide (10 volumes strength) is now evenly added on the flesh side by drops in the proportion of 0–6 cc per gram of leather. In the case of very thin leathers (weighing, say, 2 grams or less), this proportion of hydrogen peroxide is not enough to dampen the whole square evenly, and the amount is increased to 1 cc per gram of leather. The damp piece is allowed to dry for 24 hours; it is then given 5 further daily doses of hydrogen peroxide. At the end of the 7 days, the piece is inspected and its properties compared with those of the untreated leather.

Durable leathers are completely unaffected (except for some possible fading of the dyestuff); they are not darkened in any way, are perfectly supple, and do not crack on bending. Unsatisfactory leather may crack on bending, may be blackened and gelatinized especially around the edges, and in very bad cases the leather may, in addition, be eaten into holes.

Note: Normal sulfuric acid and 10 volumes strength hydrogen peroxide can be purchased usually from a drugstore, or the pharmacist will obtain it for you. An eyedropper is a convenient way of applying the solutions. (From H. J. Plenderleith, *The Preservation of Leather Bookbindings*, see under "Conservation and Restoration" in the Bibliography.)

Recipes for Paste, Egg Glair, and Leather Dressing

Wheat Flour Paste (10 tbsp)

2 tbsp. bleached flour (not self-rising)
10 tbsp. water

Mix the flour and 2 tbsp. of the water together (in a pan or bowl that can be heated) and stir to a smooth creamy consistency. Add remaining water and stir again. Place the pan holding the mixture in a larger pan of boiling water. Keep the water boiling slowly. Cook for 5 minutes, stirring constantly. Remove from the water, cover the paste with a damp cloth placed directly on the paste, and set aside to cool. When cool, transfer to a storage jar with a top. If stored in a refrigerator and removed only to take out the amount needed, this will keep satisfactorily for 5 to 7 days. It is preferable to mix fresh paste in small batches at short intervals rather than in large quantities in anticipation of keeping it over a long period of time.

Rice Starch Paste

This is made in the same way and in the same proportions as wheat paste. Substitute rice starch for the flour.

Glycerine Paste

If a prepared dry paste is used, mix together 1 part glycerine and 5 parts water. Then stir in the paste. If the paste is to be made from flour and cooked, mix the glycerine into the paste after the cooking is completed and the paste cool, in the same proportions as above.

Egg Glair

White of 1 egg
Water—1/3 volume of albumen
1 tbsp. vinegar
Pinch of salt

Mix ingredients, beat well. Cover and let stand overnight. Remove crust from top. Strain the clear liquid through 2 layers of cheesecloth, leaving sediment in bottom undisturbed. Bottle and cork. Refrigerate when not in use.

Leather Dressing

Neat's-foot oil (60%)
Lanolin, anhydrous (40%)

Melt the lanolin in the top of a double boiler and mix in the neat's-foot oil in the proper proportion. Lanolin is generally available in drugstores, and neat's-foot oil in hardware stores. This can also be bought as a prepared dressing from bookbinding supply houses (Library of Congress, Preservation Leaflet no. 3).

Metric Conversion Charts

Conversions from Metric Measures

Symbol	When You Know	Multiply By	To Find	Symbol
		Length		
mm	millimeters	0.04	inches	in
cm	centimeters	0.4	inches	in
m	meters	3.3	feet	ft
m	meters	1.1	yards	yd
km	kilometers	0.6	miles	mi
		Area		
cm^2	sq. centimeters	0.16	sq. inches	in^2
m^2	sq. meters	1.2	sq. yards	yd^2
km^2	sq. kilometers	0.4	sq. miles	mi^2
ha	hectares			
	$(10,000\ m^2)$	2.5	acres	
		Mass (weight)		
g	grams	0.035	ounces	oz
kg	kilograms	2.2	pounds	lb
t	tonnes (1,000 kg)	1.1	short tons	
		Volume		
ml	milliliters	0.03	fluid ounces	fl oz
l	liters	2.1	pints	pt
l	liters	1.06	quarts	qt
l	liters	0.26	gallons	gal
m^3	cubic meters	35	cubic feet	ft^3
m^3	cubic meters	1.3	cubic yards	yd^3
		Temperature (exact)		
°C	Celsius temp.	9/5 (°C) +32	Fahrenheit temp.	°F

Conversions to Metric Measures

Symbol	When You Know	Multiply By	To Find	Symbol
		Length		
in	inches	2.54	centimeters	cm
ft	feet	30	centimeters	cm
yd	yards	0.9	meters	m
mi	miles	1.6	kilometers	km
		Area		
in^2	sq. inches	6.5	sq. centimeters	cm^2
ft^2	sq. feet	0.09	meters	m^2
yd^2	sq. yards	0.8	sq. meters	m^2
mi^2	sq. miles	2.6	sq. kilometers	km^2
	acres	0.4	hectares	ha
		Mass (weight)		
oz	ounces	28	grams	g
lb	pounds	0.45	kilograms	kg
	short tons (2000 lb)	0.9	tonnes	t
		Volume		
tsp	teaspoons	5	milliliters	ml
tbsp	tablespoons	15	milliliters	ml
fl oz	fluid ounces	30	milliliters	ml
c	cups	0.24	liters	l
pt	pints	0.47	liters	l
qt	quarts	0.95	liters	l
gal	gallons	3.8	liters	l
ft^3	cubic feet	0.03	cubic meters	m^3
yd^3	cubic yards	0.76	cubic meters	m^3
		Temperature (exact) to Metric		
°F	Fahrenheit temp.	5/9 (°F −32°)	Celsius temp.	°C

Bibliography

Conservation and Restoration

Barrow, W. J. *Manuscripts and Documents: Their Deterioration and Restoration,* 2nd ed. (Charlottesville: University of Virginia Press, 1972).

W. J. Barrow Research Laboratory, *Permanence/Durability of the Book* (Richmond, VA: The author). no. 1, A Two-Year Research Program, 1963; no. 2, Test Data of Naturally Aged Papers, 1964, no. 3, Spray De-Acidification, 1964; no. 4, Polyvinyl Acetate Adhesives for Use in Library Bookbinding, 1965; no. 5, Strength and Other Characteristics of Book Papers 1800–1899, 1967; no. 6, Spot Testing for Unstable Modern Book and Record Papers, 1969; no. 7, Physical and Chemical Properties of Book Papers, 1507–1949, 1974.

The Causes and Prevention of the Decay of Bookbinding Leather. Interim reports of the Bookbinding Leather Committee (London: Printing Industry Research Association and British Leather Manufacturers' Research Association, 1933, 1936).

Cunha, George, and Dorothy Cunha. *Conservation of Library Materials,* 2nd ed., Vol. I, Text; Vol. II, Bibliography (Metuchen, NJ: Scarecrow Press, 1971, 1972).

Haines, Betty M. "Deterioration in Leather Bookbindings: Our Present State of Knowledge." *British Library Journal* 3, no. 1 (Spring 1977).

Horton, Carolyn. *Cleaning and Preserving Bindings and Related Materials,* 2nd ed. rev. Pamphlet no. 1 of a series, Library Technology Program Publications no. 16 (Chicago: American Library Association, 1969).

Innes, R. Faraday, "The Preservation of Bookbinding Leathers." *Library Association Record* 52 (December 1950).

Library of Congress, Preservation Office. *Polyester Film Encapsulation.* (Washington, DC: Government Printing Office, 1980). Ordering No.: Stock N—030-000-00114-1.

———Publications on Conservation of Library Materials. Conservation Workshop Notes on Evolving Procedures, Series 300. No. 1, Heat-Set Tissue Preparation and Application (May 1977). Request from Library of Congress, Attn.: Assistant Director for Preservation, Administrative Department, Washington, DC 20540.

Plenderleith, H. J. *The Preservation of Leather Bookbindings* (London: British Museum, 1946). Reprinted in new format, 1967.

———, and A. E. A. Werner. *The Conservation of Antiquities and Works of Art,* 2nd ed. (London: Oxford, 1971).

Reed, R. *Ancient Skins Parchments and Leather* (London: Seminar Press, 1972).

Report of the Committee on Leather for Bookbinding, 2nd ed. (London: George Bell, for the Society of Arts, 1905).

Swartzburg, Susan G. *Preserving Library Materials. A Manual* (Metuchen, NJ: Scarecrow Press, 1980).

Glossaries

Carter, John, *ABC for Book Collectors*, 5th ed. (London: Hart-Davis, 1972).
Glaister, Geoffrey Ashfall. *Glossary of the Book* (London: Allen & Unwin, 1960).

Historical

Cundall, Joseph, ed. *On Bookbindings Ancient and Modern* (London: George Bell, 1881).
Davenport, Cyril. *English Embroidered Bookbindings* (London: Kegan, Paul, Trench, Trubner, 1899).
The History of Bookbinding 525–1950 A.D. An Exhibition, Baltimore Museum of Art, November 12, 1957 to January 12, 1958 (Baltimore: Trustees of the Walters Art Gallery, 1957). Foreword by Dorothy Miner.
Hunter, Dard. *Papermaking. The History and Technique of an Ancient Craft*, 2nd ed. (New York: Knopf, 1947).
Lalande, Joseph J. "Art de Faire le Parchemin." *Academie Royale Des Sciences Description Des Arts et Metiers*, 3 (Paris, 1762).
Loring, Rosamond. *Decorated Book Papers*, 2nd ed. (Cambridge, MA: Harvard College Library, 1952).
Middleton, Bernard C., *A History of English Craft Bookbinding Techniques* (New York: Hafner, 1963), 2nd Supplemental Edition (London: Holland Press, 1978).
Nixon, Howard M. *Five Centuries of English Bookbinding* (London: Scolar Press, 1978).
———*Roger Powell and Peter Waters.* (Froxfield, The Slade, 1965).
Payne, John R. "An Annotated List of Works on Fine Bindings." *American Book Collector* XVIII, no. 1 (September 1967).
Peignot, Etienne Gabriel. *Essai L'Histoire Du Parchemin et Du Velin* (Paris: Chez Antoine-Augustin Renouard, 1812).
Weber, Carl J. *Fore-edge Painting: A Historical Survey of a Curious Art in Book Decoration* (Irvington, NY: Harvey House, 1966). Facsimile Edition).

Illustrated Works

Adams, Frederick B. Jr., comp. *Bookbindings by T. J. Cobden-Sanderson.* An Exhibition at the Pierpont Morgan Library, September 3–November 4, 1968 (New York: Morgan Library, 1969).
Charrière, Gérard. *The Art of Bookbinding.* An Exhibition May 26–June 20, 1970 (New York: Gimpel & Weitzenhoffer, 1970).
Designer Bookbinders. Modern British Bookbindings. An exhibition shown in New York, Chicago, Los Angeles, London, 1971. (London: Designer Bookbinders, 1971).
"Gerhard Gerlach: A Memorial Exhibition of His Bindings, and Recent

Work of the Members of the Guild of Book Workers. New York, GBW, 1971." *Guild of Book Workers Journal* X, no. 1, supplement.

Hunt Institute for Botanical Documentation. *The Tradition of Fine Bookbinding in the 20th Century*. An Exhibition (Pittsburgh: Carnegie-Mellon University, 1979).

La Reluire Originale Français. An Exhibition, January 17–February 23, 1964 (New York: Museum of Contemporary Crafts, 1964).

Masterpieces of French Modern Bindings. Exhibition held in New York, 1947 (New York: Services Culturels Français, 1947).

San Francisco Museum of Modern Art. *Hand Bookbinding Today, an International Art*. An Exhibition Organized by the San Francisco Museum in Cooperation with the Hand Bookbinders of California (San Francisco: Museum of Modern Art, 1978).

Sotheby & Co. *Catalogue of Valuable Printed Books and Fine Bindings from the Celebrated Collection of the Property of Major J. R. Abbey* (London: The author, 1965).

Wiemeler, Ignatz. *Buchbinder 1895 bis 1952*. n.p., n.d.

Instructional Manuals

Burdett, Eric. *The Craft of Bookbinding, a Practical Handbook* (London: David & Charles, 1975).

Cockerell, Douglas. *Bookbinding and the Care of Books*, 1st ed. (New York: Appleton, 1902). Has gone into many editions and been reprinted many times.

Diehl, Edith. *Bookbinding: Its Background and Technique*, 2 vols. (New York: Rinehart, 1946).

Fahey, Herbert, and Peter Fahey. *Finishing in Hand Bookbinding* (San Francisco: The authors, 1951).

Harrison, T. *Fragments of Bookbinding Technique*, from articles in *Paper & Print*, n.d.

Nicholson, James B. *A Manual of the Art of Bookbinding*, 1st ed. (Philadelphia: Baird, 1856).

Town, Laurence. *Bookbinding by Hand*, 2nd ed. (New York: Pitman, 1950).

Periodicals

AIC (American Institute for Conservation), formerly IIC-AG. *Bulletin;* 2 issues yearly, vol. I, no. 1, 1960 and continuations.

Guild of Book Workers Journal; 3 nos. to a vol, vol. I, no. 1, Fall 1962 and continuations.

IIC (International Institute for Conservation of Historic and Artistic Works). Journal, *Studies in Conservation;* issued quarterly, vol. I, no. 1, 1956 and continuations.

Restaurator: International Journal for the Preservation of Library and Archival Material. Copenhagen, Restaurator Press, vol. I, no. 1, 1969 and continuations.

Index